DIVORCING
YOUR
NARCISSIST

DIVORCING YOUR NARCISSIST

You Can't Make This Shit Up!

TRACY A. MALONE

Divorcing Your Narcissist: You Can't Make This Shit Up!
ISBN number: Paperback - 978-1-7365078-1-0
Copyright ©2021 by Tracy A. Malone
Library of Congress – Control Number: 2021910921

Copy editing: Karla Crawford
Cover design: Erica Gamet
Interior design: Erica Gamet
Illustrations: Jasmine Mann
Audible reader: Kate Parry
Author Photo: Raelene Kerner

Connect
Website: narcissistabusesupport.com
Website: tracyamalone.com
Website: divorcingyournarcissistbook.com
Instagram: instagram.com/tracyamalone/
YouTube: youtube.com/c/tracyamalone
Pinterest: pinterest.com/tracyamalone/

A WORD ABOUT THIS BOOK

LIABILITY

The author, Tracy A. Malone, is not a medical doctor, psychologist, licensed therapist, or licensed attorney.

This book is not intended to, nor is it to be interpreted as diagnosing any condition, nor is it to be interpreted as providing medical, psychological, legal, financial, or other professional advice. This book should not be used to diagnose anyone with narcissistic personality disorder. If you believe that you or a loved one is suffering from narcissistic abuse, please seek help from a trained professional familiar with narcissistic abuse. This book is not intended to provide legal advice with regard to divorcing a narcissist. The law in every state, regarding divorce, child custody, child support, alimony and property division is different. The reader is strongly encouraged to seek legal advice from an attorney in your jurisdiction who is experienced in dealing with divorce cases involving narcissists.

This book is intended solely to provide non-professional information and assistance to persons seeking information regarding common situations experienced by individuals involved in divorcing a narcissistic spouse, and to provide strategies based on anecdotal experiences shared by thousands of surTHRIVERS. The surTHRIVER stories in this book were donated for use in this book to help educate others. The names and identifying details of characters associated with events described in this book have all been changed. Any similarities to your own story would make sense because thousands of stories submitted described the common behaviors of narcissists going through divorce. Every effort has been made to rotate the sexual identity of the victims to further conceal their identities, understanding that the behavior patterns of narcissists are essentially the same, regardless of gender or sexual orientation.

REFERENCE TO INDIVIDUAL PERSONS

Nothing in this book, or any of the accounts shared herein, are intended to describe the factual circumstances of any specific person's experiences. Names of all individuals contributing information for use in this book have been changed. Any resemblance to any person, whether living or not, is purely coincidental.

REFERENCES TO SOURCES/RESOURCES

This book includes references to various websites and resources. The author, Tracy A. Malone, does not assume responsibility for the content or accuracy of these third-party sources, or for the web addresses or links contained in this book, as some may have changed since the date of publication and others may no longer be valid.

ENDORSEMENTS

"Because she has lived it, no one gets how difficult it is to divorce a narcissist the way Tracy Malone does. You can feel like you are literally under siege and trying to figure out how to escape hell. This book will give you the resources to anticipate what's coming and then the tools to handle whatever is flung your way. It's worth every word and every penny."

> ~ **Rebecca Zung**, Top 1% Divorce Attorney, Narcissist Negotiation Expert, YouTuber and Bestselling Author

"Tracy Malone's *Divorcing Your Narcissist* is packed with tons of sound advice and hard-earned wisdom that will help readers navigate the exhausting, grueling, and high-conflict terrain of divorcing a narcissist."

> ~ **Bree Bonchay**, LCSW, psychotherapist and founder of World Narcissistic Abuse Awareness Day

"Malone's *Divorcing Your Narcissist* is an invaluable tool with breaking the insidious cycle of narcissistic traumatic abuse. The wisdom Malone gleaned from her personal plights with narc abuse is evidenced in her book. Leaving no stone unturned, the reader is led to

access their inner sleuth and warrior to construct a plan of action that will dismantle a disorienting and dangerous narrative."
~ **Rev. Sheri Heller**, LCSW, Interfaith Minister, Free-lance Writer and Addiction/Trauma Therapist in private practice

"This is hands-down the most comprehensive book on divorcing a narcissist. Tracy writes the ugly truth that so many experts are too exhausted or too afraid to explain. Yet, with the truth, she brings hope, inspiration, empowerment, and a healing message to anyone brave enough to divorce a narcissist. Do not divorce without this book!"
~ **Lindsey Ellison**, author, narcissism expert, and breakup coach

"Tracy Malone has helped so many heal and recover after narcissistic abuse and her new book takes that help one step further. *Divorcing Your Narcissist* is not only an incredible read but an important one since it covers everything you need to know about protecting yourself from a narcissist during the divorce process. There is no other book like Tracy's on the market and you can't put a price on the value contained within!"
~ **Suzanna Quintana**, Founder of The Narcissist Relationship Recovery Program and bestselling author of the book, *You're Still That Girl: Get Over Your Abusive Ex for Good!*

"As a divorce attorney for more than 30 years, I have seen over and over again the devastation and powerlessness a victim experiences when divorcing a high conflict person. With *Divorcing Your Narcissist: You Can't Make This Shit Up!*, Tracy Malone has created an invaluable resource for those suffering through the process. A surTHRIVER herself, Tracy and her experts share truly actionable advice and tips for not just getting divorced, but also healing and thriving beyond narcissistic abuse!"
~ **Susan Guthrie**, Leading Family Law Attorney, Mediator and Award-Winning Host of *The Divorce & Beyond Podcast*

ENDORSEMENTS

"In *Divorcing Your Narcissist*, Tracy Malone recognizes the unique challenges of divorcing a narcissist and provides practical guidance to help you navigate the process and begin to heal. Malone offers tried-and-true tips and compassionate advice based on her personal experiences and years of educating and coaching narcissistic abuse survivors. I'm certain this much-needed resource will help many!"

~ **Sharon Martin**, MSW, LCSW, psychotherapist author of *The CBT Workbook for Perfectionism* and *The Better Boundaries Workbook*

"*Divorcing Your Narcissist* captures the terror and chaos of what this unique process is like, but Tracy's writing and expertise does it in a way that is filled with humor and authenticity. This is a must-have manual for anyone going through this experience. It was an honor to be included as a contributor."

~ **Alisa Stamps**, MSS, LCSW, founder of "Shattering the Mirror: Support and Recovery Group for Adult Children of Narcissists" and author of *The Gaslighting Recovery Journal*

"*Divorcing Your Narcissist* is a must-read book for anyone leaving a toxic relationship. Tracy A. Malone, an experienced surTHRIVER herself, has compiled a comprehensive guide to what you can expect and how to effectively plan when you know it's time to reclaim your life. This resource is a game changer as you navigate ending the relationship with your narcissist."

~ **Dr. Marni Hill Foderaro**, SurTHRIVER, Speaker and author of the award-winning Spiritual fiction, *God Came To My Garage Sale*

"Tracy is a warrior for victims of emotional abuse! *Divorcing Your Narcissist* should be in everyone's tool kit when going through the horror of ending a relationship with a narc. Tracy has brought together an amazing team of experts and knows, not only from her own experience but from the experience of thousands of victims, what it takes to survive divorcing a narcissist."

    ~ **Anne Blythe**, Founder & CEO of btr.org and host of the *Betrayal Trauma Recovery* podcast

"I first met Tracy when she was a guest on my podcast. We hit it off immediately because we both have the same approach to dealing with narcissists and divorce. This book should be your go-to divorce resource when you are looking for direction and guidance for your divorce. She takes you by the hand and walks you through everything you need to know about divorcing a narcissist. Make this book a mandatory member of your divorce team and you won't regret it."

    ~ **Jason Levoy**, J.D. a/k/a The Divorce Resource Guy, is a former divorce attorney and host of The Divorce Resource Guy Podcast

"Tracy Malone has masterfully and meticulously given you the beginning, middle, and appropriate end to a story that was never about love: Life With A Narcissist! Practical advice to help you see patterns and traits clearly, make wise decisions, and craft a detailed, successful exit plan. Refer to it often for courage and clarity, especially in those moments when you start second-guessing yourself. You can do this, and Tracy shows you how!"

    ~ **Rhoberta Shaler**, PhD, Relationship Crisis Consultant, Author, Host of Save Your Sanity: Help for Toxic Relationships podcast…and, SurThriver!

"This is an important guide for navigating the loaded minefield of divorce from a narcissist. What you don't know *can* and *will* hurt you and your children… forever. Read this book first!"

    ~ **Joyce Short**, author of "Your Consent – The Key to Conquering Sexual Assault," TEDx Talk Presenter, and Founder of the Consent Awareness Network (CAN)

ENDORSEMENTS

"Finally: a handbook for divorcing a narcissist! Tracy Malone has covered every aspect of this unbelievably difficult topic and compiled them all to create a veritable bible for victims of narcissistic abuse. This book will answer all of your questions *and* many that you didn't even know you had."

~ **Victoria McCooey,** Transformation Coach, Speaker, Creator of The Reclaim Your Power System™

DEDICATION

Thank you, God, for guiding me through the traumas of my past and showing me how, through you, to turn those lessons into a vessel to help others. At the beginning of this horrible journey, I asked you why this was happening. I now know that you had a bigger plan; I am here to help those you send to me.

Book team

Karla Crawford, editor – Karla, thank you for all of your hard work and dedication to package my run on sentences and scattered thoughts into an amazing resource for people going through a divorce with a narcissist. You are a talented editor and I will forever be grateful.

Jasmine Mann, illustrator – Jasmine, your drawings have made my book come to life! You are my kind of surTHRIVER and I thank you for putting your heart and soul on display. You have so much to offer this world; I am honored to feature your artwork.

Erica Gamet, cover and layout designer – Erica, my sweet talented friend who has always been there for me. Thank you for your beautiful cover design that perfectly captures how the covert hide their tricks. You have done such an amazing job on the layout!

Proofreaders – To all my proofreaders, thank you for your time and feedback.

Audiobook team – A very special thank you goes out to my friend, Jonathan McFadden from Prodigy Talent Training School in Florida for donating the perfect Audible book reader. Your support for the cause and generous contribution will help many people heal. Learn more about this wonderful organization by visiting the website at http://prodigytalenttraining.com.

Book contributors

I have been blessed to pull together so many talented experts who I am also proud to call friends. Thank you for sharing your knowledge about divorcing a narcissist for my readers. Together we can change the world!

Donna Andersen, Susan Ball, Anne Blythe, Bree Bonchay, Karen Covy, Lindsey Ellison, Randi Fine, Susan Guthrie, Reverend Sheri Heller, Jason Levoy, Rosemary Lombardy, Amy Marlow-MaCoy, Sharon Martin, Victoria McCooey, Jessica McCrea, Suzanna Quintana, Patricia Riley, Duane Robert, Rhoberta Shaler, Joyce Short, Debi Silber, Babita Spinelli, Alisa Stamps, Tina Swithin, Debbie Tudor, and Rebecca Zung

Facebook team

In June 2016, I started a Facebook group with a goal to bring together those in need of validation and community. I never dreamed that this part of my journey would bring the most compassionate loving souls I have ever known into my life. These international men and women have put aside their free time every day to moderate the conversations, accept new members, and put out fires. Under the management of Marie Colvin, who despite her own challenges was always there to help support the team and create a safe place for survivors, our team has built a community that we are all proud of. Without you, the group would not survive. A simple thank you cannot adequately express my gratitude.

Thank you, Marie Colvin, Donna Maree, David Emrich, Melisa St John, Renee Cisneros, and Carolyn, as well as the numerous past admins who have volunteered their time to our group for the last five years. I appreciate every one of you!

DEDICATION

Support group members

A special shout out to the ladies in my online support groups who are courageous enough to search for answers and for your continued passion to learn to heal. Thank you for sharing your journeys along with your willingness to allow your lessons to help other surTHRIV-ERs get their wings and find their voices. You each have left imprints on my heart and your friendships mean the world to me. I can't thank you enough for putting your trust in me. I look forward to the day when we can meet face-to-face.

To the men and women in my in-person support groups who were the first people I learned from: your stories showed me the struggles we all share and led me to find answers that have helped so many. Thank you for showing up and pushing me to learn more. Because of you, I am able to offer guidance to help others heal. Thank you, John, for adapting the group during COVID and taking on the leadership role.

Subscribers

Thank you to all of the millions of people who have supported my YouTube channel and listened to my Podcasts. When I began this journey, I always said that if my crazy stories could help even one person, it would all be worth it. I never imagined my reach could extend all over the world. I am humbled and grateful. Thank you.

Friends and family

Thank you to my dear friends for loving me unconditionally and understanding when I couldn't be present because I was knee deep in this book. Your support, encouragement, and patience mean the world to me. I love you all.

To my son, Chris: you make me the proudest mom. You have grown into a wonderful young man. If it weren't for your encouragement to make my first YouTube video, I am not sure I would have landed where I am today. Thank you for your support and love.

To my sister, Laureen, who struggled with a life-long battle with addiction and had finally broken free only to be taken from us in April 2020. In one of your last texts, you told me how proud you were of me for writing this book; I am proud of you for slaying your demons in time for us to reconnect and be sisters again. I will miss you forever.

My copyright attorneys

Thank you to Chester Rothstein and Olivia Harris from Amster Rothstein & Ebenstein in NYC for teaching me one more very valuable lesson: the lesson to fight for my rights to use my term surTHRIVER and for proving to me that the law *can* be on my side. Thank you for supporting surTHRIVERS everywhere.

My abusers

When you took advantage of my kind heart, you thought you could break me because I was weak for having emotions. I dedicate this book to you. Had you not been so evil and heartless, I would have never hit bottom and discovered the deep wounds I needed to heal. Because of your abuse, I will never be the same and that has changed my life for the better. I never want to be that girl who accepts gaslighting, abuse, or anything less than I deserve. Sorry to disappoint you, but the poison didn't work! I am thriving despite your attempts to ruin me.

TABLE OF CONTENTS

"Divorce is a game to narcissists." – **Tracy A. Malone**

INTRODUCTION

To a narcissist, divorce is a game of psychological warfare. To win, history must be rewritten, making them into both the victim and the hero. Conspiracies against you will escalate into false allegations and accusations that include everything they themselves have been doing all along. These claims will generate confusion because they will seem to be an alternate reality relative to what your life together was really like. Divorce literally undoes everything you thought to be true.

Almost eight years ago, I divorced my husband in a battle called by the judge, "the most tortured case in our town's history." Blindsided, smeared, falsely accused, and attacked in hearing after hearing, I was left broken and weak. It wasn't until I was in a relationship three years later that I learned about narcissistic personality disorder and narcissistic abuse. It was then the pieces fell into place, unfolding answers to every relationship I had ever had, from my family to my marriage, and even some friends throughout various stages of my life.

My journey to recovery left me with a passion to educate the world. I couldn't believe that I had never recognized or known about controlling behaviors, gaslighting, or passive-aggressive personalities. I now realize that my mother was narcissistic, which explains why I never learned boundaries. Ghosting was our family ideology and triangulation tactics were used extensively to divide all of my sisters.

Being raised in an environment where love was intermittent and conditional, I was destined to attract others who would abuse me.

Divorcing someone with a narcissistic personality disorder, or any cluster B disorder[1], is worse than you could ever imagine. There will be an advanced level of vindictiveness that you have never seen before. The false allegations will come at you in rapid fire, most holding no more than a twisted speck of truth. The person you were married to is gone, morphed into an evil stranger ready for war. They will aim missiles at your heart that first throw you into a downward spiral and then attack everything you hold dear utilizing isolation, character assassination, lies, and stonewalling. The realization that they want to destroy you is shocking to your soul.

A narcissist will leave the gate weaving elaborate tales which will immediately send you into defense mode. This is not only hard to recover from, but it also makes it more difficult to expose the truth about them. To defend against these attacks, it will be necessary to find the smoking gun that will uncover their deception. Evidence will be your savior; your job will be to gather all the materials necessary to prove your veracity.

Throughout the process, anticipate the repeated false claims to be executed with a jarring lack of empathy and zero regard for how they will affect you. Expect diversion tactics, unfounded declarations, and downright hurtful behavior to knock you off balance so that even your self-preservation becomes unstable. At no other time will you see such a huge swing in emotional detachment away from you. There is no concern for you and, in their mind, they're entitled to treat you as if you were a stranger and an enemy. And that is exactly what will happen.

The primary goal is to win; the win for them means you lose everything: financially, emotionally, socially, and parentally. Elaborate conspiracy theories will be perpetrated that detail the years of abuse they suffered at your hands: the bipolar, alcoholic, cheating, thieving,

---

1   Characterized by dramatic, overly emotional or unpredictable thinking or behavior. They include antisocial personality disorder, borderline personality disorder, histrionic personality disorder and narcissistic personality disorder.

child abuser. When asked why they had never spoken up, the fear card will be played with claims that your controlling nature made them feel unsafe. Linguistic masters, they will rarely be without the perfect response.

The need to contend with constant stonewalling and unreasonable demands will shine a spotlight on the unfairness of the family court system. Your narcissist will procrastinate during the discovery phase, hide assets, reduce their income, delay the courts, and then file endless motions to find you in contempt for any reason under the sun, such as shining the spotlight on one incomplete inconsequential detail that you submitted, all which increase your legal bill at an alarmingly accelerated rate. The glaring injustice is that they never appear to be held accountable for anything while you and your team chase your tails in response to a myriad of insignificant legal requests. Be prepared for the dishonesty you will encounter because everything about the process will feel that way. Inherent defects in their moral conscience foster their desire to promote your outrage at the iniquity – it is all part of the plan.

Divorce comes easily for a narcissist because they have no emotions to slow them down. They aren't afraid of court because they feed off of watching how they can still manipulate you. A courtroom is their stage and they relish the control, attention, and drama that will ensue. They have a hefty disdain for rules so none of the standard trepidation or anxiety normally associated with a life-altering event such as this will faze them in the least. In fact, most victims report that their narcissistic spouse appears to have fun as they turn on the charm in the courtroom and watch your attempts to steer clear of the daggers they're throwing.

The swirling of emotions often mixed with the dodging of the swift blows and lies can create a downward spiral into anxiety, fear, and depression. Your life may feel like it is falling apart; emotional irregularity is known to create a tornado that can be overwhelming. All the while, you are grieving the illusion of who you thought they were and what your entire life was really about. You may not know where you are going to land, but it doesn't mean all is lost. You are learning things at a rapid pace while juggling a plethora of issues. Keep your eye on the prize, your backbone rigid, and stoically brush off the emotional turmoil.

People with narcissistic personality disorder (NPD) have no moral compass or moral consistency in addition to an astounding lack of empathy. Reeling from the inhumane treatment they experience, victims are often heard asking, "Who is this person??" You will find yourself replaying the relationship over and over in your head and wonder "What could I have done differently?" There are no words to explain the lengths to which a NPD spouse will go to destroy their partner in divorce, but many who have been unfortunate enough to experience this type of abuse will at some point say, *"You can't make this shit up."* After three clients said this to me in one day, I knew this title would capture the essence I wanted to convey about the experience of divorcing a narcissist.

What if you could hear what others have gone through and the tricks that were pulled on them? Could you learn from their stories? With this in mind, I wrote this book as the CliffsNotes™ for divorce – sharing strategies utilized by narcissists throughout the process, as well as tips to help you avoid the foreseeable obstacles and protect your future.

Throughout my work, I have spoken with thousands of surTHRIVERs who have been where you may be now; all wished they had firsthand knowledge and a better understanding of what was to come, before being thrown to the wolves. Many of these surTHRIVERs contributed their stories to enable others to develop a solid strategic plan to outsmart their narcissistic partner in the courtroom. You will have the advantage of understanding events that have occurred to others and the best approaches to take in order to cope with the fear, threats, emotional abuse, gaslighting and, my favorite part, the hues of grey in a divorce decree, which you will find in Chapter 11. Without this foresight, ongoing abuse most often persists time after time.

Divorcing a narcissist is more than the marionette control they've exercised over you throughout your relationship; it is a contest where the winner takes all. To help you prepare for the journey, I've also gathered information from 26 experts in the field of narcissistic abuse: authors, psychologists, therapists, coaches, lawyers, mediators, and financial professionals, each sharing their top tips for surviving a divorce of this nature. All offer a varied perspective for navigating the flying debris, which will help you beat the narcissist at their own game.

Despite the generally scary prospect of what can happen during your divorce, my desire is to instill strength, not distress. I will teach you how to survive by explaining effective strategies for emotional resilience allowing you to triumph through these dark times. Our inherent survival subconscious will become our coping mechanism.

This book was written to enlighten and empower anyone going through a divorce with someone they suspect has a narcissistic personality disorder.

Ditch the conventional divorce wisdom: There's a saying that the only thing worse than being married to a narcissist is divorcing one. This is because divorce threatens to diminish the narcissist's sense of control and carefully crafted public persona, sending the narcissist's core personality traits - lack of empathy, entitlement, interpersonal exploitation - into overdrive as he or she tries to maintain their power over you and manage their public impression. It doesn't matter how much history you have, who initiated the divorce, or if the narcissist is already engaged to the new love of his or her life, the narcissist is *in it to win it*, and that means all conventional divorce wisdom does not apply. Expecting an atmosphere of compromise, decency, and civility will only cause you more pain and disappointment and can put you at a huge disadvantage tactically. Since your divorce is likely to be less conscious uncoupling and more *War of The Roses*, you must ditch the conventional divorce wisdom and any expectation of fair play. Instead, develop strategies that will not only protect you but also help prepare you mentally and emotionally for the long haul.

Bree Bonchay, author, psychotherapist, founder of World Narcissistic Abuse Awareness Day

Chapter 1

WHAT TO EXPECT WHEN YOU'RE DIVORCING

Facing the truth: you are a victim

The first time you admit the words out loud – you believe that you might be married to someone who is abusing you – it hurts almost as much as the real pain you have experienced living with it day in and day out. Arriving at the conclusion that your spouse has used gaslighting and manipulation tactics on you is hard enough to wrap your head around, but telling someone else will release tears and a new flood of emotions. For me, the realization that his actions were carefully orchestrated to trap me like a spider in a web left me feeling betrayed. The shame that I had done something wrong created doubt and spurred the "if I didn't…" and "if only I had…" thoughts which took over my mind. Since narcissists wobble between the role of victim and tormentor, the vacillation between the two can cause cognitive dissonance[2] to their victims. This is the odd thing about being

---

2   The state of having inconsistent thoughts, beliefs, or attitudes, especially as relating to behavioral decisions and attitude change.

a victim of narcissistic abuse: even though you are the one abused, it is you who feels the guilt and shame. To most, it's clear that the guilt should be owned by the abusive spouse, but that is not possible when that someone has NPD (Narcissistic Personality Disorder). They blame everyone for their failures except themselves.

Until I had a better understanding of what narcissistic abuse was, I could not admit that I was a victim. Once armed with the words and behaviors, it was all too clear. Eventually I was able to say the words: I was a victim of narcissistic abuse.

With the emerging awareness that the life you had been living was a lie, you are granted the right to claim the victim card. The different types of narcissists will soon be explained; for you, the abuse may have been obvious all along and your life was a daily dose of hell. Those of us entangled with covert narcissists have a different story. Expect to read things in this book that don't sound anything like your narcissistic spouse; others will be spot on and identical to the abuse you've suffered. Nevertheless, we are all victims and the journey to safety will be the greatest challenge of our lives. I promise you will get through it. Remember the "for better or for worse" part of your marriage vows? This is the "worse" part so hang on.

When you are a victim of abuse, your self-esteem and sense of shame can be overwhelming because the abuser's judgment still echoes in your mind. You feel damaged and unworthy, and often hopeless that you will never be able to find your way out of this emotionally abusive relationship. You believe the narrative that it was your fault and that you are bad, so you hide your shameful story, but the absence of hunger doesn't mean you are not starving. In this stage, you may feel fearful but learning strategies to overcome and let go of that fear is crucial. You may have lost trust in yourself and others, unsure if you will ever be able to find it again, but understand that you were deliberately targeted for your kindness and loving traits by someone who needed to feed off your generous heart. You were, in fact, a victim but you can be whole again.

There is only one way out of the victim stage and that is to fight like hell to defend your truth once and for all. Move through this as quickly as you can by educating yourself. When you learn the vocabulary that explains what has been happening, you will be able to shed that guilt and begin the healing process.

After suffering narcissistic abuse for years in my marriage, I wondered if I was the narcissist. I asked myself, "How do I know I'm not the narcissist?" One day, I decided to write down all the classic behaviors of a narcissist:

> Lying
> Lusting
> Pornography use
> Masturbation
> Cheating emotionally and physically
> Gaslighting
> Explosive anger
> Property damage – punching walls, throwing things
> Physical intimidation – yelling and spitting right in your face
> Hiding
> Being secretive
> Obsessing about perceived slights

Then I asked myself, "Do I engage in these behaviors?" I answered them completely honestly because I really wanted to know. The answers to my questions revealed a pattern.

I don't use porn. I don't cheat. I don't lie. I don't gaslight. I don't damage property. I don't hide things. I don't do any of these things! I am in touch with reality and I am a self-aware person. I care about bettering myself, finding peace, and forming lasting, fulfilling, and genuine relationships.

Anne Blythe, Founder & CEO of btr.org and producer and host of the *Betrayal Trauma Recovery* podcast

Discovering the detective inside you

These days, it is common to learn about narcissistic personality disorder by googling compelling articles and binging videos all night long. At this point, the obsession to find as much information as possible with what I have fondly dubbed "YouTube University" will burn brightly inside you. I remember when I first heard the stories of others and felt like they had been looking into the window of my life. It was both comforting and scary, all in the same moment. My need to understand kept me searching for more relatable stories. I quickly saw the reality of my life given voice by the strangers on my computer screen.

A part of yourself will awaken that you never knew existed. You will become a detective with one mission: to find the dirt on your spouse. Your future will depend on taking an active role to compile crucial evidence to bring to court. The type of information you will be faced with might be painful and probably shocking, but the inner fortitude you've always had will come shining through for you when you need it the most.

It can be complicated to know when you should stop gathering and begin converting your new found knowledge into an action plan. Learn to recognize when you have enough confirmation of the behaviors you have witnessed and set the healing in motion. If your life becomes consumed with videos and articles rather than rest, more harm than good will be done. Now is the time to tap into your pool of strength which will enable you to take the steps necessary to fight the upcoming battle.

Later in your recovery, your inner detective will be needed again. Then, the information you seek will be how to heal the traumas caused by betrayal, fear, abandonment, and the fight itself. In the next few chapters, I will show you the tools necessary to hone your sleuthing skills.

A warrior awaits your call

On your wedding day, never in your wildest dreams did you imagine that the best day of your life could end in divorce. You probably never thought of this person as anything other than perfect. When a divorce is imminent with a narcissist, no matter who instigated it, a narcissistic injury has been created. In their mind, you have gone from being on the highest pedestal to lower than their worst enemy. Their black and white thoughts and actions will be shocking because their self-esteem is incapable of self-repair. You will soon learn that this is not just another divorce – put away all hope that it will be civil.

You must become a warrior, ready to fight a clean battle, despite their attempts to drag you and your reputation through the gutter. A narcissist cornered can become unmoored from reality itself. The situation can get ugly fast but if you have children, you must protect them and their futures at all costs. Never stoop to the narcs level of trickery; keep your head down and do everything in your power to assist your legal team to prepare your case with all of the provable evidence that you can muster. Resist the urge to go low – trust the truth and your team. Don't get me wrong: I would never insinuate that you should roll over and die. Come to the table prepared with proof and evidence and respond to the false accusations with that documentation. Bring your warrior strength to court and call on that super power through each hearing, trial, and challenge. A warrior is honorable, brave, and willing to stand up for the truth by producing testimony that will trump any of the lies that are told. Through it all, try not to let them get to you because that is the nutrition they crave. Just prove them wrong. This is the part of you that will not allow the pain of this chapter in your life to define you.

Seeking the ultimate peace

When coming out of a divorce with a narcissist, we deserve a medal of honor for the pain endured. The tactics deployed will be unlike anything you could have imagined and this not from a stranger but rather someone to whom you gave your heart and soul. You have felt a gamut of emotions throughout the process – swinging from the initial feeling of not wanting to divorce to feeling disdain and maybe even hatred for your former spouse.

The mediation and courtroom battles may have made you feel like you would never recover. The costs associated certainly left an unexpected hole in your financial future and rebuilding appears to be an impossible task. Friendships were challenged and many possibly failed. The ensuing damage has caused trust issues which prompt you to wonder if you will ever feel safe or whole again. How can you find peace in the end? By propelling your life forward, the light will be visible at the end of the tunnel and inner peace can be attained.

You can and will find joy again once the end is in sight. No matter what material possessions you may lose along the way, always remember the price of freedom and balance it out with the benefits of peace. Next, do the work to determine what made you vulnerable by developing a better understanding of how to heal the wounds that made you a good supply in the first place. When you come through the other side, take things slowly until you are able to successfully spot another narcissist. Learn the tools to set healthy boundaries and test someone's intentions before you get involved. Relationships must always be 50/50. If you find you are giving more than you receive, reevaluate, and don't ever let yourself get stuck again.

The ultimate prize is to live a life filled with happiness and harmony. Begin by finding gratitude that the fight is over – the first step towards your new, uncomplicated, life.

What is a SurTHRIVER?

When I began my recovery journey, I never expected to find that the traumas created by the narcissistic people in my life had been there all along. Being raised by a narcissistic alcoholic mother certainly set me up to blindly entrust my future partners without ever considering their treatment to be hazardous to my mental health. I hated the word victim. Despite the heinous things that brought me to my awakening, I didn't want to live forever as a victim.

> **Victim** – According to the Merriam-Webster Internet dictionary, victim is defined as "one that is injured, destroyed, or sacrificed under any of various conditions; one that is subjected to oppression, hardship, or mistreatment." When you are a victim of a crime, people understand it wasn't your fault. You were targeted and a crime occurred. When you are the victim of abuse, the world often blames you for staying. Not having boundaries, or even being codependent, somehow makes it your fault. This causes you to feel alone, unheard,

and often lost.

I needed to be a survivor and let go of the self-labeled victim role.

Survivor – Merriam-Webster Internet dictionary defines survivor as one "to continue to function or prosper." A survivor pushes through something difficult in order to come out the other side better than before. The struggle to let go of the victim mentality is made easier with the validation of what occurred and the addition of narcissistic abuse as a new term in your vocabulary. Hope begins to peak out with the realization that you were wounded by the relationship and then seek help to learn healthy patterns and heal. Face the emotional pain instead of curling up in bed or letting the anxiety cripple you and steal another day away. You will learn that trusting yourself is the forefront of recovery. In the future, you will be more cautious to freely give trust away again without someone proving they are trustworthy with thousands of trustworthy moments. The fear of sharing the story lessens when the story starts to lose its grip on you; grieve the lost relationship and commit to doing the work so you can move on. You will then finally know and believe that you deserve to be happy.

I have had the honor to meet people who were victims and survived, but went one step further to become a surTHRIVER. I've learned to give back, to teach, and help others avoid this type of abuse. I, too, became a surTHRIVER.

SurTHRIVER – You have been through hell and back. You are a proud warrior who fought to find yourself and heal from the fallout of living in a toxic, abusive situation. You live in the present by honoring yourself, promoting healthy boundaries and self-care. Your skills have not only been honed to spot dangerous people, but you have had and passed additional tests. You now recognize and have the courage to walk away, never willing to tolerate bad behavior again, no matter how good they appear on the surface. It is the ultimate self-trust knowing that you will identify and stand up to abusive people. Finding gratitude in everything brings calm, a oneness with the universe that empowers you daily. Your heart resolves not to hide behind the trauma story enabling you to proudly stand up in support of others who are just beginning their journey. Fearlessness replaces fear. The comprehension that you had the power all along to deactivate that fear is inspiring. You have gone from hopeless to hopeful to having faith in yourself – you see the world of possibilities waiting for you ahead. The selfless gift of giving back to others makes you a surTHRIVER.

Emotional resilience begins by mapping out your fears

You have picked up this book because you want more information about divorcing a narcissist and what you can expect. The risks of what could happen will be understandably frightening. As you read through the stories of others, rather than dwelling on the fact that some of these are actual risks, use the information as preparation and protection. It's important to consider all angles so if any of these tricks are utilized, you will not be blindsided. There is control and fortitude in being prepared.

There are real fears that come into play as you face divorce. Even if the only option you face is scary, you still must learn to manage your fears to survive the process. The unknown is powerful and can be incapacitating, especially in a divorce battle with a narcissist. Your spouse knows your fears, your strengths, and what you will defend with all of your heart. They also know the truth and will do whatever it takes to twist it just so they can win. Winning is everything to a narcissist.

Exercise #1: Planning for the fear

To help you understand your trepidation, you must first identify your fears and then plan a course of action to stand up and defeat them. Grab a piece of paper and write the answers to these questions:
   » What are your biggest fears about this divorce?
   » What can you expect to happen?

» What fears keep you awake at night?
» What would happen if any of these fears came true?
» Is there any proof that these could happen?
» What can you do to minimize the possibility of any of them happening?

Our rational mind knows that we must stop thinking about the drama story, yet we don't seem to have the emotional resilience to stop our imagination from serving us up another anxiety cocktail. What can we do?

If you can prepare your reaction to these possibilities in advance, it will be much easier to develop a formula that will ease the fear. Not having a blueprint to follow is what provokes panic and misery.

Think about and plan each scenario:
» best-case
» middle of the road
» worst-case

What might your reaction be to each one of these scenarios? Planning for multiple options eliminates the unknown variable from the equation. It removes the fear and instead instills confidence that you know how to handle the situation.

It has been said that the best offense is a good defense. If you're able to avoid being blindsided, you can retain a small advantage in the courtroom. Even if your ex surprises you with a scenario you hadn't specifically prepared for, you will have thought through enough situations that you can adapt on the fly and modify your reactions accordingly. You will not be the deer in headlights that they're hoping for. You have a plan and your power is indestructible.

Be organized from jump street: The more organized you are throughout the divorce process, the less overwhelmed you will feel when things happen. Divorce is a roller coaster ride, so get your ducks in a row and the bumps won't feel as bad when you go over them.

Jason Levoy, former divorce attorney turned coach, creator of DivorceU

The secret to understanding fear is to understand the meaning you put behind it. Everyone has mental recordings of things that have happened previously that play on a loop in their heads. These tend to replay automatically when faced with fearful predicaments. We need to face the concerns head on and look at the evidence to understand that the situation has other possible outcomes.

When you begin to learn this dynamic practice, it may seem impossible to believe that it will work. It's okay to feel uncomfortable initially. You are learning a skill that will ultimately be your defense from the fear of worst-case scenarios and catastrophizing yourself into a deep depression. As with anything, practice makes perfect so be sure to put in the time and effort. It will pay off in the end.

If you get nervous, that's okay too. It's natural, but having a plan will make things easier. Act strong in front of them even if you don't feel that you are. Don't give them a reason to call you crazy, and never let the weakness you may feel show. They will feed off of your reaction so be careful to give them nothing or they win. Narcissists learn from your reactions. If they find a crack that makes you angry, like an elephant, they will remember and pull that card every time. Only you can break the cycle by presenting a strong stance that says, "I will no longer allow you to hijack my emotions."

The truth is a narcissist's nemesis. They silence you with fear to take away your capability to show who they really are. While they demand loyalty that you keep their secrets, they will do everything in their power to destroy you. Your silence is expected and intimidation tactics will be used to ensure that you do not expose them.

The emotional trauma incurred from divorcing a narcissist is not easy to explain. Chances are good that your friends and family will not understand it. Even doctors are only able to treat the symptoms, not the actual cause. It is possibly rooted in the fear of the unknown. Do you have anxiety? Here, take a pill. Can't sleep? Try two of these before bed. Depressed? Take an antidepressant. I am not saying that in many cases medication won't help balance you, because it can. Don't let the stigma of taking pharmaceuticals to help you through a rough time cause you more pain. You will not need them forever;

these medicines can stabilize your body and mind so you can keep moving forward every day. There are also many natural herbs and remedies available to help level out your system. St John's Wort, Ginseng and Chamomile are all good for depression. If you struggle with traditional medicines, talk to a holistic doctor who specializes in natural cures. Health food stores, drug stores, and online research are all viable alternatives to look for advice. Also, never discount the benefits of exercise, a healthy diet, sunshine, and plenty of sleep and fresh air. If you're in serious need, don't just poke around. Ask a specialist what are the best options for your symptoms.

The divorce – what you can expect

When divorcing a narcissistic partner, victims are filled with mixed feelings vacillating between sadness and loss, anger and betrayal, and rejection and abandonment. Divorce, by nature, is the loss of a dream, a promise, security, and the future you had planned for your family. When couples come to the consensual decision to divorce, time is allowed to process and grieve yesterday and plan for a new tomorrow. Divorcing a narcissistic spouse, however, doesn't look like a "normal" divorce where communication about the kids and assets gets discussed with a settlement decided upon and implemented amicably.

Gaslighting, stonewalling, lying, sabotage, smearing, stealing, hiding money and assets, false allegations that distort the reality of truth, projection, using kids as a weapon, parental alienation, stalking, financial abuse, physical abuse, emotional abuse, using the court system to legally abuse you, and ignoring your boundaries are some of the exhausting offenses you may experience throughout your divorce with your narcissist.

Narcissistic people see others with black-and-white thinking, commonly called "splitting." There is no grey area. This is very confusing because it feels like the narcissist changes their personality overnight – one day you are part of a happy family but you might wake up in a wildly unstable relationship with the devil incarnate the next.

Black-and-white thinking is a defense mechanism seen in people with personality disorders such as NPD or BPD (Borderline Personality Disorder). No matter who decided on the divorce, the rejection becomes a narcissistic injury and splitting is activated. You are either all good or all bad; crossing the line in many cases from bad to believing you are pure evil. Narcissists are ego hemophiliacs and they must defend themselves against the evil (you) at all costs.

This is the first place where victims get confused and wonder:

» Who is this person? I don't know them.
» How can they do this to me? They know me better than anyone in the world.

Splitting becomes a justification in the narcissist's mind to be able to utilize any and all methods to win. Most victims erroneously think that since you were married, they will treat you with respect. This never crosses their mind – your new status as the evil one drives every decision they make from this point forward. The intention is to confound and build their victim role, exerting additional control over you creating the need for you to defend your best qualities.

This manifests with you as the evil one, designed to create a smokescreen shielding their faults. Think of it as a distraction to knock the wind out of your self-protection sails causing trauma so that you don't see the other things they are doing right in front of your face.

Know your truth! Don't be affected by the false allegations. It's never easy to not take hurtful things personally. Learn survival skills to regulate your emotions. Find a good coach or therapist who understands the hazards of divorcing a narcissist to assist you with new coping capabilities.

Narcissists need to win at all costs which, in divorce, means the winner takes all. If they win, you lose, and that is their primary goal. All too often, victims voluntarily walk away from everything just to be granted freedom. By all rights you would think, "If I walk away, they will disappear, and I will start over." Sadly, the need to win drives the narcissist to come back to kick you again and again. Why won't they just go away? Victims often equate this behavior to that of a rabid dog. Build up your defenses, construct a solid team around you, and buckle down for the fight of your life.

Brace yourself for punishment: A divorce is the ultimate statement of defiance for a narcissist. You are denying the narcissist their supply and dismantling the dominance-submission dynamic they feed off of. Consequently, you will be punished in a big way. Generally, this initially takes the form of a smear campaign. Preparing yourself for the advent of a monumental smear campaign is a critical step in surviving a divorce from a narcissist. Surrounding yourself with a network of support, inclusive of friends, family, legal team and therapist is critical to bracing this storm. They may advise you to execute an exit strategy and a contingency plan if the narcissist's tactics escalate to dangerous proportions. It may be necessary to inform work colleagues of your plans to divorce as the narcissist may attempt to sabotage you in your work environment. With protective measures in place, you will have a greater ability to take measures to change your phone number, residence and social media info. It will offset the paralysis that the narcissist's punishment might induce. Be prepared!

Rev. Sheri Heller, author, Licensed Clinical Social Worker

Chapter 2

GETTING STARTED AND MAKING DECISIONS

Divorce with a narcissist is complicated which will oblige us to remember that they have varied attack strategies that focus on exploiting our fears and vulnerabilities. The first barrage of attacks will seem puzzling and insurmountable. They appear to make up their own rules with different standards set just for them.

Consider running a marathon through a minefield – that is how many have equated their experience. You will need to constantly maneuver around obstacles that get placed in your path with each calculated move designed to bring a renewed explosion of anxiety and legal damages. There will be a never-ending stream of stumbling blocks but stay strong and hold on because the game has officially begun.

> *"My divorce from a narcissist was a combination of the movies*
> *Fatal Attraction + Psycho + Twilight Zone, tossed into a*
> *tornado." – **SurTHRIVER***

Power and strength: the Discarded vs the Discarder

The decision to leave your spouse is never easy. The very idea of getting away can be hard to conceive because with this type of abuse, you can lose your confidence and strength. Most victims say that they feel like they lost themselves somewhere along the way. It also may seem impossible to move forward with the decision to get a divorce simply because you are unable to see the possibilities of a new life beyond the fear of the unknown.

In my research and interviews with thousands of people divorcing a narcissist, I've encountered those planning to leave, some currently enmeshed in the process, as well as survivors who have made it through successfully to the other side. There is always a common thread: this may be the most difficult thing they have ever faced. It makes no difference whether you are the discarded or the discarder; the gloves must come off and the battle is brutal.

When you are the blindsided "Discarded"

The non-NPD individual is often the "Discarded" – the one who has stood by their spouse through infidelity, emotional abuse, and living the role as the one who took care of everything. Many victims stay for the children or for financial reasons. Perhaps they were the stay-at-home parent, or not allowed to work, and have no financial protection or resources available to start anew. It's difficult to watch your life go from a Hallmark to a Lifetime movie; the process is bewildering and emotionally draining. Most victims have been isolated from their support system due to carefully implanted narratives designed to smear everything they hold dear leaving them helpless to fight. This tactic is deployed to confuse the victim with no one to talk to, further injuring and alienating them. Due to the amount of chaos and drama, the victim struggles to explain what they have lived through to friends and family even though most are unable to find the words to elucidate properly to begin with. Because of this uncertainty, they simply do not possess the emotional calm and often look like the crazy one.

The hardest way to find out a spouse wants to divorce is to be blindsided and completely unprepared. Being thrust into dealing with the shock, emotional abandonment, rejection, and usually some form of betrayal is often compounded by endless meetings with lawyers, all at the same time. It's overwhelming due to the lack of an adjustment period. Victims of this type of abandonment end up being treated for depression, PTSD, anxiety, and encounter many sleepless nights. An additional layer of pain comes into play through the eyes of the discarded – they did everything in the marriage, always hanging in for one reason or another and all for nothing! My husband asked for our divorce over the phone with no preamble or discussion, so this really hits home for me.

The blindsiding strategy is common with NPDs because they get bored easily, always on the hunt for a new supply. When they see a patch of greener grass, they will just pick up and leave. They are always seeking the constant adoration that new love brings; you have been uprooted and replaced with an upgrade and they have no qualms telling you so. This is a perfect example of entitlement and lack of empathy, both NPD characteristics on the DSM-5's list. The DSM-5, The Diagnostic and Statistical Manual of Mental Disorders, is the official manual for the assessment and diagnosis of mental disorders. In the NPD mind, they are permitted to leave without conversation or any effort because they've been processing it for quite some time. They don't have any real feelings for the marriage, regardless of its length. For many victims, this is the first time they clearly see the absence of compassion in such a grand way, often leading them to ask, "Who is this person?"

This paradigm of marriage dismissal is often accompanied by clearing out the bank accounts, hiding assets, the destruction of records, and character assassination. When these methods are instigated, rest assured that they were calculated to destroy their spouse emotionally, financially and spiritually. It doesn't seem fair, and it's not, but don't get stuck in the inequity of it all. Make an appointment with a lawyer and a coach or counselor as soon as you can to help you legally and emotionally navigate the unfamiliar territory.

Eleven reasons people stay; how many sound familiar to you?
  » you had no financial means to get free or support yourself
  » religious beliefs
  » the kids were under 18
  » you believed this was just them and they could be
    nice sometimes
  » for better or worse – honoring the sacred marriage vows
  » you were the stay-at-home parent and your spouse prom-
    ised that you would get nothing if you left
  » even though you knew you didn't have a perfect marriage,
    the unknown was terrifying
  » starting over on you own would be too hard
  » you got used to crumbs and it was enough
  » you had a good lifestyle and had learned to manage the
    emotional trauma
  » despite knowing your spouse was cheating, you thought
    if you kept your end of the bargain, one day they would
    love you again

The discarded experiences shame, betrayal, abandonment, and confusion. You did everything for them; you gave them everything, or you
made all the money, or you ran the house, or you raised the kids. They
might have cheated and caused emotional or physical abuse, but you
stayed. You gave them one more chance, repeatedly, and you listened
to one more promise, often. You stood by your vows – for better or
worse. You didn't know the worst was going to be a daily cascade of
trauma. You endured all of this, so how could they leave you now?

**Get rid of any illusions that your soon-to-be-ex is going to be
"nice" to you or care about you during the divorce.** This is the place
where women get into the most trouble in divorcing a narcissist.
We want so badly to believe that our ex would never do anything
on purpose to hurt us. This illusion will cost you thousands upon
thousands of dollars in attorney fees because narcissists will do
absolutely anything and everything to hurt you -- especially if you
are the one who left them. Narcissists are punishers, and you can be

sure you'll be the target of their punishment.

Stop being nice. Another mistake that women often make in the divorce process is trying to be nice and considerate about everything. The problem is that while you are trying to be nice, a narcissist has no emotional attachment to your well-being and thus will have no problem taking everything he can from you. It's imperative (though I know extremely difficult) that you take emotion out of the divorce process and look at it like a business deal, one that your future relies on.

Navigate the divorce process as if your life depends on it...because it does. One of the mistakes I made in the divorce process was not demanding what I deserved regarding our finances. I had been a stay-at-home mom during our marriage, though I worked in all of our businesses that we created together. My ex could not have achieved any of our success without my valuable contribution, but at the time of the divorce I neglected to stand up for my part in the marriage that led to our financial success and therefore came out on the losing end. Demand that you receive your worth (another reason a good lawyer is important because they will demand this with you). Don't try to be equal and fair in the very beginning of the process because then you'll end up with far less than what is equal and fair. Expect a narcissist to go for it all in the hopes of getting the most out of it. Because of that, ask for everything and then you'll have a better chance of ending up with what is actually equal and fair.

Never lose sight of your future. The biggest mistake I made in my divorce and the mistake that cost me not only tens of thousands of dollars but left me in incredible debt afterward, was that I didn't look into my future and prepare for it. Especially if you are financially well-off in the marriage, plan your future during the divorce as though you were planning your retirement, meaning that it's crucial to figure out exactly what you'll come away with after it's final, where that will put you financially, and what your financial life will look like in the first few years (Will you be buying a new house? Will you move? Will you be able to support yourself? Are you changing jobs? Are your kids' education/savings/etc. taken care of?

Will you be going back to school?) If you don't have this foresight for yourself, you're taking a huge gamble that everything will work out for the best. And if you're divorcing a narcissist, that's a gamble you don't want to take.

Suzanna Quintana, author, narcissistic abuse coach

The graceful mutual divorce

You both knew it wasn't a great marriage but agreed to make it work until the kids were off to college or some other milestone. Marriage counseling and other talk therapy were attempted but the mutual decision has been made to get a divorce. You think in this type of split that an exit plan is not necessary. Be careful: NPDs use the guise of cooperation as a mask to trick you. It's natural to trust your spouse, and if they are being amicable, why wouldn't you trust them to do the right thing? The process begins by joining forces, automatically assuming that they have your best interest at heart, so you blindly accept offers without reviewing them for minefields. There is a need for caution, however, to make sure everything is properly secured for your future and that of your children. The specific preparations needed for every divorce will be addressed in Chapter 8.

Emotions run high through this type of divorce but it may be resolved so that you have no regrets. The hope is that you can remain friends or at least amicable co-parents.

When you plan the leaving, you are the secret "Discarder"

The non-NPD spouse may be the "discarder," divorcing by choice because they are finally done living like they are walking on eggshells. Emotionally worn down, several other failed attempts later, or things have escalated and there is risk, the victim may decide to get out secretively. This type of escape may be the victim's only hope. It takes grit and financial stability to be the discarder but they are ready to be free and make the choice to leave. Having tried to get away before but promises, charm, and the reemergence of the person they "actually married" can suck the victim back in and be convincing strategies to stay. They know this never lasts, however, so they have finally made up their mind to begin anew.

If this is where you are, I suggest you map out your exit. You are in control at this point and can make the transition smoother with planning. This type of departure takes a burst of courage and can be overwhelming. Many in this situation hate the feeling that they are being dishonest by tippy toeing around with the intention to leave. The lying feels so disingenuous to them that they fear losing even more of themselves. Take comfort in the fact that this is being done because you have no choice, you are not lying to hurt someone, and you are doing what you need to do to survive. People with NPD hate being rejected or abandoned, so if you are dumping them, this will cause a narcissistic injury that will promote you to enemy status.

Keep your plans secret: When you've finally had enough, do not announce your plans to file for divorce. The minute your soon-to-be ex knows that you're done, abuse will escalate, money will disappear, and the smear campaign will accelerate. Keep your behavior the same, while you gather what you need and make your plans.
Donna Andersen, author, founder of Lovefraud Continuing Education

The top two reasons secret planner discarders leave:
» After being abused for years, the strength and financial means are finally found to get away.
» There is no other option. They will never let you go if you don't escape this way.

Throughout the planning stage, emotions run high with fear and anxiety, mixed with worry of the unknown. Navigate this with determined blind faith and remember that despite not knowing how it will work out, there is a bright future ahead.

Quick first-step checklist

To remain emotionally stable, boundaries need to be established
Setting boundaries from the very beginning of the process will help the triggers and drama from making your life an emotional mess.

You will recognize the need for a boundary when their actions create unwanted feelings. Establish and define the limits (i.e., limiting the number of texts) and introduce the rules with consequences if they do not comply. Communicate and document everything in an email. Do not waver in implementing the repercussions because if you do, they quickly adapt and will ramp up the bad behavior. Always choose an outcome that you are comfortable with. If more than three texts a day or topics other than parenting will result in their getting blocked, be prepared to have a solution to the parenting needs. Blocking them could result in emergency hearings because you are obstructing their access to the children and the handover process. A better ramification might be that if they continue to over-text, your lawyer will go into court and ask for all communications to go through a parenting app, mediator, or in extreme situations, the lawyer. Tap into their concerns over the expense by adding that you will use their texting patterns to demand that all the expenses be their responsibility.

> *"Most say setting a boundary with a narcissist rarely works. I suggest that the act of trying to set a boundary, despite its possible risk of failure, is far better for your soul, than never trying at all. When you surrender and stop trying, they win. Never stop fighting for your rights." – **Tracy A. Malone**

Don't panic! The world as you knew it is changing and it is scary facing an unknown mysterious future. It's natural for your mind to go into panic mode. Resist it. Instead, harness that energy to empower yourself to get through the divorce, protect yourself and your children, and be brave.

Your life is going to be turned completely upside down as you navigate this process; it is important to commission the help of a counselor or coach. Divorcing a narcissist is never easy and their goal will be to take you down, so you will need extra support. Most survivors don't have the funds to pay for a counselor, especially mid-divorce. If you cannot afford a therapist or coach, explore local mental health services or domestic violence (DV) programs. There may be free or low-cost options available. Alternatively, if there is a university in your area, reach out to them. They often have master's level students, supervised by a licensed professional, who might offer free help. Find community by enrolling in a local support group. To find a group near you, visit my website[3]. We try to maintain an updated listing of groups all over the world that are either peer-run or monitored by a counselor or coach.

Clear away all the debris so you can have an unobstructed view: With support, see if you can begin to bring awareness to the ways in which the narcissist sets their trap. Begin to learn what tactics like gaslighting (psychological manipulation intended to plant doubt), and projection (when the narcissist takes the parts of self they despise, places them on to someone else, and then attacks them) are so you can be prepared. If you are able, try to view the situation from the outside-in, rather than the inside-out -- kind of like watching a tornado from a distance. That vantage point will hopefully offer you a much different perspective so that you can begin to place your boundaries where you want them to be and give space to yourself and your emotional reactions.

Begin to construct your boundaries and if needed, your safety-plan: Decide what is acceptable for you and what isn't in the way in which you receive treatment from the narcissist. Perhaps make a list of exact words that the narcissist uses so that you can refer to them whenever you need a reminder of what you are no longer willing to take. Begin to practice saying "no," which can be difficult and may require a "bracing for impact" sort of mindset. An important thing to keep in mind is that just because you are changing and growing as an individual, does not mean that the narcissist is also growing and changing. In fact, I would venture to say that most of the time they are incapable of this type of transformation. That is okay. We cannot control what others do, say, or how they react, but we can continue to remain in our authentic selves and learn how to "claim our land."

---

3   https://narcissistabusesupport.com/book-resources/

Be mindful of the role(s) of your children: Often narcissists will utilize triangulation and place the child in the role of messenger to be a go-between and perform "jobs" that no child should be responsible for—"Bobby, tell your father that I can't stand his tone of voice." You have the opportunity to not allow that to happen. You get to break that cycle and offer your child protection from this, which will go a long way in your relationship with them. They will know that they can trust you to do what is best and not allow anyone else to hurt them in that way. You are also teaching them how to put in place boundaries for themselves through your example. Most importantly, you are offering to them the idea that they are worthy and deserving of love and protection from a parent.

Alisa Stamps, Licensed Clinical Social Worker

Protecting your assets must start today

Becoming financially independent is the first step to moving forward on your own. Open a checking and saving account in your name and apply for a credit card. If you have not had credit in your own name before, use this time while you are still married to get your credit and financial history started. Use the card once a month and pay it off to boost a credit score presence. A jump-start in this process could be beneficial if you need credit later to rent an apartment or purchase new furniture. If you have expensive jewelry or other valuables, secure them in a safe deposit box. Document their existence for discovery, but protect them from disappearing. If you share joint credit cards and they have no balance, ask your lawyer if you can close them. This is typically only allowed prior to the actual divorce papers being filed.

Set up your own bank account: If you don't have one already, create an account that has enough money to pay for attorney fees and other divorce expenses. When the divorce process begins, be prepared for your narcissist to move money, and claim there is none to give you.

Lindsey Ellison, author, narcissism expert, and breakup coach

Getting organized will save you money and time – start early
One of the first things that should be done is gathering and organizing all the required paperwork as advised by your attorney. Make
copies of all statements and vital documents and safeguard them outside of the marital home. On your computer, create folders for bank
statements, retirement accounts, taxes, investments, expenses, and any
communication with your spouse. Starting the organization process
early will save time and money, especially when your lawyer needs
something. It will make your life much more manageable during a
time when everything feels out of control. If this isn't done from the
beginning, the risk of becoming overly triggered and stressed is a real
possibility. Since you will be asked during discovery by the courts for
years of records, seemingly from the beginning of time, sort everything by year. Further breaking them down by folder type like bank
accounts, credit card statements, etc. will make everything so much
easier to pull them quickly when needed.

Stash cash
In most states once the divorce paperwork is filed, accounts are ordered to be frozen; neither of you will be allowed to make any large,
unusual payments or withdrawals. If you have no access to money,
look into taking a credit card cash advance or periodically take a little
extra cash on the debit card at the grocery store to accrue a growing
stash of your own. I have talked to hundreds of survivors who had all
of their accounts unknowingly closed, leaving them with no money
and no credit. Protect yourself in advance if you can. Talk to your lawyer and ask if you are allowed to take a portion of the joint accounts.

Expect the worst
When dealing with a narcissist, you must understand that they have
no empathy for you and they are done. It doesn't matter if you've been
together for 40 years. A normal person, mother, father, wife, or husband would look at that time together and be kind; you could trust
them to protect you and the kids. A narcissist, however, is a different
animal. They feel nothing and that will be shocking to you; you'll be
revictimized over and over by their acts, tricks, and consistent lack of

emotion on display.

Protect yourself
Anticipate, react, and ALWAYS protect yourself first.

If you are considering leaving your narcissistic spouse or have made up your mind to do so in the future, do not clue your abuser in: Do not threaten separation or divorce. Doing this will give your abuser a chance to try to talk you out of it and plenty of time to set up a strategy that will hurt you. If you've already mentioned separation or divorce to your spouse, just say that you've reconsidered; that you love them and have no intention of leaving, then get started planning.

Get a lawyer immediately and covertly begin planning your exit strategy: This is especially important if children are involved. Interview attorneys until you find one who is shrewd and has considerable experience with manipulators. A divorce lawyer without those two things will be no match for the manipulative behavior, lies, and stall tactics that your spouse will try to use against you.

Get everything in order: Begin saving your money and putting aside as much as you can. Locate every joint credit account that you have ever had with your spouse and close whichever ones you can. Make copies of all documents showing your spouse's income, yearly taxes, or spending records. This is not a time to be concerned about being kind, equitable, or moral. Once you leave, your abuser will be anything but those things. Keep your plans under wraps until you have everything in place, and then have the divorce papers served. From that point on, do not address any questions your spouse asks of you, or make any compromises. They are traps. Make it clear that all future inquiries will be handled through your attorneys.

Randi Fine, author, host of the blog talk-radio show, *A Fine Time for Healing: A Sanctuary for Your Emotional Wellbeing*

The gamut of scenarios in narc-world

There are many different types of narcissistic people, each with their own set of narc-individuality. The spouse that experienced only the milder personality during the relationship will be caught completely unaware when the evil rears its ugly head. The level of abuse could range from rare verbal attacks to constant and vicious.

Often when survivors listen to videos or read books on narcissistic abuse, they question whether their spouse is really a narcissist. What if they weren't the type that cheated, or stole money, or was verbally abusive? Not all narcissistic people check all the boxes; some are verbally abusive all the time and some utilize manipulation in a more stealthy manner. I often hear, "We never even fought." If this sounds familiar, you may have been blind to the covert, passive-aggressive form of control that had been festering under the surface. Maybe you got used to it, or justified the actions by thinking "this is just how they are." I was like this: my ex-husband was extremely covert and his charm and love bombing techniques always fooled me into thinking that our marriage was not abusive. My parents fought and my mother threw things and I equated these obvious actions with abuse. The lies, hiding money, and passively making me feel like I wasn't good enough was never on my radar.

The level of crazy that you endured in the relationship often equates to the level of crazy you will see in the divorce. Nothing is written in stone so go into this with an open mind and your eyes wide open, wary of unexpected attacks. Even if you feel you had a relatively easy relationship that is no guarantee that the divorce will be the same. In a million years, I could never have anticipated the behaviors that I saw during my divorce. Hope for the best but plan for the worst.

The cycle of narcissistic abuse

The traditional cycle of abuse applies to a relationship as it travels from the wonderful to the crazy ugliness that defines the journey of those unfortunate enough to have been caught in the narcissistic web of deceit. The three swirling stages are idealize, devalue, and discard. These stages will continue for the life of the relationship with each looking a bit different once you are hooked. This will make more sense later.

Idealize

When you first meet a narcissist, the attention can be overwhelming as they begin the process to determine if you will be a good "supply," or prospect, for them based on your qualities. The interview is subtle as they empathetically inquire about your life. The deep conversations cultivate a sense of trust that makes it easy to share your intimate secrets and past mistakes. The narcissist is so charming, and the charisma so intoxicating, an untrained eye will never see it coming. I believe an individual's story attracts the narcissist who can quickly determine if you would be quality prey, the strength of your boundaries or vulnerabilities, and if the grooming process is worth pursuing.

Once you pass the initial test, the seduction, commonalities will be distinguished. This phase is often described as "too good to be true." The conquest has begun and you are placed on a pedestal where you will hear things such as "I have never met anyone like you before," or "No one has ever been so perfect, where have you been my whole life?" It becomes their personal challenge to get you to believe that they are as 'perfect for you' as you are for them. Almost immediately, they will demand your every waking moment and they rush intimacy to show you how you make them feel. Grand gestures and exciting passionate days all feed the dialogue that they are who they say they are: kind, generous, empathic, trustworthy, and that perfect match you have been searching for. Proclamations ensue that you are soulmates and you must see this through because you were meant to be together. They tell you how handsome or beautiful you are and begin to talk about their future with you in it. This is called future faking.

The language of the Idealize cycle:
- » "I always dreamt of someone as perfect as you. You are the best thing that has ever happened to me."
- » "I knew right away that we are soulmates." (or Twin Flames)
- » "Your ex was crazy to let you go, you are amazing. I will never leave you."
- » "No one has ever been this good to me."

Devalue

Once you are ensnared and fall for the persona they have been selling, the narcissist begins to lose interest. It was the chase that they desired. If you dare question them about their behavior or challenge a boundary, you quickly get moved into the next stage of this abuse cycle: devalue. Little things start to come up and the tension begins to build. They may nit-pick your habits or complain about the lack of attention you are paying them and proclaim that you are not the same person they thought you were. This falling from grace is extremely hurtful and the victim is quickly conditioned to 'try harder' to make them happy so that you can once again be the person they fell in love with.

The confusing parts to the victim are that their behaviors start to change; they no longer want to spend every waking moment with you and instead pull away. Things they say don't add up. The charm that you saw in the beginning becomes something they only do in public. Behind closed doors, they pick at you and begin to say things to hurt or confuse you. They often get angry if you want to do things with your friends and project jealousy in an attempt to isolate you for better control. The devaluing tactics used with a narcissist are brutal.

The language of the Devalue cycle:
- » "The more I get to know you, the more I don't like you. My ex's were much better, nicer, prettier, smarter and/or more responsible than you."
- » "You were never good enough for me. I can't believe you tricked me into believing you were someone else."
- » "I can see why everyone leaves you. You never listen to anyone and you always need to be right."
- » "You are an emotional mess. I can't keep picking up your pieces."

Discard

The discard stage can of course mean they leave you, but it can also be part of the cycle where they ghost you or claim they need their space. During this stage, the victim will see a side of the narcissist that they have been completely oblivious to – a heartless and non-empathic person who displays cruel verbal and emotional actions. Victims often feel like they are being punished but struggle to figure out why everything has changed. What did they do wrong? When the narcissist decides to leave, they are thoughtless and merciless as they wreck the heart of their victim. For this reason, once the divorce process has begun, the narcissist shows no empathy to you or your children and they feel entitled to use any means available to break you because you are now public enemy #1. The thing is, you now know the truth about them, and they must destroy you before you disclose it and blow the false persona (mask[4]) they have built out of the water.

The language of the Discard cycle:

> » "I have never cheated on you; you are the cheater and I am not sticking around to be abused anymore."
> » "I am honest and everyone knows it. No one will ever believe what you say because you are a pathological liar."
> » "I was never like this before you came into my life. I hate drama and you thrive on it."
> » "You are crazy and need professional help."

This stage feels like a punishment and it can be mystifying. I have heard tales of spouses disappearing for months on end, completely radio silent, with no indication of where they are or when they'll return. The imagination has a tendency to run wild from panic that something may have happened to anger for what they are putting you through. Once they return, if you take them back, the cycle will begin again.

---

4   The masks of a narcissistic person will be fully explained in Chapter 3.

Chapter 3

UNDERSTANDING THE PLAYERS

Narc-education and the DSM-5 guidelines

In the game of divorce, it is important to understand the enemies who will place the landmines and idiosyncrasies in your path. I will share a few of the players to help you identify who you will be coming up against.

Narcissistic Personality Disorder (NPD) falls under the category of Cluster B Personality Disorders within the DSM-5[5]. To be clear, NPD is a personality disorder that typically displays on a spectrum. A narcissism spectrum means people can present with just a few traits (low) such as healthy self-love or self-centeredness to the opposite extreme with full blown personality disorder (high) and a larger number of the more dangerous traits and malevolent behaviors. A very rudimentary explanation of the spectrum could be the differences between rum raisin and pink bubblegum ice creams. They are both ice cream but they sit on opposite ends of the (ice cream) spectrum. The

---

5   The Diagnostic and Statistical Manual of Mental Disorders, introduced in Chapter 2

narcissist that constantly belittles you is as dangerous as the one who covertly ebbs away your sense of self. While these two flavors of narcissists present themselves differently in marriage, during divorce they overlap. Those with NPD can appear mild, sweet, and kind until the narc-injury of a divorce threatens the image they have been portraying, at which point they could instantly morph to straight up devious. You will wonder how you could have possibly missed that side of their personality. Not all narcissistic people will go as far as my examples – the descriptions throughout this book are to be used as a guide of common behaviors only – and if your spouse isn't pulling these types of tricks on you, consider yourself lucky. Having the awareness of what they are capable of will empower you to recognize situations as they are happening and adjust accordingly.

It is technically and medically incorrect to call someone the name of their personality disorder. There is not a separate type of human called a narcissist. Just like you would never say, "My mother is a bi-polar," the same holds true for "I am married to a narcissist," since it is technically their personality disorder. You would be correct if you said, "My husband is bi-polar," or "My wife has Narcissistic Personality Disorder." With this said, for the ease in understanding when I refer to narcissists in this book, I will sometimes refer to them as a narcissist or a person with NPD.

Narcissists can be male or female and they traditionally display telltale behaviors by late childhood. It is estimated that 6.2% of the United States population has Narcissistic Personality Disorder (NPD). That equates to approximately 20 million people – 62% men and 38% women (Stinson et al. 2008). If we assume that each person with NPD negatively impacts three people, 60 million victims would be accounted for in the USA alone. Many experts believe that number to be extremely low and feel a more realistic multiplier would be at least ten (or 200 million victims). These numbers are staggering: there are over 325 million people in the US and the victim count grows daily.

According to the DSM-5, a person can be professionally diagnosed with narcissistic personality disorder by having at least five of the following characteristics:

» A grandiose sense of self-importance (e.g. exaggerates achievements and talents, expects to be recognized as superior without commensurate achievements)
» Preoccupied with fantasies of unlimited success, power, brilliance, beauty, or ideal love
» Beliefs that they are "special" and unique and can only be understood by, or should associate with, other special or high-status people (or institutions)
» Requires excessive admiration
» A sense of entitlement (i.e., unreasonable expectations of especially favorable treatment or automatic compliance with their expectations)
» Interpersonally exploitative tendencies (i.e., takes advantage of others to achieve their own ends)
» Lacks empathy: is unwilling to recognize or identify with the feelings and needs of others
» Often envious of others or believes that others are envious of them
» Shows arrogant, haughty behaviors or attitudes

While these characteristics outline the DSM's criteria, the way narcissistic personality disorder presents is not always reflective of this list.

> **Never tell them they are a narcissist or that they have a personality disorder:** They will turn on you like a rabid dog and you will become their target of blame. They have no ability to empathize or see their own flaws. This does not exist within them. You only jeopardize yourself and you will not change them. The best you can do is manage them.
>
> **Susan Guthrie,** nationally recognized top family law and mediation attorney

Covert (or Fragile) Narcissist

If you put a frog in a pot of cold water and steadily turn up the heat, the frog will adjust to the raising temperature and will boil to death.

Narcissistic covert abuse is often compared to this analogy because it happens slowly. Once caught, the heat (abuse) gets turned up. Most victims of covert narcissists report that they felt something was off, but it didn't feel like abuse because it was subtle and hard to put their fingers on the changes. The typical pattern of a covert narcissist is to come on fast and intense, claim their soulmate, and propose quickly. It's the idealize phase of the relationship where the victim is placed high on a pedestal and not allowed the chance to really get to know the person or see their true self. The intensity of being the center of someone's world sounds like a fairy tale; but then there is a noticeable change in availability and the victim is no longer the priority…the first of many confusing moments that showcase reality. At first the narcissist will blame the change in attention on the need to get back to real life. That seems like a good excuse so the first crumb offered is accepted. Later, the blame gets pointed at you, the victim. It's all your fault things changed and the internalized "if only you…" or "if you had just done…" taunts are released. This is the devalue stage test. You are being graded for your reaction to the withdrawn attention. If you continue to accept the justification as moving back to normal life, they know they have a low bar to meet and you are controllable.

These tactics are common from a covert narcissist. They are unoriginal, often cowardly, and exceptionally low on the emotional intelligence scale. Most victims don't notice these methods or understand their meaning. They don't see the person as they really are until they leave. The strategies are stealthy and designed to confuse.

Covert narcissists are exceedingly difficult to recognize and even harder to expose because they have built a fake persona with everyone they know. Most that are unaware of the covert traits see a charming, helpful, caring, compassionate, and often enlightened individual. However, this type tends to stick with the same tricks and methods, don't learn from them, and are extremely persistent.

Covert traits you may have seen:
   » rushes relationships with very intense love bombing (idealizing phase) that "prove" how much they cherish you

» charming yet socially awkward and less skilled than the grandiose or malignant narcissist
» introvert – withdrawn and self-centered
» lack of empathy for you or others – fake empathy can be exhibited as a technique to get something they want or to find new supply. It is an act to make people think they have true empathy.
» Passive-aggressive communication and behaviors, usually done behind closed doors:
  › guilt
  › subtle insults
  › shaming
  › blaming
  › gaslighting
  › passive-aggressive anger
  › procrastination
  › ghosting
  › ignoring your concerns
  › silent treatment
  › stubbornness
  › sullenness
  › a sarcastic or argumentative attitude
  › deliberately not doing the things they say they will do
» low self-worth – secretly depressed with exceptionally low self-esteem
» victimized – they play the victim, the world is out to get them, in divorce you are out to get them, they use their victimhood to trap victims, and they share stories of trauma and neglect.
» sullen, angry, and never content with a quiet rage simmering just below the surface
» overly critical and always believe they are better and smarter than everyone else, even their boss
» needy and vulnerable
» anxious

» resentful and jealous

» hostile and argumentative; must always must be right

» not typically good in social situations – if they do go to events, they will ruin them with passive-aggressive behavior.

» no genuine friends – only admirers and people they can use for supply

» constantly seek validation – always bragging to convince others how great they are. In extreme cases this manifests as a God-like mask to be the savior to those lucky enough to be in their presence.

» arrogant and dismiss other's opinions because they believe they are better

» entitled and believe that they deserve the best of everything and seek those who will give it to them, even though they are not worthy of it.

» hypersensitive to feedback or criticism – they react with rage: "How could you!"

» need to control everyone around you – the need for control controls them.

» smug with an air of superiority: they don't need you

» expert justifier of their behaviors and usually present it by turning the mirror on you. If you catch them cheating, it was because you weren't being a good partner to give them what they wanted.

» intense need to win and prove they did nothing wrong so they point fingers at you to deflect the accusations

» no remorse – able to apologize, but the apology is not genuine. They never learn from their actions. The apology is an act to give hope. They will turn around and pull the rug of hope out from under you again at another time.

» emotional actors to control the victim. Crying on demand creates drama, sells them as a sensitive person, moves the attention to them and garners sympathy.

» pathological liars – if their lips are moving, they're lying.

Even when the truth would serve them better, they lie. They can't help themselves and you will wonder how they keep all the fake facts straight.

Weapons of passive-aggressive covert behaviors:

» the silent treatment – to punish and abuse their victims. When the covert narcissist goes dark (ghosting) and refuses to engage, the victim feels rejected and wonders what they did to provoke this behavior, making them feel like they did something wrong. Ultimately, the victim will get angry causing resentment from the narcissist because they believe they are entitled to treat people this way.

» ignoring you – pretending not to hear you or understand your request, completely aware that this is aggravating behavior.

» reactive abuse – pushing the victim to react with anger and then placing blame regarding their anger issues

» playing the victim – a control tool to garner emotions and evoke sympathy by always having a sad story about past mistreatment or making others believe they are team players by consistently accepting the short end of the stick.

» the joke is on you – off-handed jokes are designed to make the victim feel bad. Humor to tease and belittle someone is followed by a "just kidding" in an insincere attempt to ease the pain, but the objective is achieved.

» name calling and constant verbal abuse – typically done in private but sometimes the line is crossed and it's done in front of family or friends.

» pretending to forget the things they promised to do – intentionally not doing something after they said they would and expressing anger or exasperation if it is mentioned.

Grandiose Narcissist

The grandiose narcissist is the poster child of what is characteristically described in the DSM-5 – charming, charismatic, confident, attractive, and entitled. This is how most imagine narcissists to present themselves as the "constant mirror gazing" or "let's take a selfie" type. They tend to hold jobs that put them in a place of power and marry easy-to-control people who will also boost their image and careers. In order to be in a relationship with them, they require someone who appears worthy of being on their arm. Status is necessary but even that cannot outshine them. Usually soon after marriage, the devalue stage will begin to knock their partner down a peg or two from the status that originally attracted them. It is important that the victim have insecurities so that they need the narcissist.

Grandiose narcissist traits you may have seen:
- » superiority
- » entitlement
- » flamboyance
- » pompous
- » brash
- » forcefulness
- » never plays the victim
- » charming
- » extravert
- » controlling
- » rages quickly if they don't get their way
- » hypersensitive to feedback
- » unable to accept that they are not perfect, so they deny criticism and put anyone down that does not get fully on board idealizing them.

Malignant Narcissist

Malignant narcissists are on the higher end of the narcissistic spectrum because they usually exhibit an evil side, possibly with sadistic traits. They share the lack of empathy and the poor sense of self-worth with their lesser narcissistic comrades but because of this darkness, they tend to be the ones who derive joy from taking down their enemies. In a divorce, they make the false allegations of criminal behavior in order to have their spouses arrested. They will never stop litigation and will prolong everything in the legal arena simply to ramp up the torture-factor.

Where a narcissistic injury often launches other types of narcissists into black-and-white thinking, a malignant narcissist always sees people as friend or foe. Anyone they determine as lesser than them automatically falls into the enemy camp and they are not shy about voicing their opinions. Their amplified lack of empathy will be evident in everything they do.

Malignant narcissistic traits you may have seen:
- » limited capacity to show empathy
- » pathological liars
- » power and social influence – motivated by the greed of power, they hang with successful people, have great jobs, lead companies, and throw their weight around against their victims.
- » grandiosity
- » demand validation
- » exploitative
- » evil tendencies – straddle the line that other types of narcissists only touch
- » stalkers
- » dangerous – more so than other types as they are more calculated in planning attacks
- » manipulate the victim and court system breaking all the rules – in their minds they are entitled to use the legal system because they are smarter.
- » more likely to have criminal charges brought against their victim
- » takes pleasure in humiliating and causing pain
- » master of all skills – unlike the other types of narcissists, they learn from their efforts. They test a strategy, evaluate its success, and then look for additional ways to serve up endless abuse.

Rich Narcissist

There is no type of narcissist that is rich by default but any could be. However, with financial success, the privilege that they believe they are entitled to will be actively sought. A grandstanding performance in the courtroom to allege that you are just in it for the money should be expected as the spouse is often painted as a gold digger. Rich narcissists take the worst pieces of all the various types and create a hybrid of a covert malignant robot with one mission – to destroy you. Narcissists with assets feel they are entitled to everything even if you are legally entitled to half. It is not uncommon that they will spend more than what you would have gotten originally just so you get nothing. Doctors, lawyers, and businessmen and women who could easily afford to give a fair share will make false allegations, stonewall and change lawyers repeatedly, all to drag out the process and run up the expenses. A wealthy narcissist will go to any lengths to ruin you, and your children too, for the mere pleasure of it. I opted to add this category to alert victims who may be divorcing a powerful and afflu-ent narcissist that the difference between them and the other types is that the abuse likely won't stop once the divorce is final.

When dealing with a narcissist with money or influence, the rules will constantly change simply because of the unlevel playing field. The potential of losing part of what they believe to be their assets will manifest as a wound – no matter how long you were married and what the division of property laws are in your state, they believe that you have no right to anything that they perceive as theirs. The battle lines are drawn to protect their money and assets at any cost; the cost usually being the destruction of their spouse and children. The party with the money will do anything to prove that the other has no legal rights to anything. Additional court costs and legal fees will amplify the destruction of your financial situation.

The spouse knows they have access to more money than you. The goal is to create as many diversions as possible, overextending your financial risk causing you to run out of funds. I have friends whose di-vorce bills totaled over 3 million dollars, while others got away cheap at only one million dollars. I have heard horror stories of post-divorce abuse where the rich narcissist comes back to court to sue you for their legal fees. This journey is likely in the cards for you if you're divorcing someone with money.

The narcissist's access to unlimited resources to hire lawyers and expert witnesses will begin to devalue and destroy your reputation. This is vital to their case because they stand on the pillar of being successful, wealthy, and untouchable. They first claim that you are money hungry, out to take everything from them. This victim role they create plucks at the heart strings of anyone who will listen. Hearing that you married them for money, compounded with the lies of your abusive nature towards them and the children will turn life-long friends against you and begin the isolation process.

To the victim of the senseless legal waste of money, you will feel sick that this could have been your nest egg to move into the next chapter of your life, but the narcissist wants you to start again with nothing. They would rather pay millions of dollars to legal teams than to give you one penny. Sadly, this backwards thought process applies to your children too. The narcissist will blow through what could have been the children's college fund for the smallest reason. I want you to know that you can rebuild despite how hopeless it may appear in that moment when you are in the fire pit of divorce hell.

Your parenting skills will be questioned and expert witnesses called to show the children are unstable and that it is your fault. The years of being a girl scout leader and volunteer at the school will be tossed aside because these false allegations become the conversation.

Family and friends will be summoned to testify against you. The power of money often creates a chasm as they are tempted to pick the side with the money and influence. If you aren't aware: money does influence people. In this high society world, you have seen it – the true gold diggers, the fake friends, and the crowd surrounding your wealthy spouse who only wants to be on the inside. The daggers shot by those once welcomed at your dinner table will induce magnified pain because you honestly believed that their friendships were true.

The false allegations described will rip at your very core because the attacks are so far from who you really are. They assault your greatest strengths knowing that they are what you will predominantly defend. Don't waste time ruminating over the fact that they know these claims aren't true because the truth simply does not matter. Once the defamation against you is set into motion, the narcissist will take it as gospel with not a care in the world as to how it will affect you. Distorted statements that insinuate depression or mental instability typically are established early to demonstrate that you are an unfit parent, if there are children involved. A rich spouse will take this declaration to the furthest degree possible and have you committed into rehab or a mental institution, fabricating a much more convincing story to tell the judge.

If the children prefer being with you because you are loving and sensitive to their needs, this will anger the narcissist into making parental alienation claims against you. The money brings a parade of false witnesses to show the court that you are an unstable, abusive, alcoholic, bi-polar, angry parent that the children must be saved from. Buying off the children is common. First, they will be fed disturbing lies to make them afraid of you, and then the money begins to flow. Offers to buy phones, new clothes, fancy cars, ritzy vacations, Ivy League educations, computers, and even homes are designed to keep the children on a short leash and in their debt. These things will be held over the children for control, convincing them to not have a relationship with you. The unspoken truth behind the spending spree has been covertly planted in the children's minds: "You talk to mom (or dad) and I will cut you off." In my recollection, the most extreme example was a 12-year-old receiving a $100,000 car. The child had no driver's license but was forced to remain loyal under threat of losing the car, all at the dad's discretion.

Family phone plans allow the narcissistic parent to see all the kids' texts, including those with you. With this control, phone access can be shut down when the kids are with them, leaving you incommunicado. If you're sending the children messages while they are in the care of your ex with no response, print screen shots of both message threads to prove they were deleted leaving the children with no knowledge that you were trying to check in. Using the knowledge of what they've done, the narcissistic parent will build mistrust by telling the kids that you don't really care about them, planting seeds of hatred in their minds. Substantiating that your ex is censoring your messages will be something a judge will want to see.

Car or insurance payments are normal buy offs as well, keeping the kids firmly under the narcissist's thumb. They can have a new vehicle of their choice as long as they don't go to the opposing parent's house with it. The intention is to have the 16-year-old want the car so badly that all they need to do is decide they want to stay with the parent with the money.

You have heard of the Disneyland dad/mom where everything is fun and rule-free at their house, making it harder for you to give equally or enforce discipline at yours. The dangling carrot of inheritance is a big one. Be on my side and you stay in the will; don't and I cut you off. Where does the loyalty lie? Making the children pick between two parents based on money should be illegal but it's not. The legal and financial abuse will continue amplifying the alienation of your children until they want nothing to do with you. This is the reality of divorcing a rich narcissist.

As with any narcissist, expect everything to be a struggle, from them not producing the discovery paperwork or vital pieces of their financial portfolio, to closing accounts, or hiding money online with crypto currency. With money comes the added ability to hire legal advice to instruct them how to move money and retirement accounts into trusts and corporations so that they are no longer part of your familial property or out of the country and impossible to track in American courtrooms. This is similar to the ruse where a coin is hidden under a shell and shuffled around so its location is a continuous guessing game. When the narcissist has more money than you, get a good lawyer who knows which battles to fight and which to walk away from.

Remember, the drama of divorcing a person with money and assets rarely ends just because the divorce process is over. They keep the legal battle in the court system for years to come. Why? Because they can. If they were ordered to pay you something, you can bet you will not see that compensation in a timely manner causing you to go back to court to fight for what you were already awarded. In Chapter 11, I will share the secret money-saving clause that should always be added to every divorce decree that, if done correctly, will save you thousands of dollars in post-divorce legal abuse.

Poor Narcissist

When you are the breadwinner, or you have assets, there is a unique type of narcissist who is more like a conman (or woman). Simply put, they choose a mark and they go after it. They have no wealth of their own and are unable or unwilling to hold down a job but they have grandiose visions of what they would like to do – they just lack the motivation or the financial means to get it done. They often represent themselves as the helpful one, able to fix things around the house or whatever you need; they will morph into anything to suit you.

The initial love bombing hooks the target as they share their victim-hood story. They focus on empathic, non-boundary enforcing people pleasers who are looking for affection, or possibly tired of being alone, to exploit. Always about the money and affluence, they latch onto their victims with an artificial shame that makes you more willing to give. You believe them to be genuine and get sucked in.

Their grift starts out small to deflect the fact that you are being conned. They test your boundaries to see if you will buy them dinner or take them on a trip. The speed at which they move is like lightning. In an effort to isolate you and maintain control, they usually avoid meeting your friends and family as they literally become your entire life. If you are permitted to see friends, it is only to hook those friends into believing how much they love you. They move into your home and start to help as they methodically commence to manage your money and assets. Marrying this type of narcissist happens rapidly but the divorce will take an exceptionally long time as they make claims against everything that is yours.

No matter what type of narcissist you have been married to, they are often described as emotional vampires who guzzle the life force out of their victims. I like to suggest that they are emotional porcupines ready to launch hypothetical quills at whoever they perceive as dangerous to their persona.

I often ask my coaching clients for the profession of their ex-husband or ex-wife because this provides incredible insight into the inner workings of their minds: It is critical to "profile" your ex-narcissist almost like the FBI would profile a criminal. If they are in the sales industry, it means they are incredibly skilled at "impression management" because they have been trained to speak smoothly, say all of the right things and throw out a hook to make the sale. If they are in law enforcement or a military position, there are generally more control issues that come with these professions. If they are lawyers, they litigate.

While I am talking to clients or those I meet doing my volunteer work, I am often seen scribbling notes in a desperate attempt to understand the inner workings of the narcissist in question: Are they exhibitionists who crave attention and the spotlight, or are they the covert, introverted type who often fly under the radar, but are incredibly calculating in their approach? Are they the elitist, cutthroat, opportunist-type constantly hunting for their next kill in an effort to elevate themselves financially or in status? Do they fall into the amorous, Casanova category, ready to seduce the pants or skirt right off their next conquest? Or do they exhibit several categories? Many individuals with personality disorders also suffer from addiction problems such as drugs, alcohol or pornography.

The narcissists who have exhibitionist qualities will typically cancel their parenting time for social events providing you with documentation that their words in court are not in alignment with their actions: The narcissists with introverted qualities are generally smarter about what they put in writing. On the other hand, I have seen some who are so disconnected from reality that they provide mountains of documentation for court due to their bizarre, rambling diatribes. The cut-throat opportunist is typically so preoccupied with business and lifestyle choices that they will be distracted by the mundane task of caring for a child until an opportunity arises to showcase the child for attention. The romantic, seductive type is easily distracted by the next blonde that walks by but many times, will use the child to paint an idyllic picture if the new woman craves children and a white picket fence lifestyle. When addiction issues are in play, the narcissist is not operating at their full potential and this situation often provides opportunity for court documentation. Knowing thine enemy is critical in any battle; a custody battle is no exception.

Tina Swithin, author, founder of One Mom's Battle

The narcissistic masks

Narcissistic traits can overlap, or your narcissist may only have a few, because everything NPD-related is on a spectrum, which is as wide as it is long. While behaviors do converge, your spouse might be a hybrid with combination characteristics. Not everyone yells, not everyone gaslights, not everyone is charming, but they all wear masks. Don't bog yourself down trying to label your narcissist spouse because chances are good that you have only seen the tip of the malevolent iceberg. Your diagnoses will continually change as you see the various mannerisms displayed during your divorce. It really doesn't matter what we call them; what matters is the tricks they pull, the behaviors they exhibit and how they make you feel.

While I have outlined the definitions of the different types of narcissists earlier in this chapter, I want to remind you that the same behaviors are often not shared from one covert narcissist to another. Narcissists have created many masks throughout their lives that they present to the world. Imagine a mask as a character, role, or a false persona that they play. Masks of normalcy are routinely invoked to create the illusion to the world that they are normal and not disordered. Designed to entice the people they want to attract for various supply, it's ultimately all about the status, services, money, accolades, dedication, sex, and servitude. The masks are interchangeable so you may identify or cross-identify with several depending on the target of their influence. Narcissists don't need friends or partners; they need an audience so the mask must be selected very carefully.

The narcissistic mask is used as a tool to build a carefully tailored persona in order to friend people who they will later use for supply. When you see a contradiction to what they do in public and what they say in private, you are observing the public mask being removed behind closed doors. The masks may seem familiar to you but look a bit deeper and observe other relationships they have and the way the "show" might have always been interchangeable depending on the crowd. Once an actor, always an actor and this performance theater will carry over in every social circle in their lives.

A quote from one of my favorite movies, *Sabrina*, is apropos – *"Illusions are dangerous people. They have no flaws."* The mask chosen for you is customized to your needs; they made themselves your dream illusion. The role was defined by your own imagination and carefully orchestrated to trap you. I envision the mask being removed at the door and placed on a hook like a hat. Once you see thru the fantasy and catch a glimpse of the real person, you can't unsee it. It's scary and the sense of betrayal may be overwhelming.

Narcissists do not want to be exposed. After their mask falls and they realize you have seen the truth, a narcissistic injury usually occurs. To reduce the risk of being unmasked, they know when the gig is up and begin planning their exit. How do these masks relate to your ex?

The Charmer
Covert narcissists are infamous for their charming mask, even though all narcissists can manifest charm on demand. When in use, charm can ooze thick and gooey but it is easily recognized after-the-fact as fake. In the beginning, they attract a person to them by finding commonalities to show the new victim how perfect they are for each other. If you like yoga, horses, and classical music, they do too. The passive-aggressive behaviors are more stealth than the more aggressive abusive behaviors we have come to know. It's a slow drip that makes recognizing the coercive control difficult to see. As soon as the victim questions annoying or bad behavior, they are immediately shut down and accused of being wounded by past relationships and projecting

that on them. Your ability to trust them will be probed as they doubt your loyalty, simply because you had the nerve to raise a concern. This gaslighting technique, followed by promises, makes it easy to give the impropriety a pass. You are charmed again, and they are back in control. The confusing dual personalities, mixed with intermittent charm, forms the victim's trauma bond like prey in a spider's web.

This is how your relationship began, with a persona you believed was the person you had fallen in love with. Until you are completely infatuated, the charming mask will be used both in public and in private; then they are free to act differently behind closed doors. The slippage of the mask can be gradual or immediate; the narcissist has studied and tested your reactions. The decision on how fast you are transported to narc-world is guided by your toleration tipping point. It took five years and a 2,000-mile household move before my ex-husband flipped to show his true colors. Inside your home, you start to see little things that are confusing. My husband's public mantra was "Do the right thing," however, he did not practice what he preached. I only knew his public mask, so I was confused when his words and actions clashed. I did not understand masks yet.

The victim of the charming mask struggles to let go of the public persona because they believe that to be the real person. Holding onto the better version of the person will keep victims trapped for years as they try to love the narcissist more to help them find that charming happy person they believe to be deep inside. As the fog dissipates and the victim can see the narcissist clearly for whom they really are, they are no longer fooled. This is the real them; the charm was just an act.

Everyone called my husband Prince Charming. He tediously built his persona which made it hard for our friends to accept the truth about him. Over time, the charming passive-aggressive mask appeared and I was gaslit to believe that I was being unreasonable to question the contrast in his actions. He said he needed to be able to relax at home and not have to be 'on' all the time. I didn't understand what he meant until I learned about NPD and deduced that being 'on' alluded to maintaining the mask he had so painstakingly created. I was sold on the fairy tale and it wasn't until my divorce that a friend made the observation that "every fairy tale has its villains and betrayals."

The charming and generous masks pair perfectly together to impress and buy companionship. They are not giving to give; they are giving to show the range of their generosity and charm. Behind closed doors the narcissist will complain and call these people takers. Deep inside, they feel like people should be giving to them even though they never really give them a chance.

Generous

Narcissists love being in the limelight. Being seen by everyone as kind and giving, they bestow money and material things on people to buy the title of the generous one. Someone who is truly magnanimous feels no need to divulge their actions or the charities they support. Narcissists, however, do because they only do it for the accolades. This false self can be addicting to the point of confusion. Despite sometimes not being able to afford the grander maneuvers they take part in, they acknowledge that they must pay to play to remain in character and will do whatever it takes. The generous mask can be used to shower the victims with gifts to buy their love only to withdraw the affection in the discard stage. During divorce, the victim's betrayal can be magnified as they trusted their partner to be generous. They had watched so much be given so freely to others that they erroneously believed that even through it all, their narcissist would still take care of them.

The Privileged

The narcissists who wear this mask outwardly appear to believe that they're better than everyone, but inwardly live in fear, behind closed doors, of the act they're playing. This role takes extra work to weasel into the crowd they are seeking, all the while knowing they are out of their league. Due to the complexity of this mask, it can be more tiring than the others. The privileged mask demands an audience with a higher status than themselves. They can only hope they are able to con their way into a relationship and be accepted. Because they are playing this role with people who could easily learn the truth, the generous mask is often borrowed to buy their way into this club of friends.

When wearing this mask, narcissists become huge self-promoters who must tell outright lies regarding their status and lives. Legitimate people of privilege are much more low-key as their legacy precedes them.

The privileged mask chooses partners who make them look good: eye candy and those with status, money, or power. With a "Look who I am married to" attitude, they turn their unfortunate other half into the bait to help trap those whose attention they seek. Who was your narcissist trying to impress and did they ride your coattails to get there? You may remember being briefed on the importance of certain people before an event and instructed to treat them differently if they were on the A-list. If you were the one who had the status and privilege, you were sought out to assist getting them into a particular circle. Initially you were praised and they told everyone how amazing you were. Slowly, as they wormed their way into your inner circle, little cracks began appearing to zap your confidence and put you in your place – beneath them.

The Arrogant Intellectual

There are many brilliant narcissists so the difference between smart narcissists and those who simply wear the arrogant intellectual mask is important to understand. Narcissists who sport this mask are always searching for prey. Cracks will begin to appear shortly after the love bombing stage because they cannot maintain this false persona without an attentive audience. They are always right and will argue a point regardless of its veracity. Others will often surrender because it simply isn't worth the fight – they are like a dog with a bone and will not give up until they have met their objective.

Sensitive

This mask is used to convince a narcissist's victims into believing they are sensitive, fragile, and capable of empathy. While the true feelings aren't there, they can play the role of an empathic person using manipulative tears as their weapon of choice. If your narcissist showed you this mask in the beginning, it was a ploy to get you to trust them and feel safe. Review the rest of your life with them and you will see that the compassionate card was always an act, just like it will be throughout the divorce process.

The Rescuer

Narcissists play on people's wounded nature and it is common to prey on those with vulnerabilities like those recently divorced, financially needy, lonely, or with low self-esteem. They will jump in to be your rescuer when you need help, thus securing a connection and an instant bond. Once the victim becomes indebted to the narcissist, they become trapped. They step in to be a knight in shining armor; financial assistance never lasts beyond the love bombing stage, however, but they are often targeted because they have something that the narcissist wants.

Vulnerable

Narcissists incapable of caring for themselves or doing adult things like chores, paying bills, or being able to hold a job will wear the vulnerable mask. You were intentionally selected as a caregiver; they are so helpless that you become responsible for not only caring for them but basically being their parent. To someone who makes a habit of rescuing others, this role might seem sweet in a weird codependent way initially, but overtime you will realize that your spouse is never there for you. All the house and family tasks get dumped on you. Over the years, you have realized that they couldn't be trained as you originally thought they could. Crocodile tears are a mechanism you may witness with this type of mask. Their life story always blames the people from their past who didn't support them, causing them to be the way they are now – helpless. When they feel you pulling away, the water works will be turned on instantly to create the guilt needed to get you back under control. The tears hold a secondary value: the vulnerability shown makes the victims believe that they are sensitive and caring. Even when victims finally see the truth, that this was an act and a lie, they often still get sucked back in a few more times because the pullback story and pity party are expertly crafted. Most who marry the vulnerable mask end up not only being dumped but also tasked with all the heavy lifting throughout the divorce to produce the evidence and tedious paperwork.

The Victim

This mask is chosen by narcissists who have exceptionally low self-esteem and lack the confidence to pull off a more exciting mask. Their victimhood is embellished to find empathic people to control. Compassionate people pleasers with poor boundaries help the narcissists sing their victim song. Altruistic individuals only want to help, to fix things, and they have the empathy necessary to become engaged in the drama the narcissists create. If you ever considered yourself a narc-magnet, be assured it was your kindness that was targeted. They tug on the heartstrings of a kind person with stories of how they have been wronged; the crazy ex who cheated on them, the boss who doesn't understand how smart they are, and the injustice of everything in their life. Their narrative steadfastly remains "Everyone always leaves me and you will too!" but take no accountability or responsibility for their role. It's always someone else's fault, they are the blameless victim. During divorce, this mask can be pulled out of the closet making them the victim of a lifetime of abuse at your hand.

The Spiritual/Religious

The spiritual/religious mask is the choice around people who care about God and spirituality. They will often rise to the occasion becoming spiritual leaders and influencers. On the surface, they appear upstanding and trustworthy as they profess their love for God and humanity. In reality, they lie, cheat, and abuse their partners and children. The confusion lies in the vast difference between their public persona and not living the spiritual life. When narcissists choose this, it is a commitment to the audience and to the role. It will be the overlying facade that governs the role they play and the public persona they portray. They may or may not actually believe in God or spirituality but the mask gives them the unbridled power to judge others and believe that they are better than them. Since this public face is of the highest status in the eyes of their patrons, it is harder for the victims to see the truth even when they know it to be accurate. When someone plays this role, they are craving an automatic trust level that comes to people who are spiritually connected.

Deep down, darkness surrounds them that only the victims can see. The rest of the world identifies with the front-facing act, confusing the victims when they question the morality of their actions. If done right, this mask is one of the strongest to overcome the believability of the act.

The Great Team Parent

In their efforts to join the parental club, the narcissist must step into the closet and don the mask for the public persona that embodies everything necessary to show the world what a great parent and team player that they are. The rules of this mask are to be an active and loving parent so they must publicly display their adoration which can be quite confusing to the kids. In front of everyone, the child is praised and cherished but as soon as they get in the car, the attacks begin for anything that the parent felt embarrassed about, like missing the game winning point. That embarrassment is projected onto the child as the cause of their anger. The narcissist will step up to volunteer by being the soccer coach, Girl Scout leader or chief party planner, charming the other parents with the solitary goal to establish how wonderful they are. The compliments they receive are the supply they crave. Like a trophy, they can proudly use this mask to better their status in other circles. However, not unlike the other masks, once the lights go out on the public face, they become evil and indignant. The good parent role doesn't appear again until the front door opens. They aren't there for the kids, so shooting hoops in the driveway or helping with a school project will only occur if they can show off to an audience. Children observe the cruel inconsistent messaging which can leave them wounded, physically and emotionally, for life. To the narcissist, children are used as a tool to gain status and nothing more.

The Dedicated Parent

This mask attempts to show the world how great they are through their kids by being a dedicated parent. They may homeschool, or be the mom who is the classroom volunteer, or the dad who makes the chili for every class dinner. They often ignore their children only using them as objects when they meet the standards and play along with the role they are assigned. This mask includes self-promotion; sending out the Christmas cards with pictures and the letter sharing what they did all year, giving people the script to agree that they are a great parent. There is little truth in those letters, however; they may have taken that vacation, but they ignored their family and only focused on themselves. The family, in this case, was used as a stage prop to help them present the dedicated parent mask.

The Good Neighbor

Have you ever noticed your spouse pretend to love your neighbors when they are with them but talk badly about them as soon as the door closes? Complaints abound about having to go to the block party but as soon as they walk outside, their face changes: a big smile appears and they hug everyone, peppering in jovial conversation. This mask ingratiates the neighbor to them to manipulate later in the smear campaign against you. When you need help, they will look at you funny and abandon you quickly because of the implanted narratives that they choose to believe. This maneuver is used to isolate you.

But wait! There's more!

The martyr, the lover, the workaholic, the fake self-improvement, the playful, and the self-sacrificing masks are others you may have witnessed throughout your marriage. There are so many that can be used to ensnare a victim and the narcissist has perfected ways to customize exactly what they need to do that determines which they pull off the shelf. The romantic, trustworthy, fun-loving, charismatic, love at first sight, bring you soup when you're sick, and surprising you with gifts for no reason gestures were all just an act. This awareness in hindsight is when most victims are able to finally see that their entire marriage was a sham.

Gaslighting occurs when you begin to question the inconsistencies and the cracks in the mask(s). Over time, the victim surrenders to the fight because it just isn't worth the effort and the good, kind, and charming masks get put back on the shelf until the doorbell rings. The masks are only designed to close the sale – they were never real.

Combination masks are common – narcissists can rock a professional-family-spiritual mask. Examine the masks your ex wore throughout your marriage. Were they varied for different groups of people? Were they different in front of family members, friends, or coworkers? Write down all the different masks you saw. This will help you prepare for what you might see during the divorce.

How long did it take before you saw your narcissist's mask fall?

Chapter 4

EMOTIONAL PROCESSING

My "dumbass" theory

During our time as a married couple, my husband and I loved taking photos. We kept a bulletin board plastered with pictures of friends and memories of our fun times. As time went on, more things were added like mementos from trips and special items we had collected along the way. When my husband left, I had to dismantle memory lane and in doing so, I found a postcard that he had apparently liked so much, he saved it. It was black with a cartoon and the word "dumbass." The irony did not escape me; I laugh because this is the way I feel about him now thus forever coining my "dumbass" theory. The concept: when you learn how not to let their behavior bother you, they lose their power over you and become nothing more than an annoying mosquito buzzing around your head.

Do you know anyone who displays the same mannerisms every time you are with them? Maybe they always find someone to flirt with at the bar, they forget their wallet, or they are always late. Eventually, you learn to accept this type of behavior because "it's just them" and it's no big deal in the grand scheme of things. You and your friends might chuckle and subconsciously think "dumbass," there he goes again. This is not to say that you would keep these friends if they were exhibiting quirks that were truly offensive but we all know people whose behavior is as predictable as that of a dumbass. It's freeing to not give their behaviors any emotional juice.

Your narcissist will behave badly. Count on it. You will begin to see patterns and learn to expect them. We feel triggered by their exploits because we are amazed that they are trying that trick again. However, you have the ability to prevent their actions from controlling your emotions. My theory is meant to deactivate their power to shock and trigger you. This will allow your emotional roller coaster to flatten out because the things they do won't hold the same energy to confound you. Rather than feeling upset, think to yourself, "of course they are doing this, dumbass!" This is a group effort: I will outline many of the common behaviors that narcissists use during divorce; your job is to laugh at how unoriginal they are.

To build your emotional resilience and letting go skills, compare the dumb things your friends do to your "dumbass" narcissistic ex. In no way am I inferring that what the narcissist did is ok because there is no justification. I am also not downplaying the severity of their actions. However, we cannot change the narcissist; all we can change is ourselves and how we let their antics affect us. They feed off your reactions and when they lose the power to control and trigger you, the game gets boring. They will then, hopefully, find a new focus and stop abusing you.

I have shared this theory with many survivors and it has empowered them to have a safe word. It can be used as a shield that stops the narcissist's actions from annoying or controlling them. Instead, they are granted the freedom to laugh and realize how pathetic the narcissists life will be if they continue to be such a "dumbass." When in court, every time you look at them, envision "dumbass" written across their forehead. Think "dumbass" whenever they do something stupid. Before long, you will realize that the space they had rented in your head is gone.

There is a great deal left to life after admitting, "I don't give a shit." What would your life look like if your narcissist lost all of their triggering powers and you legitimately couldn't care less?

All aboard the emotional rollercoaster!

Fear = False Evidence Appearing Real. Fear is generally the first emotion felt as the reality of divorce hits and thoughts begin percolating of an unknown future. This causes overwhelming anxiety and hopelessness, shutting down your emotional resilience. It feels like you are standing in one spot as the world around you accelerates to fast forward.

If you allow yourself to be consumed with worry of the unknown, the fear will amplify, lie to you, and rob you of being present today. The complicated thoughts that your internal fears feed on will only serve to make you weaker unless you learn to identify and control them.

The only thing you can control in the whirlwind of divorcing a narcissist is yourself. It can feel like the end of the world, but it's not. The shock of learning the truth about your marriage, the lies and betrayals, throws most victims into a psychological tailspin as they ask the question, "What the heck is happening?" Depending on your role in this divorce, whether you're the discarded or the discarder, you'll know your emotional strength and what you need to do to proceed.

If you are the discarded, you'll deal with rejection, shame, anger, abandonment, and fear of your uncertain financial outlook and future. If you are the discarder, your emotions will include relief that you finally found the courage to plan and execute the separation and divorce. Most victims who initiate the divorce have carefully planned their exit so they've already faced diverse emotions. However, they may experience resentment at themselves for waiting so long to make their escape a reality.

The stages of discovery and recovery when you go through a divorce with a narcissist are not static and do not fall in a specific order. Instead, expect to rotate in and out of these stages, much like a washing machine in a spin cycle. We all have a fight-flight-freeze response which is the body's built-in system designed to protect us from threat or danger. During the divorce process, most will experience them all.

Anti-fear is a powerful weapon: When divorcing a narcissist it is natural that fears are activated: the fear of loss such as loved ones, financial stability and your life as you knew it, to name a few. Narcissists feed on power and your fear feeds them that power. Face your fears by working with a strong attorney to stay proactive and not reactive. Keep calm and set boundaries to ensure the narcissist does not see your fear and use it as a weapon to manipulate you during the divorce process. Stand firm and do not let them push your fear buttons during negotiations or otherwise.

Babita Spinelli, psychotherapist and certified coach

Stages of recovery

Shock – If there was no warning that your partner was ready to discard you, without a single word or therapy session, you may be in shock. If it was you who finally found the courage to file for divorce, faced with the lies and cruelty of your ex, you may be thrust into the "freeze" state, much like a deer in headlights. You will wonder who this person is as the pain burns to your core. The shock and often accompanying feelings of betrayal may indicate treatment for PTSD would be in order, especially if you find you are unable to sleep, eat, or be productive.

Abandonment – When a marriage gets ugly and turns to divorce, it is easy to sustain an emotional abandonment wound. When the internal message is "You were not good enough," the rejection is compounded by shame because of the deception that breaks your trust in your partner. Even though you deserve to be free from this type of abuse, many falter due to the strong emotional ties until they come to the conclusion that life will go on after the marriage.

Anger – If you were the one who filed for divorce, you were probably thrust forward to make the decision because you finally got angry. Did you know that anger is a secondary emotion? We use anger as a response to something someone does to us. If we feel unheard, we get angry. If we're lied to, we get angry. If the children are used against us, we get angry. It is unhealthy to keep anger bottled up; it is, however, also a catalyst to change. It is a deep response that is natural, healthy, and part of being human. Simply put, anger is hurt that has not yet been dealt with. You can ignore your emotions, but they will catch up to you one day. If you were the discarded, you may have been swirling in exasperation at what was happening. You stayed, a virtual slave to this person, and now you've been discarded; indignation is mixed with confusion and pain because you do not understand what you did wrong.

Anger is a tricky emotion. Without tapping into it, victims tend to stay with their abuser and settle for crumbs. This stage is an important part of recovery because without it, we are stuck. In our day to day lives, if someone upsets us, we should be able to express our disappointment in healthy ways rather than immediately feeling irritated. With a narcissistic person, once we get piqued, the conflict will escalate. They enjoy pushing the buttons that cause anger since they know how difficult it is for you to express your feelings. This will also provide their supply because they have broken you. They want to control how you feel. It is only when we finally get mad that we gain the inner fortitude necessary to get out of an abusive relationship. However, if you allow yourself to remain angry, your mind will not be able to focus on what is necessary to move forward with the divorce. Causing upset is designed to rattle you and keep you in defense mode.

Letting go of the anger during divorce is difficult. You may even find that you have a case of Post Traumatic Divorce Syndrome (PTDS). Ultimately, in order to fully heal, you will need to get to a place where you can forgive the vile and painful things that were done throughout your marriage, and forget the need for revenge or justice. It is okay to get vexed but living with the monkey on your back for years will hinder your growth and prevent you from moving on. Unhealthy anger is not where you want to live; please talk to someone who can help you manage this emotion. Seek the help of a professional if you feel rage for prolonged periods of time.

Anger is a stage all victims need to pass through in order to heal; it

empowers you and launches change. Without it, you are left suscep-
tible to hoovering and returning to the scene of the crime. Get angry
in healthy ways: use it as fuel to cauterize your wounds, allowing
them to scab over and heal. This is when you will find the courage and
strength to push through the fight. For now, use it to propel yourself
to learn the truth, fight the good fight, and find that courage to create
a better life.

Keep Your Cool: You're going to want to keep your emotions in
check, because if you don't, you're playing right into their hands. As
soon as you lose it, they're already winning. Now, their manipulation
is working. Keep your cool, keep your emotions in check, and don't
let them get the best of you.
Rebecca Zung, author, nation's top 1% divorce attorney, high
conflict negotiation coach

Depression – The heavy sentiment that creeps in with rejection,
the self-imposed feeling of being a failure at love, can be formidable
and usually grabs ahold of you quickly. The stories in your head that
convince you that you did something wrong and are unlovable are
common thoughts and all part of the healing journey. They can still
make you sad. Sadness is temporary, but when coupled with depression, you may start to lose interest in activities or life in general. If you
can't get out of bed or don't want to handle your responsibilities, get
help. Talk to your doctor about going on a short-term anti-depressant
treatment, as mentioned in Chapter 1. This is not the time to give
up the fight. A narcissist's goal is to cause upset so that you freeze
and give up.

You may ask yourself, "Do I still love them?"

Most victims struggle with this. If you were the discarded, it will be
more difficult than if you decided to break free on your own. When I
talk with survivors in this stage, it is clear that they are trauma bonded to an illusion – the illusion of how perfect the relationship was in
the beginning (the love bombing stage). They tend to attach to the
positive ideas they were fed as what they will later learn was intermit-

tent reinforcement. I equate this to occasional momentary glimpses into the person they had impersonated from the beginning.

The person they pretended to be was just an illusion, a carefully created mask representing everything you were looking for. The mask they wear or role they play can be very convincing and feel genuine because they have perfected the art of morphing into exactly what you wanted in a partner. Thus the confusion, do you still love them? You long for this person to be real, to see the light, and try again; you vow to yourself that this time you will do everything right. When the relationship was good, it was over-the-top good. It's those moments we remember and want to hold onto as we ask ourselves: "Am I making a mistake?" or "Can they change?" or "Can I help them change?" Your mind says things like, "It wasn't always bad" and "I have everything I'd ever wanted because of them," and, my favorite, "If I try harder, they will go back to being the person I fell in love with; only with my love will they be able to feel safe being themselves."

My suggestion to clients who are struggling with this question is to do a simple exercise. Make a list of all the things you love about them, and a second list of things you don't like, a rudimentary pros and cons list, if you will. Be sure to include even the little annoying things. Usually the column of negative things is quite long. Then ask yourself, "What percentage of the time did you feel unconditionally loved?" "Did they ever confuse or frighten you?" "Do you feel comfortable with your kids in their care?"

The final step is to write down the things they did that pushed your boundaries. Dig deep to ensure this is a fair, robust list. Label each line; ask yourself, "How did that make you feel?" I often suggest carrying a slip of paper with you that details all they put you through. Take care of it like the life line that it is. Every time you wonder if you may still love them, pull it out and remember, "I deserve someone who loves me unconditionally, all the time. Not someone who could ever do these things."

Did they ever really love you?

I was haunted by doubts because it sure felt like love to me. When my recovery journey first began, this question came up often and the answer I kept seeing was, "No, Tracy, he can only pretend to love you." Initially this really made me angry. "Who can do that for ten years? How could it have been just an act?" Many survivors of this type of abuse have a difficult time accepting the concept that their life as they knew it was a lie.

In my recovery after the divorce, I studied NPD and learned that my family of origin was very dysfunctional. My bar for real unconditional love was low, nothing like real love, so I held on to the ways he showed his affection and thought it was authentic. He constantly showered me with cards and gifts; he appeared to be so proud of me and was always the perfect gentleman in public. I bought into the Prince Charming storyline and was sure that I was the luckiest girl in the world. I basked in the public attention and compliments as proof of how much he loved me. I never recognized the things he did behind closed doors to control and isolate me, or saw his need to be better than me at everything from cooking to photography. I ignored every red flag and declared that this was "good enough." The endless lies, secrets, and betrayals I was fed for ten years got blindly swept under my carpet of disillusion.

The hardest part to accept is that the crumbs of goodness you are offered are not as you actually see them. You probably witnessed these kind gestures and happily thought, "This is the person I married." Giving you crumbs, or intermittent reinforcement, is another manipulation tactic to keep you hooked, to placate you to stay so your abuser can get their needs met.

If you wonder whether they ever really loved you, be prepared to experience the answer in living color throughout the divorce. Someone who ever loved you, even a little, would be kind and respectful. I have never seen those sentiments in any narcissistic divorce. Actions speak louder than words. The behaviors that they display as the relationship ends will tell you everything you need to know.

Guilt, shame, and self-blame

Divorce can carry a stigma that you are not capable of nurturing a relationship for fifty years, thus raising the question, "What is wrong with me?" A gray line exists between guilt and shame of which most have a hard time finding clarity. Guilt is the feeling you get when you do something bad. You might feel guilty if you said something hurtful to your spouse – it is human to make a mistake after all. Guilt's purpose is to alert us when we do something that causes injury to someone else. With the knowledge, you can then change a behavior, or apologize for your bad choice, make amends, and move on.

Shame tends to shine a spotlight on what we may have done better, opening us up to ruminate over the guilt-fueled "what ifs" because we're sure we didn't do enough. You may beat yourself up with shame from the failure of an unsuccessful marriage. Mine was multiplied because it was my second divorce. It is an intensely painful emotion that announces "I am bad and profoundly flawed." I tried to make light of it by holding my hand in the shape of an "L" on my forehead; jokes made me feel like I was in control. Self-blame was my way of understanding and justifying the shame I felt. I look back now and realize that while I opted for the self-deprecating angle as my coping mechanism, I was actually only adding an additional layer of self-inflicted cruelty.

When you hold onto guilt for something you did (I *did something* bad), it often internalizes to become shame (I *am* bad).

The narcissist's goal is to trigger a reaction. They want control and by deftly pushing the right buttons, instigating arguments for example, they get the supply they seek. The victim's reaction will correlate with the type and intensity of abuse they received. Details may get twisted, the lines blurred, and the victim will time and again end up being accused of being the abuser. This is often internalized causing guilt for reacting followed by shame and a sensation similar to drowning. It is hard to function when you feel lost because no one believes you. The important thing to remember is to give yourself permission to move past any shame associated with reactive abuse because, as the old saying goes, "the devil made you do it." The narcissist is throwing down a victim card – they foster this victimhood to gain sympathy and turn the people and the courts against you.

Narcissists lack of empathy makes them exempt from experiencing guilt or shame. This should answer the question, "Do they know what they are doing to me?" The bigger question is "Do they care?" They can't introspect that they did something bad (guilt) or that they are bad (shame); they will lose no sleep over the havoc being wrecked in your life.

Last ditch emotional effort: couples counseling

If you are able to get your spouse to agree to counseling, don't set high expectations. Most victims agree that therapy with a narcissist is a disaster. Charming the therapist or playing the blame game and taking no responsibility for anything are the two angles primarily seen. The narcissists natural ability to charm makes some therapists who are untrained in NPD believe that change is imminent and you should give the relationship another shot. Or, upon calling the narcissist out for bad or inappropriate behavior, they refuse to go back and label the therapist every derogatory name imaginable. Narcissists don't want to be told the truth; they don't believe they've done anything wrong, so no therapist will be paid more than once if they don't take their side. The demand for loyalty is always there.

If you do decide to try counseling, look for someone who specializes in couple's therapy. It is critical that they are qualified to identify abusive behaviors, have a deep understanding of all personality disorder types, and be unbiased to either side. If they are not properly trained, the narcissist will hijack the session and turn it around to focus on your problems.

It is vital to realize that there are therapists whose singular goal is to repair ALL relationships – no matter the risk or danger associated with your abusive partner. The horror stories that I have heard made my skin crawl. Be certain: if the couples counselor you find doesn't have the knowledge of abusive personality types, resume your search until you find one that does. Your life may depend on it.

How to assess if a therapist understands NPD abuse: It is imperative that a therapist in your team of support during harrowing divorce proceedings is completely versed in narcissistic abuse syndrome. Ideally, they will specialize in treating complex trauma, as narcissistic abuse is a subset of relational trauma and culminates in Stockholm syndrome. You can request a brief phone call to query the therapist prior to setting up an initial consultation. In a few minutes time, you can inquire about the therapist's understanding of gaslighting, smear campaigns, flying monkeys and the absence of empathy. You can determine if they understand the necessity of no-to-minimal contact or abide by contraindicated directives to 'negotiate' differences. A seasoned therapist versed in NPD abuse will immediately know the lexicon of narcissistic abuse and how imperative it is to detach with an ex.

Rev. Sheri Heller, author, Licensed Clinical Social Worker

Someone with NPD cannot change. They can promise, misrepresent themselves, and fake change for a little while, but will soon unconsciously revert back to their bad behaviors. When it is a spouse, once they know you aren't happy and that their mask has fallen, they will begin the discard process.

Recognizing the onset of the discard process may be obvious because the passive-aggressive manners escalate. If your abuse was physical, the mistreatment will surge as well because the gig is up and there is no reason for them to pretend to be nice anymore. If you are married to a covert narcissist, a more stealth discard may begin in the background. On the hunt for new supply, detachment from you will be quick. You may find them not being present for you or your family because in their mind, they have already moved on. If this is happening, don't be surprised by their sudden exit; the therapy showed them that you have figured them out.

Ditch the couples counseling and invest in individual counseling or coaching for yourself. You will gain the strength to leave when you are validated and given the proper tools to get through the next stage of your divorce. The writing is on the wall after couples counseling fails.

Make plans and prepare to proceed on your own.

Counseling: the Trojan horse – my story

After my husband asked for a divorce, we tried therapy even though he had moved 2,000 miles away a few months earlier. To get started, he agreed to a multi-hour session; he flew in the night before, rented a car, and stayed at a hotel steps away from the parking lot of my new apartment complex. Of all the hotels he could have chosen, I couldn't understand at the time why he picked that one. I assumed it was a fear tactic to make me obsess about seeing him – it certainly worked that way. It wasn't until court that I fully understood his covert mission.

My ex was absent when it came time to pack up and sell our 4,500 square foot house. I was given two weeks to find new owners for 90% of our belongings. He wasn't interested in keeping anything: his clothes, electronics, or even childhood mementos. He simply walked away without as much as a backward glance. I reached out multiple times when I found things I thought he would want. His reply was always the same: "get rid of it." Those emails ended up benefiting me later in court, although that was not the original intention – I had sent them because I felt it was the right thing to do. I couldn't fathom how someone could walk away from everything in their life as if it meant nothing.

That was the first time I was able to acknowledge that he was methodically erasing our life together.

He never asked what I had kept or gotten rid of from our home. I moved into a 1,100 square foot apartment so I was extremely limited, spatially. After our first therapy session, he offered to take me to dinner. I accepted because I honestly thought we were trying to work it out. After dinner, he expressed an interest in my new apartment so I stupidly invited the fox into the hen house, my pretty prison. He was sent there on a mission, I found out later, because his lawyers wanted him to take inventory of which items I had kept. Their determination was that I owed him half of the proceeds from the garage sale and that I wasn't being truthful about the amount I had collected. They intended to evaluate everything from our home in order to petition the court to remove that portion from my half of the 50/50 split.

He surveyed everything, unbeknownst to me. Our dining table sat eight forcing me to purchase a smaller secondhand table that fit in my new apartment. Our outdoor furniture gone, replaced with two single chairs from Home Depot. From these two items alone, they tried to claim that I was frivolously spending the marital money. They wanted to place the value in the tens of thousands when in reality, I made $350 at the one garage sale I had been given time to hold.

Therapy day was a grand narcissistic stage production, an act for him to prove to the world that he was willing to give it another try. He was able to wear the victim AND hero masks at the same time.

I was leery to see him since he had lacked the courage to even ask for the divorce in person. A friend suggested I get a portable recorder to document the session knowing I was an emotional mess and likely wouldn't remember anything. By law in Colorado, only one party is required to know of the recording so I borrowed a recorder and brought it to the therapy appointment; it sat in my purse on the floor.

I am grateful I recorded our session that day and the reason is this: I listened to his fake dialogue of false promises over and over throughout our divorce and it renewed my strength each time. At first, when I heard him say, "Of course I will take care of her, she is family," I had hope that things really would be okay and that everything would go smoothly. I see now that I was still in denial. Later, as things got crazy, I would replay the vile lies and I got angry. It was that anger that propelled me to let go of the dream and delusions I had been hiding behind since we first met. I pulled myself together and set out to reveal the cracks in his defense.

He was dishonest that day in therapy. There I was, holding on to hope and believing that he wanted to give us another try, when he was actually giving himself a head start to prepare for battle. Doesn't this remind you of a Trojan horse in a therapist's office? Beware of other possible manipulations involving therapy with a narcissist.

Resisting coercive control to get you to stay

This may seem counterintuitive to the process, but often when divorcing a narcissist, they might try "hoovering" to get you back. Hoovering is a strategy meant to "suck" a partner back into the relationship. This could happen if you instigated the divorce because they were caught unaware and need to get their financial house in order. Or they may have seen a lawyer and discovered that you are entitled to half of everything they own. Promises to work harder to be the person you fell in love with will be made to get you back as well as offers to finally go to couples counseling.

The charm will be amped up to full strength reminding you of the way it used to be, slowly introducing guilt and manipulation to get you to drop the divorce case. The problem is their behavior will backslide to the way it was before with one distinct difference: they now know you are onto them and will drop the mask. With no reason to pretend to be kind any longer, the abuse will increase quickly. If you fall for the ploy, they just learned a very important fact about you: a carrot can be dangled and you will reach for it.

Their efforts to get you back can be powerful and hard to resist. Did you know a victim will go back to their abuser an average of seven times? You may be sure it can work this time, you believe in second chances, but rest assured that they will abuse you even more if you stay. Your objective should be to resist their efforts to stop it from going forward. It will take courage and anger to stay the course. Recognize that they are again crossing your boundaries and trying to establish control by not respecting the fact that you want a divorce.

Daily acts of courage: After years of living with a narcissist, partners are still reeling from the trauma of the relationship. From the initiation of a divorce with a narcissist to the conclusion, I recommend finding ways to ground yourself during the process. Daily acts of courage can help build emotional resilience. Recognize how far you have come and set a daily reminder each day of forward progress. Other daily acts of courage can include stepping boldly into action to build your new life; face your challenges by staying the course; resist the temptation to "give-in" on what you deserve to receive in the divorce despite the emotional roller-coaster (and it will be); or find something that brings you joy or makes your spirit soar even if it is small. You will need this to balance the challenges that may come your way during the divorce process.

Reconnect with friends and family you know will support you: Narcissists usually have cut you off from friends and family. You may have become distant from the people you were close to before your marriage and the narcissist may have kept you from connecting with them. Do not let fear or shame stop you from reaching out to those you were close with during your divorce. Allow yourself to be vulnerable with them and let them support you. It is important to surround yourself with an understanding support system. This can also help in the healing process.

Ensure self-compassion and self-care: Recovering from a narcissistic abusive marriage may feel like PTSD and requires the same work through; otherwise the divorce will take over your life. Reclaim the person you were by reminding yourself of all those positive and amazing qualities. Be gentle and patient with yourself. Recharging and incorporating self-care and taking a pause to catch your breath are important during what can be an emotionally draining and long process.

Babita Spinelli, psychotherapist and certified coach

The day you realized that your triggers are your superpower...

In a perfect world, your best defense would be to know upfront what to expect, except the divorce process with a narcissist is often one of the most unpredictable things you can experience. Your spouse knows you, sometimes better than you know yourself, and their goal will be to provoke and draw damaging responses from you to sabotage your case. No one could possibly be prepared for every stupid little thing that will be hurled at them but if you understand your own triggers, you can better prepare to hold your emotional stability in check.

What are triggers? Triggers are reminders of or feelings derived from past events that can spur a reaction of fear, anger, sadness, or unworthiness. A flashback can trigger not only the memory of the event but also the emotion of how you felt at that moment. Learning skills to separate the emotion from that memory will help you recover faster because you can catch yourself before you spiral down into the emotional rabbit hole.

Possible triggers:
- » constant reminders of your imperfections or an over-generalization: "You always do that wrong!"
- » name calling or negative juxtapositions, i.e., comparison to your abusive mom
- » rejection
- » loss of freedom / being told what to do
- » false allegations and lies
- » bad or abusive parenting accusations
- » broken promises
- » feeling unsafe or scared
- » financially unsafe and vulnerable
- » a violation, physical, emotional, or financial
- » lack of follow through
- » no respect of your schedule
- » last minute cancellations / plan changes
- » disrespect

Do you find any of these trigger you? Write down your provocations to learn how to manage your reaction when they occur.

Make no mistake that when your narcissistic spouse attacks you on a personal level, they know exactly which buttons to push to cause the desired reaction. During the divorce, this will be proven repeatedly to weaken your resolve and drum up unfavorable emotions to knock you off balance.

Common sentiments from a trigger (I feel):
- » unloved / unlovable
- » betrayed
- » unworthy
- » disrespected
- » judged

- » blamed
- » controlled
- » left out
- » ignored
- » powerless
- » trapped
- » feeling unheard (you have no voice)
- » manipulated
- » unsafe / in danger

Our reactions, good or bad, are fuel for our narcissist (supply). When they see that they can still evoke emotions, they will continue to push past the point of no return. If a particular memory triggers fear, ask yourself if you are safe in that moment. As you feel a reaction boiling to the surface, ask yourself, "Am I reacting to a trigger? Is it possible to slow down my reaction because it is what they are trying to incite?" What emotion(s) do you feel? Where is it derived from in your body? Learning to tune into your body permits you to slow down the reactions generated.

What are your narcissist's triggers? Everyone has triggers to some degree. They might not be overwhelming and others may seem to have nearly no reactions to anything. If you can identify them, however, you can better plan to avoid that minefield and not poke the bear which would only cause more drama.

Exercise #2: List your spouse's triggers

Make a list – and be very honest with yourself – regarding the common triggers of your soon-to-be ex-spouse.

- » What triggers them? How do they react?
- » Do their responses affect the children?
- » Do they utilize passive-aggressive measures? What types of things do they do?
- » Are the children used as pawns?
- » How do you react to their behavior?
- » How does it get resolved?

» Did they ever apologize or take any responsibility? Do you end up apologizing to stop the insanity?
» How often do you see their bad behavior?
» Recall a situation when they were angry or unreasonable about something specific. How did they express their anger? Did they yell? Throw things? Did they ever get violent and hurt you or the children? How long did they stay angry?

Most survivors of this type of abuse report that the angry events in their relationships would never get resolved until they surrendered simply to keep the peace. Victims are groomed early in every relationship to do this very thing. When the anger erupts, the mind games and passive-aggressive behaviors will continue until you acquiesce. This is an effective way to strip the victim of their soul; they are not allowed to have opinions, emotions, or be able to discuss anything of importance. When you are always walking on eggshells, knowing these unreasonable behaviors might not stop or begin all over again, it becomes easier and easier to throw down the white flag.

I cannot emphasize enough the importance of writing down and examining patterns. By seeing them in print, we can navigate away from them and find different strategies to cope. You are heading into war and every piece of data you can analyze will empower you to be stronger.

The emotional attachments to possessions

Everything collected as a couple has a story behind it. Remember that Christmas you got the Lladró© you treasured? Or the painting on the wall from that wonderful vacation together? There are memories of the kids' childhood that have deep significance for us. The separation of stuff during a divorce can cause negative responses and flashbacks.

Emotional attachments to property and assets can be tricky. Our "stuff" holds meaning, stirs emotions, and binds us energetically to a particular memory. When I first understood that our home was to be sold, I was faced with the tedious and heartbreaking task of going through ten years of memories and I was only given two weeks to make it happen. Our home was large; we had four living room sets; the unused formal living room, a family room, loft and a basement with a full home theater. Everywhere I looked, I was bombarded by painful reminders of the times we had together that I thought were happy. I was moving into an apartment a quarter of the size of our house which meant decisions had to be made. When my husband abandoned our life, he left with a carload of his essential items and nothing else.

The task of downsizing was daunting and if not for the help of my two dear friends, Karla and Naomi, I don't think I could have done it. I had a fire sale, selling $200 items for five dollars but due to the accelerated moving date, I ended up giving away nearly everything. I was heartbroken, magnified by the fact that I felt like my memories and everything I treasured had no value. I had to face and process these emotions simultaneously and it was painful. I was allowed no time to clearly see what I would need or want; I had to pack it in a box or get rid of it. I would have limited space so unless it was essential, it had to go.

Dealing with all the losses during a divorce is hard but letting go of belongings that hold fond memories adds another layer of the abuse. This type of abandonment of everything, like my ex displayed, is not a typical pattern of a narcissist because they usually feel entitled to everything and will fight tooth and nail to keep you from getting anything that is important to you. They could not care less about that statue but, because you want it, it becomes valuable to them as well. When your grandmother died and left you her silver, it's yours and you want it; it holds emotion for you. Narcissistic people don't attach to things but they often *pretend* to want something and will fight to the death to get it simply to manipulate you. It's hard to process but if you expect the fight, it will be less shocking because your mind can adjust and allow you to come up with ideas and negotiate plans. The trick is to not let them know how important something is to you. Evaluate what is most important to them and use it as leverage in exchange for grandma's silver.

It's hard to fathom that your spouse could be so cruel to keep your mother's china or your high school yearbooks or all of your children's photographs and you repeat the mantra: "Who does that!" One way to look at the losses could be to correlate it to if your house burns down. You would grieve the treasures and remember them fondly understanding that you must accept the fact that they are gone and there is no chance to get them back. And then you will heal.

As I look around now, eight years later, I see few items that remain from my previous life. Due to legal bills, I was initially unable to afford to replace things like sheets and towels, much less artwork or furniture. It took more than five years until I was able to begin reestablishing my household. I remained attached to things that I really didn't want but I had no resources to replace.

If you can afford to get rid of everything, it is certainly a viable option. I have a friend who was just a few months ahead of me in the divorce process. She did not want any remembrances of her ex so she called on a local non-profit that sent a truck – it collected everything from the towels to the dining room furniture. She had the means to buy everything new and that worked for her. I'm sure her healing process was accelerated because she didn't have to look at triggering souvenirs every day. I recall feeling slightly envious of the way she was able to start over with a clean slate.

I am a firm believer in objects holding energy. One thing I did to help release the emotional attachment to the items brought from my marriage was to smudge my new apartment. Burning Sage, an evergreen shrub, is used to release negative energy including past traumas and bad experiences. I was willing to try anything to make my transition easier, so I embraced this ancient spiritual ritual.

In case using the cleansing power of sage is a new concept to you, let me share what I learned and how I implemented it. Dried sage can be found tied up in little bunches at health food stores and specialty shops. Smudging is conducted by lighting the bundle and blowing the smoke into every corner, or by blowing it directly onto items to transform their energy field. I was told that this ritual can purify a house of its negative history, or banish the effects of conflict in the environment, or simply revitalize the home's energy. Why wouldn't I try it? I live in Boulder, Colorado where we are blessed to have many new age options. A friend also suggested I soak items in saltwater overnight. While I couldn't soak my towels or linens, I could soak glassware and the vase we got as a wedding gift. I believe it worked: I am now able to look at the few once-shared belongings that remain without the emotional attachment I had before these processes. Belief in the practices was enough to bring me peace; I could let go of the associated feelings and move on.

I love antiques and bargain shopping so in my effort to start re-claiming my space, I made myself happy by walking around thrift stores to find new-to-me pieces that could replace objects from my past life. It was affordable and enjoyable and if I looked often, I always found treasures. It gave me a feeling of freedom and this new apartment slowly became "my home" with joyful memories that were all mine. I repeated the smudging ritual with all my new purchases as well, just to keep the energy clear.

In many instances, one party remains in the marital home which can be difficult when memories are attached not only to belongings but also to every single room. If you are haunted by the memories, there is no escape from that prison until you can find the key to break free. Many things can be done to fashion a new environment. I have helped people rearrange their furniture so rooms feel different. If you are unsure what to do because the sofa has always been under the window, call a friend and ask for help. Creating a new space with the same stuff can be fun. Move things around, take pictures down and rehang them in different rooms, or transfer the guest room towels into the master. Little changes can make a big difference. As soon as you can, remove those family photos – seeing the remnants of your happy wedding daily on the mantle is not healthy and will impede your healing.

Often people who stay in the marital home do so for the kids and don't want to cause additional trauma by taking down all the fam-ily photos. There are other ways to protect the children's feelings while remaining true to yourself. Slowly start replacing photos in the frames. The kids may or may not notice but if they do, explain that change is healthy and you wanted something updated and fresh. Don't let them see that you made the modifications out of sadness. Be mindful of the hurt the kids are experiencing too and offer a photo of the other parent for their room. This will help them feel more secure as everything around them is changing.

I believe we go through various stages of attachment to "stuff" and they often depend on which side of the decision you are on. If you are the discarded, you might first go through an angry phase. Every time you see something that is a reminder of being a couple, you may be triggered which, in turn, spurs anger. Emotionally, you're powerless. As the anger subsides, you might encounter sadness. You may be so sad that it takes a valiant effort to drag yourself out of bed; your own home is like a carnival house of mirrors taunting you and prompting the tears. Once you come to terms with the reality that what was once yours together is now only yours, the items begin to lose their power over you. I can now look at special pieces around my home that we purchased together and appreciate their beauty without any negative remembrances associated with them.

If you are the discarder and you want your narcissistic spouse out, you possibly won't have the same attachment to material things. You were fortunate enough to be in control of your own destiny so the periods of anger and sadness were probably stages you experienced prior to the decision to file. Don't take this to mean that there are no memories but the sense of dominance enabled the release of bad energy much faster.

Dividing personal belongings

One of the biggest mistakes couples make when going through a divorce is to hold value to "stuff." So much money is wasted fighting for the mixer that by the time the fight is over, three new ones could have been purchased. I liken it to selling a car: it was a great car. You taught your daughter to drive in that car. It holds fond memories for you and, thus, you might inadvertently overinflate the selling price. It's not a special car to anyone but you. It's called a "story car" which serves no purpose to anyone interested in buying it. If you can focus on the important things, the money saved in legal fees will be astounding. That said, remember that narcissists hate to lose; they want you to lose. Please use caution when establishing what is most important or they will ramp up the fight just to take it from you. They don't care about the item; they just don't want you to have it. My first husband wanted our formal set of dishes that served twenty. He rarely cooked much less entertained, but I determined that this was not a worthwhile fight. Pick your battles and be willing to negotiate.

Personal items, like jewelry and wedding rings, are another matter. I was shocked to learn that an engagement ring is considered a gift since it was given prior to the marriage. However, if the ring was upgraded during the marriage, it could be considered marital property and be included in the division of community assets. If you were given jewelry as a gift during your marriage, hopefully you saved the card or note that accompanied it. It is then a gift and cannot be touched. I was gifted a pair of earrings from my in-laws that they claimed were quite valuable. They had tucked a note into the jewelry box saying that grandma would have wanted me to have them. This was all the evidence I needed – I got to keep them. Not everyone is so lucky to have saved a note in a box for ten years. If you have valuable pieces that your soon-to-be ex wants to add as community property, without proper documentation, you may get to keep them but only half of their worth might be added to your column of the financial division.

In situations like this, updated appraisals are worth their weight in gold. This does not hold true for all items – secondhand jewelry holds a value on the open market at only a fraction of the appraised value. My special earrings were one-of-a-kind by a famous German designer. I reached out to him and he was able to track down the one store in the USA that ever sold his pieces. I contacted that store, who determined that the earrings were originally bought for $18,000. The current value, at that time, was close to $40,000. The reality was that he could sell them to someone else for $40,000 but he offered me $3,000. The moral of this story is appraised value is not what you would get on the street so be sure to do your due diligence. In this case, my ex could have claimed the value at $18,000 to $40,000 had

I not had that little note inside the box that defined them as a gift. If he wanted them so badly, his attorneys could have added $40,000 to his total or we could agree to sell them to a dealer and split the proceeds. In this case, it would have been $1,500 for each of us which was not a huge loss over the imaginary price tag.

Removing the ring from your finger is a personal choice, but I can confidently predict that one day you will take it off. If wearing your wedding ring holds sad reminders, take it off when you feel the time is right. The sooner you can look at your hand without sadness, the faster you will heal. If you pull the Band-Aid off quickly, the pain is short and sweet; the faster you can get the ring off your hand, the quicker your recovery starts but it is important to move at your own pace and do what works for you. There is no right or wrong time to remove your ring.

My finger felt very strange when I first stopped wearing my ring. Every time I washed my hands, I looked at my naked finger like it was a foreign object. It was a constant reminder of my loss. A friend suggested I buy a "freedom ring," which is simply a new one to re-place the old. I followed her advice and that weird, empty, naked-fin-ger feeling disappeared. This granted me the reprieve to think forward to my new future and freedom rather than live in the past.

Work on your emotional recovery: Recovery from a narcissist or other exploiter involves two tracks: rebuilding your life and emo-tional recovery. You can, and should, work both tracks at the same time. Don't think you must finish your divorce before you can start to heal. Choose to work on your recovery -- and you'll find that it helps you handle the divorce.

Donna Andersen, author, founder of Lovefraud Continu-ing Education

Chapter 5

DECIDING TO LEAVE – PREPARING YOUR EXIT

If you are the one secretly strategizing to leave, be as careful as possible to keep your intentions under wraps until you have a solid plan in place.

Every divorce is different based on factors such as children, the assets that you share as opposed to what you each came into the marriage with, marriage length, and the extent of narcissistic injury incurred by your spouse. Review the exit plan suggestions below and determine the best course of action driven by what is the most important to do first for your situation. Develop a safety strategy and discuss it with your children, if they are age appropriate.

There is a multitude of scenarios people encounter when navigating a divorce with narcissists that cause them to feel unsafe:

» coexistence in the marital home (until someone is ordered to get out)
» tracking technology left behind
» your physical safety (if you are the one to move out)

> » the need for restraining orders to protect one of the parties from domestic violence

Security needs must always be considered a high priority no matter the circumstances. You may have a false sense of security that you are safe, but that isn't always true. Precautions for yourself and your children should always be taken.

Personal safety

Not all narcissists are physically abusive. Many show no signs of violence until the decision is made to terminate the marriage. Never hesitate to call the police if you ever feel vulnerable or physically threatened. File for a restraining order if you feel unsafe now or if you fear you will be unsafe after leaving. In some states, a temporary restraining order is the first step and is typically granted immediately.

Keep a journal of the abusive or threatening behaviors and keep it safe! Maintain a comprehensive record on your phone or computer, providing they do not have access to your cloud account or device.

Pack an emergency exit bag for you and the kids and hide it well. While you always hope it won't end this way, plan for the worst-case scenario to ensure security. "To fail to prepare is to prepare to fail" is well suited advice here as there may come a time when you must leave quickly and the preparations need to already be in place to flawlessly enact your full exit plan.

Pick a specific exit day. This makes the decision real and gives you a timeline to take the actions necessary. Create lists – things you need to do, to collect and to protect; dedicate time every day to reach that deadline goal.

Confide in a trusted family member or friend about the situation and create a code word that you can text if you are in distress.

Keep a list of important phone numbers in your wallet in case of an emergency. Most of us rely heavily on our phones to store these numbers but if it is shut off by your spouse or otherwise compromised, you could end up without vital information.

Plan a safe place (i.e., a neighbor's house) where the children can run to in case things get heated. Impress upon them that their job is to stay safe, not to protect you. Teach them about 911 and encourage them to memorize your name and address if they are younger.

Secure a place where you can stay without notice (i.e., a friend or family member) in the event your timeline gets accelerated unexpectedly. This person should not be your mom or best friend or any other acquaintance where your spouse might think to look. If possible, pull your car into their garage or park it out of sight.

Identify a family member or friend who can loan you money if needed although, as I mentioned earlier, it is important to begin to accumulate funds of your own as soon as possible.

Plan for your pets to be cared for and safe. Do not leave a pet alone with your narcissist if it is avoidable. They may injure or ignore the pet's needs just to hurt you. My friend learned from Instagram that her cat, Efini, passed away while in her husband's custody and there was no explanation. To avoid trusting them with your pet, make sure you include them in your plan. Did you know pets are considered to be a joint asset in a divorce?

Duplicate your house key and give it to a friend (or two) to hold. This may come in handy if they need to get you something or if you get locked out.

Documents and records safety

Move all personal records out of the house. Make copies of important documents (see below) and store them somewhere safe, like in your emergency exit bag. Pack all of this in advance in case you need to leave immediately.

Secure important documents:
   » Remove anything important from your joint safety deposit box and open a box of your own. Request to have your name removed from the joint box or close it if you haven't filed the divorce papers yet.
   » Birth certificates for you and your children
   » Green cards or other immigration papers
   » Passports
   » Car title and insurance information

» Deeds (or copies) to your home and other properties, lease, or rental agreements as well as property insurance policies
» List of account numbers, bank books, debit and credit cards, and passwords
» Social security card(s)
» Business records and tax returns
» Copies of loan and investment records, life insurance policies, income tax returns, and pay stubs
» School, medical, and insurance records
» Marriage license
» Copy of restraining order(s)
» Power of Attorney (POA) – update and record your end-of-life instructions to accurately reflect who you wish to make your health decisions in the event you are unable.

Alert your team

When you have set your escape date, notify your lawyer and close friends. Only include those you are confident will not reveal your new location to anyone. Your spouse will try to access any information about you, even tapping into your friends and family to find you.

Verify that your children's school, day care center, after school program, or camp understands who is and is not authorized to pick up your children. If your spouse no longer lives with you, ask your neighbors and landlord to call you or the police if they see them near your home.

Inform any organization that you have financial responsibilities to such as credit card companies, insurance, and car payment companies of your new address once you have relocated. If the bills continue to go to your marital home, you can count on them not reaching you which could risk adversely affecting your credit.

Packing to leave (if you are leaving covertly)

Perform multiple walk-throughs around your house, room by room, and make a list of items you need to be sure to take with you. Plan accordingly, based on your exit day, packing as much as you are able to, safely. If yours is a covert exit, avoid removing anything too early that might raise a red flag if it goes missing. Boxing up the coffee maker in advance is not worth the risk of exposure but be sure to keep it on your list so you don't forget it later.

Protecting your assets against false allegations

To protect your assets properly, I suggest taking photos and video of anything valuable in your marital home. Check every room of the house: open doors, drawers, and cabinets. Verbally state the dates and complete descriptions of everything you see as you film. This footage could very well be useful in the future. The most important thing is to cover yourself: plan ahead so you are able to prove if your ex took marital property or that you did not. A common tactic that narcissists pull is to accuse you of stealing money, property, and other jointly owned objects. This is usually a smokescreen leaving the victim to defend themselves of these false allegations while diverting attention away from them.

From the entire home being cleared out to only a few small baubles disappearing here and there, it is imperative to catalog everything. Video documentation allows you to hold them accountable. Without it, there is no proof. If they have access to the house and you suspect things are missing, record a new video. Compare the two, looking for items that may have vanished, and report any discrepancies to your lawyer. If big ticket items go missing, ask your lawyer if he advises placing a call to the police to file a criminal claim.

Family court can order belongings to be returned or the judge can level the playing field later with financial compensation to you. The risk is the zenith of your spouse's denials of any wrong doing or reversing the claims peppering in false information that the items were theirs prior to your marriage. If a narcissistic injury has damaged their fragile ego, they could go as far as filing a report with the police that accuses you of theft. When either party walks into family court with police reports, more veracity will be added to their overall case, regardless of their legitimacy.

Once a case gets past the initial stages, both sides will go through a period of discovery. This is when a list of all property is made and delineated to one side or the other. If you are the organized type, create an excel spreadsheet with item details and folders of images and videos of each room to protect yourself.

I recently suggested to a friend that she record everything prior to her husband vacating the marital home. Much to her surprise, items were already missing: the vacuum, security cameras, some electronics, and some of her jewelry! Because she caught it early, her lawyer filed motions for the return of these items until the division of assets could be completed through mediation or the court system.

This preventative strategy may never see the light of a courtroom unless they take unauthorized property and you are pushed into defense mode. Without necessary proof, you will be forced to defend yourself from any and all charges filed against you with little to back up your claims.

Two scenarios where this might be used:

1) If your spouse claims something has disappeared, video recordings can support your defense that the painting (for example) that you are being accused of stealing, was in fact on the wall where it had always been the date you departed. Conversely, if they took something that didn't belong to them and they deny its existence, go back to your photo library and find a picture that shows you wearing that missing ring or the image of that oriental area rug on the floor. This detective work will help you find the evidence of their deception. Don't waste your time digging into anything in particular unless your lawyer says it's worthwhile – they can advise you what is most important. Warning: it's not easy to review photos of the past during this time. It will likely trigger you so only do this as a last resort.

2) If you are accused of removing something that you know never existed, hold onto your truth and don't panic. Instead of playing defense, throw the ball back into

their court – ask for receipts and images to be shared of the items in question. My ex accused me of stealing his antique cufflink collection. In ten years of marriage, I never saw anything that resembled an antique cufflink collection. However, it became a talking point that he could use to engage the sympathy of friends and family. It criminalized me and again tapped into his gold digger portrayal of me. Of course, the items were never located and the statements were never proven because *lies aren't true.*

Protecting your financial security

It is recommended to check your credit report one time per year, closing anything outstanding and correcting any errors. This is important advice for everyone to take. With the continued development of the internet and nefarious people making a living off of others hard work, it should not be a surprise to hear that identities are stolen regularly. New credit lines are opened and the assurances you took to maintain a good credit score will be the last of their concerns. Along this same vein, this would be the time to pull a current credit report for yourself to confirm that your spouse has not opened anything new in your name. You can get a free credit report from websites like Credit Karma[6] that will not show up as a hit against your credit. If you choose to, you can sign up for credit monitoring which will alert you if any new accounts are opened. This could be helpful if your spouse knows your social security number – they can open new accounts in your name without your knowledge.

One of the worst cases I have seen was when an excessively hateful individual opened ten credit cards in their spouse's name and proceeded to run up over $100,000 in debt. When the bills weren't paid, her credit was ruined.

Sadly, these are common examples of financial abuse. Please make monitoring your credit a habit, starting today.

As I mentioned in Chapter 1, opening your own bank account is

---

6   https://www.creditkarma.com

the first step to establishing financial security. It also prevents your ex from being privy to your purchases or account balances. However, despite this being your personal account, you still will need to disclose it and all of your statements for financial discovery which means any monetary additions to the account will be tracked from the source. For example, if your parents loan you $10,000, be sure to have that check or transfer validated to avoid your narc-spouse investigating you for hiding secret accounts. Ask your parents to draw up a promissory note for the loan so you can show it as debt to be repaid rather than a gift. Work overtime to keep detailed receipts and pristine records to avoid unnecessary drama.

Suggestions for starting your financial journey:
- » Open a credit card in only your name.
- » Rent a mailbox at a UPS store that offers an actual address versus a PO Box. When you open any new accounts, use this PO Box *address* to receive your cards and statements.
- » Start saving money but please do not hide it in the house. Some have stashed cash for their escape only to find that their narcissistic spouse had combed through everything and robbed them blind. This could delay your exit if you are forced to start saving from scratch.
- » Transfer or withdraw half from any joint bank accounts and deposit the funds into your own new account. Take only what you are legally entitled to based on the laws of your state or country. Ask your lawyer before you do this via a protected email, so the answer is on paper. This is an added protection for if thievery allegations begin.

How to protect your personal safety

The person you married is not the same person you are divorcing. Bad behavior may have begun to manifest at this point. Part of the process is to become well versed in personal safety measures for protection. Even though they may never have raised a hand to you, do not blindly assume that you are safe. There are plenty of examples where that is not the case. As I mentioned earlier in this chapter, not all narcissists display physical violence but that does not mean that they won't. Also, not all abuse is physical; narcissists want to get to you any way that they can. They are not above spying or fictionalizing horrible stories about you to family, friends, and coworkers. These attacks can come via social media, phone calls, texts, or emails.

Remember that everything you post on social media is traceable, including locations, so be careful. Turn off all tracking services. Try to avoid using social media during this time. If you feel you are being stalked, report it or any threatening behavior to the police. Mix up your daily routine since they undoubtedly know where you will be at specific times. Don't be ashamed to get out your phone and brazenly take video of them following you, just in case you need to report them or press charges. Being bold while you film puts them on notice that you are on to them. It may slow them down if they think there could be police intervention, especially with photo or video proof.

Sometimes spouses will hire private investigators to watch you. Always be aware of your surroundings – if you fear a car is following you, change lanes to confirm your suspicion. If you're able to confirm it, make note of the vehicle details and drive directly to the closest police station, calling them on your way to give them notice of your arrival. Ask for a police officer to meet you at your car. Professionals are stealth and often change cars daily. Be aware, document and report it if you become afraid or feel like you are in danger. If you are still on their phone plan (you shouldn't be – get your own plan now!), download the images off your phone or they will likely go missing and your documentation along with them. Courts generally need proof of multiple stalking attempts before they will grant a restraining order.

A typical trick a toxic narcissistic ex will pull during divorce is the use of fear tactics: When a narcissist uses fear, it throws you off balance and causes you to become emotionally dysregulated. The goal for this tactic is to encourage you to make mistakes. It is easy for fear tactics to work because you are in a state of fear with the process and uncertainty, especially in family court. The reality is your future is at risk and you worry about your children, retirement, security and your fundamental stability.

Slow yourself down: Although there is real fear associated with this, by slowing yourself down you can take an objective look at what your ex is trying to make you believe. Oftentimes a narcissistic toxic ex will target your fears. When you can take an objective and realistic view at the situation, you will realize most of the time their version of reality just isn't realistic. You can only do this when you slow yourself down!

Constantly remind yourself that the divorce process is slow. When you are in the middle of the nightmare, you want the pain and fear to just "go away." The reality is the process is slow; there are multiple hearings, mediations, and procedural processes that take time. You can use these "built-in" delays to your advantage. Use this time to slow yourself down and really process what is going on. Giving yourself that moment to breathe and slow down can help you realize your ex is just using fear to control you.

Duane Robert, host of the Podcast, *Break the Cycle with DSD* and YouTube Channel, *Dad Surviving Divorce*

Important safety tips to plan on

A storage unit is a great option that will enable you to start moving important things out of the house prior to physically vacating it. This is a possibility only if the divorce papers haven't been served yet. Once they are, the rules change. Then, removing things from the house can get complicated and could possibly result in criminal charges if what you take is considered joint property. Ask your lawyer to be sure. Document everything you claim as your own to show that you are above board.

Take note of your spouse's schedule to be confident when would be a safe time to leave. Notify neighbors that you trust if you have a moving truck planned so they don't panic and call your spouse with questions.

If at any time you feel that you are in physical danger, know the phone number and address of the closest shelter. Call 911 without hesitation to protect yourself and your family. I realize I have reiterated this point many times but I cannot stress its importance enough.

If your spouse is the one who is leaving, immediately change the locks, Wi-Fi password, and garage door and security alarm codes. Call the alarm company to adjust your call-in password and ensure they have your cell number. Instruct them to delete the narcissist's name and phone number so that they no longer have access to your account.

There is a method to this madness: I know a woman who remained in her marital home and only changed the keypad code thinking it was sufficient. Her not-quite ex-husband attempted to access the house, the alarm was triggered, and he answered the house phone. He said who he was, verified the voice password, and said he typed the password incorrectly because he was carrying groceries and the dog was jumping on him. With no reason to know they shouldn't, they turned off the alarm and he was in. Since they were still married, he had not been deleted from the account, and as there were no restraining orders against him, the police had no jurisdiction. This is a valuable lesson: ensure that your contact information is current to reflect all modifications. This wouldn't have been an issue had she contracted a locksmith promptly after he moved out.

I cannot express adequately the importance of creating a new password for the modem. Allowing access to your network could possibly allow access to your data. I have talked to so many survivors who forgot this critical step. Unbeknownst to them, the narc-spouse would sit in their driveway late at night, tap into the Wi-Fi settings, and access their computer. They opened emails, deleted important papers, and checked the browser history – all in an attempt to stay one step ahead. To avoid this sabotage, *change the Wi-Fi password*. If you are not tech savvy, call the internet/cable company and ask them to help you change it immediately upon their final exit from your home.

Put the utilities in your name to avoid coming home one day to no power or heat. Become the master of your domain with the sole discretion to make account adjustments.

If your ex-spouse is court-ordered to stay away from the house, have a motion sensor camera professionally installed and be sure the data is being sent to a secure cloud storage service. You don't have to buy the best camera but it does need to have cloud storage.

Start an inventory of all the things you need to do, preferably in priority order. Depending on how fast you want/need to move out, dedicate time each day to see it through. If you move out without gathering the paperwork, you will be at a huge disadvantage and it could cost you a lot of money. You can plan the actual move *while* you do the important things. More prepared now equals less drama later. If you need to rent a new apartment before you leave the home, do it. It takes time to set up a new household. If you juggle this step in conjunction with getting the paperwork in order, you can safely make your exit and have a much easier transition when you have a place to go that feels safe already established.

Depending on your situation, some things I mention may not apply to you. If you're still cohabitating, you may not be able to perform certain actions without arousing suspicion. Either way, one thing you should do immediately is set up a new email account so you have a way to communicate privately with your lawyer.

Change passwords on your current account(s):
» email accounts, phones, computers, and all devices, like iPads, which are often forgotten allowing the spouse open access to private emails and messages
» social media
» accounts like Google, Audible, PayPal, and Amazon – remember to open your own if you shared one as a couple and stop using the joint account. Please don't buy books about divorcing a narcissist on a shared account. If you escape and accidentally send yourself something via any online business that they have access to, they can learn your address without even trying.
» loyalty cards for the supermarket and drugstore or you risk allowing them access to see how you spend your money.

» the children's phones – make sure that the tracking is
turned off when you escape if they are on the family plan.

Consider investing in a password management program for securely storing and managing your new passwords.

If you are planning your escape while still sharing a computer with your spouse, be vigilant with your computer use. Always open an incognito or private window before searching any website. This is a function of every browser but they all call it something different. To find it, go to the file menu and type "opening a private window." This is perfect for checking online email as no cookies are tracked, no history is memorized, and no passwords are saved. Your goal is not to be paranoid with your safety guidelines, but to be proactive and do what you can to ensure nothing can be used against you. If tech stuff is scary to you and you don't really understand it, ask a knowledgeable friend to help you set up the new passwords and get things locked down properly. You do not need to go through this alone.

Computer monitoring and key logging software can easily be installed which would allow your soon-to-be ex to view all your computer activity. Many are surprised by the intel their spouse can attain on them and this type of tracking is typically responsible.

Back up all important data to a physical external hard drive and safeguard that device offsite, possibly with a friend or trusted family member.

If your spouse holds the contract on your cell phone, get a new phone for yourself so they cannot trace your every move and call. If you don't have the money to buy a new phone, get a no-contract "burner" phone for calling lawyers, potential landlords, or any divorce-related activity. They are available at electronics stores, office supply store chains, and even grocery stores. Everyone always gets hung up on losing the phone number that they've had for twenty years; this resistance is often their rationale to not do what needs to be done. You do not need to cancel that number and can transfer it to your new phone plan once you are free, but for now, it is smart to use a second phone for security purposes. It is easy to log into a cell phone account and view text messages and phone calls. Take screen shots of all your text messages and send them to your cloud account. Messages tend to disappear if proper care is not taken. Stop this possibility from becoming your reality. The most important thing to remember will be to turn off location services if you are unable to get a new phone and are forced to remain on the same plan.

A survivor shared the following story: He was divorcing his narcissistic wife who always seemed to be one step ahead of him. A friend suggested that perhaps she was watching him through his phone activity, so he got a burner phone. He would leave the one he suspected she was tracking at home when he went to meet his lawyer. He gained a new sense of freedom and his anxiety and fears were eliminated.

When the need for a protection order arrives

Victims of narcissistic abuse often begin to fear their partners as they travel down the divorce road because the person they married is not the same individual they have become throughout the process. The prospect of calling the police can be overwhelming and many worry about the ramifications if they go forward with a restraining order. How do they keep themselves and the children safe if their spouse is volatile and the victim is afraid of retribution?

Restraining orders, or orders of protection, are court orders issued by the state to protect you if you feel you are in danger of potential harm. There are temporary restraining orders (TRO) which vary in length, depending on the state, and permanent restraining orders (PRO) which are valid forever. If you need to consider a restraining order on your spouse, you would be applying for a temporary civil restraining order. You are the victim and they are the perpetrator; judges will usually grant an order immediately if they believe the victim is in danger and reasonable grounds of your unease can be explained. Judges historically don't give a restraining order simply because you have a feeling or you are fearful something *might* happen; they need evidence. Voice message threats, phone records, texts, and videos can offer ample evidence to get a restraining order approved.

To get a civil restraining order, you may be required to go to a courthouse, fill out paperwork, and possibly pay a fee. Depending on the circumstances, a same day meeting with a judge is often arranged. Paperwork will be presented and the judge will ask relevant questions – a decision will be made on the spot as to whether or not there is enough evidence to grant your request; if not, it will be denied. Your spouse does not usually need to be present for this temporary hearing. Every state has a different process so the duration of each order may vary but another hearing is typically scheduled at a later date to extend the order, if need be. Your spouse will also be given the opportunity to speak on his behalf if he chooses to exercise that right.

Once the judge grants the restraining order, it will need to be served by a police officer or sheriff. In domestic violence situations, the fees are oftentimes waived. Once they have been served, you will be given a copy to carry with you in case anything happens. Of course, if you call the police, they can easily look it up but having a copy on your person might save valuable time.

Videos may or may not be admissible in court, depending on where you live. Ask your lawyer about the laws in your state. If your intuition tells you tensions are escalating and an altercation might be on the horizon, arm yourself with your fully charged phone. When the time comes, turn on the video, even if you don't hold it up where their face is clearly visible. Say their name and stay calm so you don't look like the instigator. Get evidence by saying things like, "Joe, I am asking you to leave," or "Joe, you are frightening me," but don't bait them. Do not add fuel to the fire just to capture the event.

If the police are called and your spouse is arrested, the court may automatically issue a criminal restraining order. These orders usually have a specific time period based on the offense and the court's decision but they do carry the same weight in the system to protect you. If your spouse still lives in the house with you, they will be ordered to vacate immediately upon being served a restraining order. The court will dictate that they cannot be within a certain distance from you, the home, or your place of business. No calls, texts, emails, social stalking, or any type of harassing behaviors are accepted. In some circumstances, other people can often be added to the restraining order if they are also in danger, like your children or family members. Once it is put into place, block your spouse from your phone and all social media. If you are in a co-parenting situation, seek advice from the courts, your lawyer, or police to arrange for a solution to communicate if they are still allowed to see the kids.

Once a restraining order is in place, do not permit your narcissistic spouse to convince you that it's okay to liaise. There have been too many cases where the love bombing tactic gets deployed and despite the restraining order, the victim lets the spouse come over to "talk." Now *you* are violating the restraining order and risk it being dropped or a judge refusing to issue another when you need it. Be incredibly careful with texts as well. If you engage, you could be in breach and expose yourself to the same dangers with the court system.

Once you stop responding, watch your back for the flying monkeys to begin circling, whispering in your ear to drop the restraining order. Their friends, your friends, family members on both sides, neighbors, and even your pastor will hear horror stories from your spouse. They'll let everyone know that they feel terrible and would never hurt you but they are the victim and it's all simply a big misunderstanding. These people will then be tasked to change your mind. Inner fortitude and keeping your eye on the prize is always key.

The questions people ask you will act as a good barometer of how to move forward. Are your friends asking you what really happened? Or are they assuming because your spouse got to them first that you acted impulsively and they are indeed the victim? Determine from tone and gestures whether they have been manipulated and recruited knowingly or unwittingly sent to do the bidding of the narcissist. Please note that you should not feel obligated to explain any details at all to anyone. If you question their loyalty, don't think of them as your best man or the godmother of your children but rather as potential spies sharing your thoughts and plans with the one person who should not be privy to them. Stop accepting their calls and tread lightly until they have proven themselves trustworthy. Your spouse's end goal will always be to get you to drop the restraining order. With this said, if a situation resulted in the police being called and your spouse was arrested, a criminal restraining order would have been put into place and you cannot retract it. It has fallen into the state's jurisdiction and it is now the state against them, not you against them as a civil order would be.

What happens if the restraining order is violated? Call the police, and use your phone to take pictures or record a video, but *get proof.* Evidence makes it easier for the police to do their job and make an arrest if one is warranted. Without proof, you can imagine the excuses that the narcissist will engineer, such as asking the flying monkeys to lie and provide them with an alibi. Most states carry a misdemeanor offense if the order is violated along with fines or jail time. If the violation becomes habitual, a judge will often add fines or extend its duration.

When you return to get a permanent order secured, any violations will be used as evidence to show the judge how the narcissist was unwilling to obey the law. This might make obtaining the permanent order a faster process. On the flip side, if *you* agree to talk or meet, violating the order, it will be used against *you* and a judge might not believe you are in as much danger as you claim. Be very strong and mindful to keep the narcissist at arm's length.

Case in point: Michele had a restraining order on her husband, John, but he was savvy and used guilt and fear to manipulate her to meet him at a coffee shop. It was a public location so she felt as safe as she thought she could. He planted someone in the coffee shop to take a picture of their meeting and then used the images to show how she had violated the restraining order; he was able to convince the court that her safety was never in jeopardy. She underestimated the level of how low he would go to hurt her.

In a perfect world, a restraining order keeps you out of harm's way but I don't want to give you the false hope that it offers total safety or that the police, when called, will do anything about the violation. I have spoken to survivors who have shared stories where they called the police and nothing happened. This leaves the victim helpless, now in a fight with the police to change the situation. It's frustrating and abusive. Do not be discouraged from taking the proper steps to protect yourself, but be aware that the system is not perfect, and narcissists are the same sneaky liars who manage to evade police and your accusations.

The reverse restraining order is when your narcissistic spouse makes it their life's work to cause you harm, including calling the police and falsifying proof to show that *they* are the one in danger. You might get arrested or a restraining order placed on you. Many who experience this are innocent victims, too afraid of retaliation to fight. No matter what, if you feel like you are in danger and have proof to show a judge, call the police or visit a courthouse for help.

The rage that the victim of this type of false arrest experiences, the injustice of it all, is so immense that they ask, "How can they get away with this? Should I file one against them now since I am the one who really needs the protection?" This might get tricky because it can be looked at by the judge as tit-for-tat retaliation. Technically, you are now not allowed to go near them so as long as you follow the law, they assume you will be safe. Sadly, we know that isn't always true.

If the need for a restraining order can be proven and the appearance of retaliation can be discredited, your legal team can assist your effort to obtain a reverse restraining order. One fact to realize first is that this action will make narcissists incredibly angry. It provokes a narcissistic injury that will cause the reprisal to lurch into full swing, escalating the entire divorce into a higher conflict case. If you are not in immediate danger, speak with your lawyer prior to making this decision. Together, you can weigh out other solutions that may be equally effective.

The police should never be called out of spite, revenge, or as a custody ploy – this never ends well. You are dealing with the law and court systems – falsifying reports could land you in jail. The legal ramifications of having a restraining order filed against someone can have a great impact on their life going forward as well. If their job has security clearance, a restraining order could risk their employment and ability to pay support. If their industry requires special licensing, this could also be jeopardized. They will lose the ability to legally buy a firearm, which is especially important for victims of domestic violence; if they already own a gun, it will be removed from their posses-sion, potentially causing an even greater narcissistic injury. Restrain-ing orders can show up on background checks, limiting their means to rent an apartment and negatively affecting them when applying for work. A potential landlord or employer will see a criminal record, with no background story, and possibly make a decision that can be long lasting.

I have personal experience with this: I have placed restraining orders on people and I have also been falsely arrested by a narcissistic ex-boyfriend after my divorce. Since there was an arrest, there was a criminal restraining order put into place. Until it was released, I constantly looked over my shoulder to feel confident that he wasn't, for example, already in the movie theater before I sat down, or I could violate the order and go back to jail. After sharing this on my You-Tube channel, I ironically became the poster child for false arrests. People continue to call to tell me their stories and get support. I have met and talked to hundreds of victims of this type of attack. Please be careful; you, too, can be the object of this form of deviousness.

The risk of dropping a civil restraining order

Once you have gone through the process of getting a civil restraining order and dodged all of the flying monkeys, your resolve may waver and you might think about dropping the order. The danger in this difficult decision is something you must seriously consider before tak-ing any action. The pressure from others will echo the wishes of your spouse – that this was a terrible mistake – and they want to work with you. If you give into the coercion and guilt, it will be used against you in court to claim that they are, for example, safe parents and deserve equal time. Dropping the restraining order would be used as a pawn to show that you are irrational and angry and that they pose no real threat to you or your children. If they did, why would you have ap-proved its removal? Discuss the legal ramifications with your lawyer as it relates to the divorce process and custody issues.

The myth about family court and restraining orders

Restraining orders are not the job of the family court system. Their task is to split your assets, define custody and support, and legally terminate the marriage contract. If you feel you're in danger, call the police or go to a courthouse and file the papers necessary to begin the process of getting a restraining order. It is the criminal court's responsibility to keep you safe. Many have the wrong impression that the court system is there to help them get justice so they save all of their allegations and complaints until they are in front of a family judge. This is incorrect and you will not get the results you hope for there. If there is violence or if you are in danger, you *must* take this information to the police in order for the criminal system to do its job and protect you. *That paperwork can then be submitted as evidence to the family court to prove that you are in danger.*

Cameras and monitoring devices: to film or not to film?

If you do not live under the same roof as your soon-to-be ex but fear that they may try to enter your house illegally, a camera or two would be far less expensive than an alarm system. Look for one with motion sensors that send video to a cloud and an alert to your mobile device when activated. Do this with the understanding that a monitored security system, when tripped, would send law enforcement officers to ensure you are safe. Follow your gut – do what you think would be the best option based on the temperament of both parties.

An example: Carol, a survivor, moved out of her house to get free of her husband. At the beginning of the divorce process while he was in that love bombing, suspiciously nice phase, he invited her over to sign some papers and review what items in the house that she wanted. Things hadn't gotten ugly, so she agreed since there were some things she did wish to have. When she arrived, he suggested that they go down to the basement to sign the papers. This seemed extremely odd because they never used that space when she lived there. He made up a lie that he wanted to show her something that he thought she would like; she slowly followed even though the hair on the back of her neck was standing at attention and her intuition was telling her something was not right. He had been physical before and she felt trapped as if she was marching into the devil's lair. There was lemonade on the coffee table and he invited her to sit in a specific seat. She complied, knowing all of this was crossing a dangerous line. As she signed the paperwork, he began peppering her with questions. Suspicious, she decided to cut the meeting short and go back another day to review the property. Carol found out later that her ex had bugged the entire basement with microphones and cameras in an attempt to use the resulting file against her in court. This occurred in a state where one-party-consent for recording was allowed. Be aware that this is a possibility and always keep your guard on high alert.

Another example: If your spouse is allowed continued access to your home, they can take things or set up cameras to spy on you, like what happened with Debra and Rick. When Rick moved out, Debra assumed he would respect her space and leave her alone. Unbeknownst to her, he did not honor her wishes. Rick would track her movements and as soon as she would leave the house, he would let himself in and move things around. His goal was to keep her in fear and to make her think she was losing her mind. Classic gaslighting compounded with actual break-ins that allowed him to manipulate her mental security. Her intuition told her that something didn't seem quite right when she would get home and eventually, she did call the police. Nothing was taken so the assumption was made that she was simply forgetting where she put things. No charges were filed because she had no evidence. In hindsight, she knew she had made it too easy for him by not changing the locks as soon as he left or installing cameras after her original suspicion.

While this could have happened without tracking her phone, in this case it made it easy for him to feel secure knowing she was at work. Disable all tracking capability on your phone. Visit your phone store right away if you are unsure how to turn off these services. Changing the locks on your doors can be costly depending on where you live and you may think it is an unnecessary expense but it is one of the most important. Call a locksmith to see if they can rekey each lock.

It's usually cheaper and the locksmith can make new keys right in your driveway. You cannot put a price on peace of mind and the money spent will pay for itself three-fold if you end up needing to involve your lawyer to get a restraining order later. Please make it a priority and give yourself the gift of security before it becomes an urgent situation.

Going no contact: it's a safety thing, so do it right

Let me explain to those new to this narcissistic abuse world what the term "no contact" means. It means just like it sounds – no contact – not seeing them – not talking to them – not texting them and disconnecting them from all your social media.

If I had to pick one word that succinctly explains no contact, it would be "block." Block them anywhere that you were connected to them in the past. To be successful, it's best to block all your friends that were their friends first, unless you are completely confident of their loyalty. This must include any of their family. Unfriending them is not good enough. Why? Most importantly, if you unfriend someone, they can still see all your posts. Also, you can still peek to see what they are doing and trust me, this never ends well. When you see that they are taking their new love interest to Bermuda, it will break your heart. If they blocked you, please don't think this means you are safe. Return the favor and block them, too. This ensures they will not get the opportunity to spy on you and offers you more protection – if they comment on a mutual friend's post, you will never have to even see it.

The discarded victims may still love their spouse so they leave the door open by opting to not go "no contact." The idea of completely cutting off all communication is extremely painful and it can be scary.

Beliefs a victim holds onto:
- » If my spouse could just see what they did was wrong, then it might be worth giving it another try.
- » If they would go to counseling, it could be better.
- » If they knew how much you were hurting, they would feel bad and come back. Are they hurting like you are?

>> If the door stays open, they may reach out when they realize that they miss you.

These reasons are common in trauma bonded situations.

Important thoughts to consider:

>> What if they don't reach out? How will you feel?

>> What will you do if they do reach out? Will you meet with them? Would you consider giving them another chance? Has this happened before?

Remember the multiple times you tried to get away in the past: did they ever change or fulfill the promises they made as a condition for you to come back? Be honest with yourself. Dig deep and find the courage to go forward with your plan despite the hoovering and love bombing being tossed at you.

How do we draw the strength and self-love to walk away, even if they might want to come back? If they call and you don't answer, will they ever try to call again? Your mind will work overtime to question the decision to go no contact. Everyone in this situation struggles with these same concerns. You are not alone.

The five challenges of going no contact:

1) There is no rulebook. Life would be so much easier if there were rules and detailed instructions for every tough situation. When your spouse pulls something unexpected (like sending flowers), it can be confusing and might lead you to wonder, "Am I making the right decision?"

2) Flying monkeys are real. As if this isn't already a big enough challenge, you will now be bombarded by their best friend or mother to tell you how much they are hurting. Claims will be forced down your throat that they really miss you or they'll go to counseling – anything that you want them to do – to prove they are different and willing to work on it. These are intended to make you second guess yourself and slow down the divorce process while they work to get their things in order.

3) Shut out your own mind. The memories of the good times start to flood in causing you to doubt your decision

to walk away from someone you professed to love. Are you giving up too soon? Why can't we just try again? Relationships with narcissists are so much more complicated but victims of this type of abuse continue to try to shove an uncaring relationship into a normal relationship box. A round peg does not fit into a square hole just like this can never fit into the normal human behavior of relationship rules.

4) You against your phone. Most understand the importance to "block" them but struggle to delete the photos and videos. The images of good times take over which makes your mind wonder if the images on the screen were the real person. "Look at how sweet he was with our daughter," or "She was so loving that day." Your mind softly tells you, "I want this again." You then start to doubt yourself, "Will I ever love again?" "Am I making a mistake? It wasn't always bad; I can tolerate the bad times..." These feelings get triggered with every photo, over and over.

Narcissists are certainly capable of having a good time. Don't be blinded by a great day because it didn't mean the same thing to them as it did to you. Do you think they have pictures of you on their phone?

Do yourself a favor: back up the photos and get them off of your phone and computer. Every time you look at them is damaging and you are setting yourself up to fail at going no contact. Delete!

If I had a dollar for every person I know who held on to texts or voicemails, I would be rich. I understand how if a loved one has passed away, being able to listen to that last message on demand is priceless. Saving them from your ex, however, is dangerous and those memories are harmful to keep. Each one is another dagger that reopens that abandonment wound; only you have the power to eliminate this pain. When the loss becomes too much to bear, our mind will offer relief: "Just one quick peek." One day, a special day, a holiday, a birthday, or maybe after a few drinks, temptation will stare you in the face. Do you trust yourself to stay away?

5) Unfinished business. This is the most overlooked challenge. Terminate everything that connects you. Closure is king. Are you still on the same phone plan? Is he "being nice" and letting you continue to store items at his house? Every piece of unfinished business brings them back into your safe space and interrupts your healing and peace. Clean it up.

A SurTHRIVER's Story: When Sally moved in with Jim years ago, he secured a storage space for her excess possessions and always paid the rent. After the divorce, he logically wanted to end that obligation, so he reached out to her. He called her, he texted her and, after not getting any response, he eventually stopped by her house.

Taking over the storage space payment was something that had not occurred to Sally. She hadn't blocked Jim so she saw his messages, read his emails, and listened to his voice messages but she was no contact, so she didn't respond. She did call the storage facility to give them her credit card for future charges, but since she didn't share her intentions with him, his anger kicked in. He felt ignored and narcissists hate that. Things escalated when he went to her house; they argued and the police were called. This could have been avoided. She could have stayed no contact but asked a friend to tell him she took care of it. She could have asked the storage company to notify him. This type of connection leaves their foot in the door. You cannot succeed in going no contact if they have clothes at your house or your bike is still in their garage.

Think about your own situation. How would you react if your calls went unanswered and you had no interest in continuing the payments? The unfinished business must be dealt with in a smart and safe manner. Establish a clean break in every possible aspect so you may go on with your life unmolested.

Be honest with yourself: are you unconsciously or deliberately not closing these doors with hope they will come back? I knew someone who was so worried that she would never see her ex again that she hid his phone charger. This was at the beginning of the breakup but she wanted to get him back, get him to call, or to create an excuse to call him. It sounds innocent enough, but it was manipulative and prolonged her pain. She eventually saw the error in her ways and then got mad at herself for stooping so low just in an attempt to hold on to someone who wasn't worth holding on to from the beginning.

As morbid as it sounds, I believe the best way to handle no contact is to imagine that the person is dead. I didn't know my mom was a narcissist when she died. I loved her despite her abusive behavior and my need to gain her acceptance. Now that she is gone, every time I think of something, I wish I could call her but I can't because she is dead. True no contact can work the same way for you. It's a disconnection that leaves you with no choice but to *not* talk to them.

When you feel emotional or memories bubble to the surface and you wish you could talk to them, pick up a notebook and put your thoughts on paper. Get them out of your head; that will help bring you closure. Journaling is extremely cathartic and healthy. If it's helpful, invite your friends over for a letter burning party. Get it out and get rid of it.

Those of you who are co-parenting have quite a different situation because you must still coordinate your children. Despite that piece of connection for the kids, you can still close out any other unfinished business.

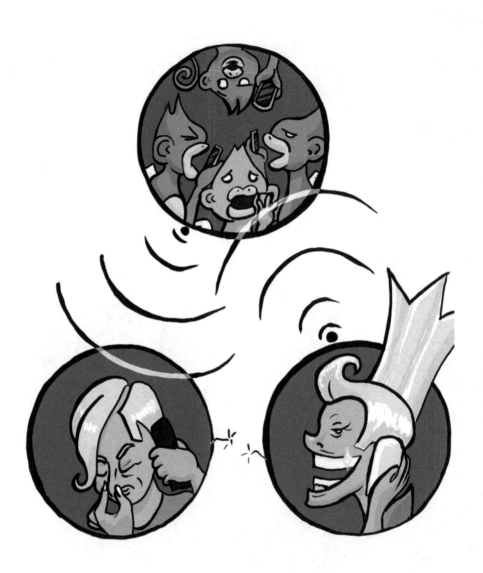

Chapter 6

IS COMMUNICATION DURING DIVORCE EVEN POSSIBLE?

While you are going through your divorce, you may be able to be civil and communicate about the boxes that are still in the attic or the needs of the children. If this sounds like you, that's great, but set boundaries – like when and how often you will answer a call or text. Agree on a plan upfront that can prevent emotions from escalating. If the narcissistic spouse learns that you will respond every time they reach out, they will take advantage of this and text you at all hours. Constant demanding texts will eventually trigger you to feel fear every time you hear the phone buzz. Unless it's an emergency, don't acknowledge immediately and gather your thoughts. Since you realize that this is all about control, take it back, set limits, and answer respectfully in your own time. Be aware that if you ignore them for too long, you are tickling a sleeping dragon and the smooth communication will go downhill fast.

Allow their calls to go to voicemail so you honor yourself by listening and responding on your timeline. Time is a gift that you should allow yourself. I know a narcissist who deliberately ignored his ex-wife's calls and texts until she got so mad that she would leave him terrible messages that he was able to use in court to validate his claims that she was the eruptive person that he had portrayed. Don't give them anything that can be used against you to prove that you are angry, hostile, or crazy. These are conjecture until you leave that voicemail. Don't hand them the evidence on a silver platter. The fact that they provoked you unfairly may be brought up in court to justify the scary voicemail, but now you are paying a lawyer hundreds of dollars to defend something that could have been avoided. If you are fighting for parenting time, it is even more important to be vigilant and remain calm.

Regularly recharge your batteries: Divorcing a narcissist is exhausting and time-consuming. Your ex drama queen or king will be sure to exploit every opportunity to turn molehills into mountains, paint you as the abuser while playing the victim, violate court orders, use the children as pawns, wage a nasty smear campaign against you and keep you on the defensive with bogus allegations, which is why establishing good divorce hygiene is key. In addition to ensuring your sleep, eating and exercise habits are up to par, you must schedule yourself regular divorce-free chunks of time of at least a couple hours a day to reset and recharge your batteries. This means not responding right away to non-urgent messages from your ex, postponing divorce-related paperwork, and refraining from researching or reading anything related to divorce or narcissistic personality disorder. If you go out with friends for a fun evening, definitely don't talk about your divorce or your narcissistic ex. Good habits and structure will help avoid burn out, maintain your composure, think clearly, and make good decisions that can determine the outcome of your divorce. Taking the necessary time to reset and recharge will also help you be less emotional and make it easier to resist the temptation to defend yourself, reactively retaliate, or respond with sarcasm or rage when baited by your ex.

Bree Bonchay, author, psychotherapist, founder of World Narcissistic Abuse Awareness Day

Divorce with a narcissist often becomes so toxic that calm interaction is not even possible, where every communication with your soon-to-be ex must go through the lawyer's office. This is the expensive way to navigate communication but sometimes it is the only way.

If communication with your ex does get ugly, if it is lawful, consider recording the harassing phone calls. As was discussed in Chapter 4, they may not end up as part of the divorce, but if you decide it would be best to get a restraining order, these threatening recordings would have great value. Check our resource page[7] to find the recording laws in your state.

Always maintain your cool and resist sending inflammatory texts or emails regardless of how much they egg you on. It's hard to hold your tongue because you want to give them a piece of your mind. They will try to trigger a reaction in you and it is human nature to react in self-defense. Instead, walk away and take a breath before answering. There is no rush. If you feel emotions bubbling up and you need a release, grab your journal and put your thoughts on paper. Use caution that you don't use any media (email, social media) where you might accidentally send it. Revisit your ideas later and try to remove the vehemence from your reply. Continue the revisions, pulling out all emotions, until only the bare bones remain. Any time they see that they can still control your emotions, they gain supply and plan future use of this strategy. With patience and practice, this effort will soon become a failed attempt, sending them back to the drawing board to come up with something new.

For the sake of the children, avoid putting them in the middle of conversations with your ex. It is best not to ask them to relay messages or tell you what happened when they were with the other parent. Reassure them that if they have anything they ever want to talk about, you are always available, but use common sense and don't push.

There are several online communication tools that can be used

---

7   https://narcissistabusesupport.com/book-resources/

to converse and work out parenting time. *Our Family Wizard*[8] and *Talking Parents*[9] are two of the more popular platforms. These services have monthly service charges and usually need to be included in your divorce decree establishing them as the mode of communication going forward, as well as whose responsibility it is to pay for it. Ask your lawyer to request this solution at the first hearing, but you are at the mercy of the judge whether or not it will be approved. If your lawyer can show that the communication has broken down between the two of you, you will have a better chance of getting it ordered. Continue to gather evidence of harassing emails, the frequency of texts as well as their delayed response times to have more ammunition for the judge to understand your plight.

Most narcissistic spouses will never voluntarily agree to this form of communication. Everything that happens on these platforms is admissible in court as evidence because the messages cannot be altered and are indisputable so you shouldn't expect them to give in without a fight. If your communication during the divorce is volatile, insist that once it's finalized, all communication goes through one of these services. Even with the court order, anticipate pushback. Don't expect them to respond to your messages in a timely manner unless guidelines are set in the decree indicating the parameters. Follow the ruling closely as engaging in texts or emails on any platform outside of what is ordered will cause you to be held in contempt of court.

Document everything: Narcissists lie all the time. They are not going to miraculously start telling the truth just because they're in court! If you want to show that your narcissistic spouse is lying, you will need to prove it! That means that you've got to document everything. Put all your conversations with your spouse in writing. Use email and text messaging as much as possible. Both of those forms of communication leave trails behind. Make sure that you're not only documenting things, but you're organizing them as well. All the documentation in the world is useless if you can't find the

---

8   ourfamilywizard.com
9   talkingparents.com/home

documents you want when you need them.

Do your best to limit your court time: The legal system is a narcissist's Disneyland. They thrive on conflict and court room drama. The same legal hearing that has your stomach tied in knots for weeks in advance, gives them an emotional high. The more you can limit your court time, the more you can start to dial down some of the divorce drama. If you can get your spouse to agree to go to mediation or use Collaborative Divorce that would be ideal. While your narcissistic spouse will still be a narcissist in those arenas too, at least those divorce processes are designed to help people resolve disputes, instead of encouraging them to fight.

Make sure everything you write down is detailed and specific: Narcissists will push the envelope every chance they get. If you want to maintain your sanity, you have to write agreements and court orders that are very specific. For example, when you're divorcing a low-conflict person, you can enter a court order that says, "My spouse gets time with the kids from Friday after school until Sunday evening." That's usually good enough. When you're divorcing a narcissist your court order needs to say, "My spouse gets time with the kids from Friday at 3:00 p.m. until Sunday at 8:00 p.m. My spouse will pick up the kids from school on Friday and I will pick them up on Sunday. If there is no school on Friday, then my spouse will pick up the kids from my house on Friday at 3:00pm." While drilling down into that level of detail may seem like overkill, if you don't have that much detail, your spouse will have all kinds of "wiggle room" to change the rules and make you crazy in the process.

Karen Covy, author, divorce advisor, attorney, coach

I want a divorce – how to break the news

Knowing you want a divorce isn't easy but saying it out loud is when the real difficulty begins. Once you have made the decision to leave, at some point you will need to tell your spouse. Despite it being your choice, this conversation is usually what victims fear the most. All your triggers will be activated at the prospect of your spouse's reaction. How rational they may or may not be is always at the forefront of your mind.

Each case and everyone's emotional attachment varies, yet it's never easy to end a marriage. You need a strategy to avoid escalating the situation. Your emotional resilience will be tested as you face the fear of a potentially ugly confrontation. The thought of hurting your spouse will tempt you to just leave, have them served papers, and avoid the entire mess.

It is helpful to know in advance what you want to say. Keep in mind, less is more; you don't owe them an explanation for your decision, despite their insistence that you do. Give them as little information as possible and walk away.

Carefully write out your script, review it, and then scale it back, removing any emotions or accusations. Never call them a narcissist. If the conversation focuses on the things they did to make you want to leave, a narcissistic injury will be initiated and the divorce will become contentious right away. Instead, prepare a few statements with very vague comments like, "I'm not happy anymore," or "I want something different," or "We are not compatible any longer." These are statements about you and your feelings, giving them no clues as to their behavior.

You will want to get closure and tell them exactly why you are leaving but the short amount of satisfaction derived will not be worth the complications created when your partner has NPD. Resist the urge; this is not the time or place. Your mission is to get in and get out without traumatizing yourself or stirring the pot and opening yourself up to further abuse.

Once you have your conversation planned out on paper, imagine their reactions. If you can think of three different reactions, you'll be able to anticipate their receptivity more accurately. You can then map out your responses accordingly. Having this forethought will empower you to not freeze or get walked on during the conversation. Prepare for an angry response, the victim (pity or sad) card, and create a third scenario that you know your spouse may use. Imagine what they might say and write it down.

What will you do if they get angry or start becoming verbally abusive? Work out an outline for this by figuring out a boundary such as, "If you don't calm down, I will leave." How will you handle the situation if they try pulling on your heartstrings? What if they bring up the kids?

Devise a safe word to end the conversation. If things get heated and they won't calm down or if you fear for your safety, you must be prepared. Know your limits and have an effective way to excuse yourself in your back pocket. You could tell them that you will contact them later to finish the conversation. Self-preservation is key – do what you need to do to allow yourself to get away safely. Advanced planning of possible scenarios for any encounter will always make it easier.

The conversation may or may not go the direction you want, but being prepared for the worst will empower you further than if you hadn't planned at all and most importantly, you won't get blindsided. To instill an extra boost of confidence, try role playing with a trusted family member, friend, or coach.

At the end of the conversation, inform your spouse that you have already spoken to a lawyer and your mind is made up to help dissuade any hoovering attempts. Know your audience: if they are being confrontational at this juncture, save the discussion about the bedroom set and KitchenAid for later. Do not pour gasoline on the fire. This will be hard enough and your mission is to get through it safely with as little trauma as possible. If the situation gets inflamed talking about lawyers, money, and the kids all at the same time, it will never yield good results. Throw down the white flag and talk details at another time.

Be prepared: they will promise to change and go to counseling. It is natural for them to play this card first if they are taken by surprise. They feel entitled to be the discarder so they need to take back control. A narcissist cannot change and soon after you drop the divorce bomb, the devalue process will start over again.

Never apologize: They will use it against you later -- always! You can say, "I am disappointed that . . ." or "I wish it could be different but. . ." but never give into an urge to take the easy way out with them and apologize.

Susan Guthrie, nationally recognized top family law and mediation attorney

Rules for follow-up conversations

Once you have told your spouse that you want a divorce, many more conversations will be in your future with the hope that they can be accomplished civilly without much lawyer intervention. You'll need to pre-plan those, too.

It's important to establish conditions with yourself before each call. Ask yourself:

» How long will the call last?
» What are the rules and boundaries for the call?
» What is my goal for this call?
» What are the consequences if they get angry or mean?

Do not offer them any indication of your emotional state. They may appear genuine and pretend to worry about you, but be assured that it is a ploy to get information that they should never have. They will use this knowledge against you later and it could put you at a huge disadvantage.

Tread lightly when they ask, "How you are feeling?" or "How are you dealing with all these big decisions?" Answer slowly and carefully. They may assert that you do not need to worry about the money because they will be fair. Please don't be fooled by this manipulation either. If you tell them you are afraid of money issues, they will do everything in their power to make it a reality. Never let them see your emotions or get access to your intentions. Keep your game face on point.

Communicating with your spouse via phone

When it comes to communicating with your soon-to-be ex, there are many scenarios in which you need to prepare, and these don't just start in court. In the example below, I am sharing a story of Pam and her husband, Ken. Read through the case and apply the strategy to your situation.

Case: Pam has been planning her escape for months, working with a therapist to find the courage to finally leave Ken. For her safety, she opted to leave a note so she could avoid telling him to his face. Previous attempts to get away were unsuccessful; she was love bombed and promises were made, only to be broken. She simply couldn't stay any longer. It took incredible strength to leave this way but she knew she had no other choice. He would never let her go if she confronted him. Pam didn't want half the business or the 401k or even money from the house. She just wanted to be free from his constant abuse. After speaking with a lawyer, she discovered that what she wanted was a simple transaction; the cost of a divorce wasn't worth it since she wasn't fighting for anything but her sanity. An annulment would be the simplest, quickest solution and it would save them a bunch of money. She explained this in her note and told him she would call that following weekend. She had concerns about the phone call.

Reminder: If you are ever in a situation like this where you are concerned for your safety and you are still on the same cellular plan, turn off all your tracking services. If you have a new phone and you don't want your abuser to know the number, dial *67 before the number. The display will read "unknown caller" on the receiving end so they won't be able to capture your number or track you.

Case (con't): Pam was finally safe and setting up her new apartment, but her emotions were worn thin. She worried about facing Ken, even if just for a phone call. As the time grew closer, she planned her call strategy using the following techniques:
1)   Set goals
2)   Set objectives
3)   Set rules and boundaries
4)   Explore possible reactions
5)   Think through your reactions

It is not unusual to be afraid of the unknown. When we don't know what to expect, layers of unnerving possibilities are built by fear. Your job is to make the unknown known by organizing possible responses and conversation deviations in advance.

Goals for the call: What would you like to accomplish? Set your goals for the call and write them down. To allay your fears, examine and plan for a range of possibilities to avoid being caught off guard. Like the other situations, hope for the best but plan for the worst.

What might be their goals for the call? They could want to understand what happened or just be terribly cross and want you to come home.

Call objective: In this case, Pam knows Ken will want an explanation which is the root of her fear. For 20 years, Ken has manipulated her and she isn't confident that he won't continue. Her objective is to be as brief as possible and answer some of his questions but be empowered to not answer any questions that trigger her fears. If he steers the conversation in a direction that she doesn't want to address, she could say something like, "Ken, I am not comfortable answering that right now. Let's discuss that on another call. For now, I want to stick with this topic."

Look at the reason for the call and think of what your narc-spouse's objective might be. Example: In this case, Ken will have questions and will most likely be incensed. The anxiety about the tone of the conversation can be crippling. Pam had been coached and trained for this moment, but the "what if he says…" concerns were keeping her up at night.

You do not need to give your spouse all the details nor do you need to answer all of their questions. Stick to your goals. Take no abuse and plan the next step. Time is going to make this process easier, so keeping the calls short will help you get through them one by one. Over time, you will get stronger and exceed your own expectations with each encounter. Acting in this manner may seem heartless and unlike you, but protecting yourself is critical.

Setting call rules and boundaries:

Rule #1: Set a time limit – "this call will last no more than 30 minutes." This is *your* rule and there are no expectations that any details should be explained, especially that 30 minutes may be all you can handle; a narcissist will get too much intel on you with even a benign explanation. Communicate the call time limit at the beginning and, as you get close to the end, give him a ten-minute warning. End the call when you said you would. Let them see your strength with your new ability to set boundaries rather than your vulnerabilities.

Rule #2: Do not tolerate yelling or belittling. Explain, up front, that the consequence will be the termination of the phone call. If, as the number of calls progress, this becomes a repeated offense, you can set a higher consequence such as, "If you yell one more time, I will block you and then you will only be able to contact me through my lawyer." *Only set consequences that you can or will follow through with.* If you are co-parenting and you still need to communicate about the children, threatening to block them and go through the lawyers will likely end up costing you both more than a college education. Be smart when setting consequences because if you say you are going to do something and then don't follow through, the narcissist will know your threats are empty. You open yourself up to them pushing harder to make your life difficult. Mean what you say and stand your ground or your narcissist will figure out that they can get away with anything.

Rule #3: If you find yourself getting angry, stop, slow it down, and/or end the call. Everything that happens via phone can be recorded. Check the book resource[10] page on our website to see if recording is allowed in your state. While some courts accept voice recordings, some do not. Worrying about them using recordings in court is, of course, a fear, but *knowing what they can use the recordings for* is the power here.

It's not the call itself but rather the fact that a pattern can be shown of your angry responses or crazy actions for their gain. When a narcissist records a call, the part where they baited you will get deleted so you look like the lunatic. That said, check the recording laws and record them if you can, if only to defend yourself in case they accuse you of anything.

Smearing you to friends and family might be another way recordings could be utilized. The narcissists can craft a story that intricately explains how frightened they have been of your rages for years. They finally had enough and recorded you to "prove their point." This will

10   https://narcissistabusesupport.com/book-resources/

help them design their victim mask to leverage sympathy from those close to you.

Turning friends, family, coworkers, and neighbors against you is a standard modus operandi and it is a painful one to swallow. Isolating you from your support system is always a narcissist's first line of attack. Having this demented-ex narrative now supported with "evidence" only solidifies their storyline. Be smart and hang up when you start to feel the telltale bubble of rage rising to the surface. The regret felt for losing your temper will only be further compounded as the video or audio evidence you handed them becomes the weapon being used against you. The reality is that now you risk losing what's important, your children for example, or at best you now need to fight an unnecessary uphill battle.

Explore possible reactions: Prior to initiating the call, map out any of your spouse's possible reactions. Try to highlight at least three potential emotional responses that you might encounter. In Pam's case, she anticipated Ken's anger over the way she left. Could he also feel hurt and betrayed? That might stir the anger she feared since we know that narcissistic injuries are prevalent in situations like this. Worst case scenario, he might display anger, middle scenario hurt, and the lowest reaction may be him not upset that she left and ready to move forward with his life without her.

Think through your reactions: Let's consider the various reactions that your spouse may have and how they relate to you and your feelings. Using Pam and Ken's situation, let's begin with the least likely reaction and build upward on the emotional scale. If your ex was not upset that you left, how would that make you feel? What if they were hurt? How would you handle it if they were really irate? What emotions and reactions would be prevalent for you? Knowing the possibilities, how would you handle the initial conversation?

Least likely scenario – He is relieved

Ken – Pam, I am so relieved that all the cards are on the table. I'm surprised that you would sneak off in the middle of the night like that but at least we are on the same page.

Pam – It was easier for me to leave that way; I hope you can respect my choice.

Ken –Do you want to get a divorce? This can be very easy; I can get a lawyer that we could both use. If we mutually agree on things, we can get through this faster.

Pam – That would be great because I also want to keep the cost down. I have already gotten some advice and I know that we will be asked to fill out a financial affidavit. Are you willing to get that started?

Ken – You are rushing me.

Pam – The court system requires both of us to fill out this paper-work. We can go through a mediator or each of us can do it separately and have a lawyer review it.

Ken – Are you planning to fight me for the house or my retirement?

Pam – I hope that we will both be fair to each other in light of our 20-year marriage. You are getting too far ahead with that question – let's start by filling out the financial paperwork and plan another call in two weeks. I have to run, I have another call.

Middle scenario – He is hurt

Ken – I can't believe you would walk away from 20 years of mar-riage without even talking to me. I feel completely blindsided. I haven't been able to eat or sleep since you left. Why would you do this to our family?

Pam – Ken, I understand that you may be surprised by my decision to leave. I'm sorry but it feels like you get upset with me so often and I was afraid that if I told you to your face, I might not have had the courage to leave. (**By validating his feelings, the conversation will be less likely to elevate to anger.**)

Ken – When are you coming home? I miss you and so does our cat.

Pam – I am not coming home. I would like to talk about getting a divorce.

Ken – No counseling, no discussion, nothing?! You made this de-cision without even talking to me. This is so typical of you, Pam. All you care about is yourself.

Pam – I know you are hurting but my decision is final. I want you to take the time you need to digest this. Can we schedule a call on Saturday and you can ask me more questions then?

Worst case scenario – He is enraged

Ken – How dare you leave me, you crazy bitch! What do you think you are going to do now? You can't do anything without me. I am going to ruin you and you will get nothing!

Pam – Ken, I would like to talk with you about this but I have some ground rules. If you call me names again, this call is over. As long as you can control your anger, I will continue the call. If you can't, we will need to try again another time.

Ken – You actually think I am going to give you a divorce? You will never get away from me. I made all the money and your name isn't even on the house! You will be homeless if you leave me.

Pam – I have spoken to a lawyer already and I know my rights. Perhaps it would be best if we continue this call after you speak to your lawyer. If we want this to be civil, you will need to cooperate with me so we can work out as much as possible without a lawyer. Since the kids are grown, the main thing we will need to focus on is the initial financial paperwork for the court system. Can I send it over?

Ken – I am not looking at any paperwork from you. Expect to hear from my lawyer.

Pam – Okay, goodbye. (There is no need to go into any explanations about your plans or intentions at this point.)

By planning out conversations, or even taking it one step further and role playing them with a friend, you can work through scenarios and empower yourself to be stronger on every call. Feeling and sounding confident will make the first steps go much smoother for you.

*"Whenever you are communicating with the narcissist in a child custody situation, you need to be of the mindset that you are not communicating with him/her, you are communicating with the court. Pretend that everything that you write is to the judge (because it is!) and that you are just cc'ing your ex. The goal is to show yourself to be the healthy co-parent despite the actions of the other party." – **Tina Swithin**

Telling the children

When the time comes to break the news of an impending divorce to children, no matter their ages, it will be hard. Unless they are older and have experienced the complexity of the relationship and understand why it should be severed, there could be many sleepless and tear-filled nights. Separating couples wonder when the best time is to deliver the news. Would it be best to do it together?

Many factors weigh in regarding the optimal way this should be handled and as with all things, it should be tailored to your specific situation. Is yours an amicable split or is there animosity? The worst thing that could happen would be for one to place blame on the other claiming "Mommy doesn't want us to be a family anymore," or "Daddy loves someone else more than us and would rather have a new family." Agreeing prior to having the discussion and sticking to the plan is critical – not necessarily for either of you but certainly for the mental health of your children.

Who can you trust?

Friends? Family? Neighbors? Co-workers? Members of your church? Every relationship is different and understanding who is on your team is important to survive a high-conflict divorce. Do not try to do this alone; if you do decide to divulge intimate details of your divorce, be sure you trust the right people. As much of a temptation as it may be to reveal the behind-the-scenes drama to a work friend, you must be incredibly careful. If your neighbors were friends with both of you, restrict all information with the assumption that they could be carrier pigeons (flying monkeys) sharing details with your soon-to-be ex. During my divorce, I was repeatedly betrayed by my husband's family, who pretended to be on my side, as well as some work friends. When it came to the great division of friends, I was confused at who he recruited for his team. His first draft choices were my co-workers, people he regularly proclaimed his dislike. He didn't really want them as friends but he did want to handicap my support system from all sides. That is the goal of an abusive person.

If a friend or family member is empathic to your ex, it is a red flag that should not be overlooked. You must do your best to set boundaries and if necessary, go no contact with them. If they are not willing to block your ex, then you must temporarily block that person for self-preservation. Outsiders may think this is just another divorce and not understand the urgency of your ex not knowing what is going on in your life. This, however, is not "just another divorce" and you must put on your armor to protect your future. Share your thought process with trusted friends and family only. Ask them to be on high alert and notify you of any contact your soon-to-be ex tries to have with them.

Anytime you start to feel that internal intuition flutter telling you something isn't right, believe it. Accept that this person has drunk the Kool-Aid© and move them onto a 'hostiles' list – this is a war and should be treated as such. A true friend would pick up the phone and immediately share that an infiltration was attempted and failed.

The narcissist will not be above love bombing your friends and family in an effort to gain additional intel. Your ex might reach out to your friend expressing concern, and follow up by asking how you are doing. Mixing concern with the inquiry will lower your friend's guard since he/she is also worried about you. It all seems innocent enough. The safest thing might be to self-isolate to prevent any conscious or unconscious attacks from the flying monkeys. This doesn't mean you'll lose your friends forever; it just means that right now, trusting others who may have been compromised is dangerous to your wellbeing.

If there is any takeaway from this book, I hope it is that you should never underestimate the lengths to which your narcissist will go to destroy everything about you. The lies will be extreme, the smears about your character will shock you, and your strengths will become weapons. Knowing it is all hyperbole is the best way to ground yourself from the runaway self-destruction cycle that they are counting on.

Know that they will get more fragmented, and more enraged, through the divorce process: It's not about you; this is just their limited coping skills and poor affect regulation.

Stay neutral and sustain your boundaries with calm assertiveness: Getting reactive with them, no matter how provocative they may be, will only make things worse.

Secure as much emotional support as possible: Enlist a therapist who can support you emotionally through the process. It's critical that you stay connected with someone who you can share your feelings with and trust, who understands personality disorders, and who will provide you a clear mirror of yourself, in contrast to the distorted version you will receive from the partner you are divorcing.

Jessica McCrea, psychologist and business coach

How to explain a crazy divorce

Depending on where you are in the process, you may have already been called the unstable one. If not, you have that to look forward to! Welcome to the Crazy Ex Club! With the amount of madness that you are being exposed to, you probably will begin to sound unhinged to your friends and family. As much as they love you, they honestly won't know what to believe. Your friends might stop taking your calls because you have become a deranged person that they no longer recognize. The stories sound ludicrous but you can't make this shit up. Unless they have been through a similar situation with a narcissist, there is no chance they will understand and you really shouldn't hold it against them. If you haven't already, you will soon realize that by repeatedly telling your wild story, fear and anxiety will be triggered. Up front, define a strategy to protect yourself from these triggers. It negatively affects you to where you are unable to sufficiently defend yourself or help build your case and win.

The Three Bucket Strategy: crafting your story

We are going to use the three-bucket strategy to properly prepare ourselves for questions that may arise about the divorce. Treat this like the life-or-death situation that it is: information should be disseminated on a "need to know" basis. As with previous scenarios that have the capability of going south fast, it is crucial to get your buckets in order for future conversations to avoid any missteps.

Step #1

Group people into three buckets to determine how to address their inquiries:

Highest bucket (safe to tell anything) – best friends and safe family, someone you can trust without question with no judgment

Medium bucket (guarded information) – friends and family

Lowest bucket (briefest story) – acquaintances, mailman, church people, coworkers, and neighbors

If someone from a particular group can't support you or isn't equipped to understand what is happening, downgrade them to a lesser bucket temporarily. If you feel some friends might have open communication with your ex or be a flying monkey, move them to the lowest bucket and give them no information that could be detrimental to you in a courtroom.

Step #2

Craft a story for each group:

Highest bucket – You should be able to share all the gory details with your besties and others who are always there for you. They steadfastly hold your hand and despite never having dealt with anything remotely similar, they believe you without question. Your therapist, coach, or if you are lucky, a supportive family member are safe to share everything with. You need unwavering support and no judgements so if they can handle the truth, add them to this bucket without reservation.

Medium bucket – You can share what makes you comfortable with these friends, but if they were connected to the ex, use your best judgement. "We have decided to get a divorce and things are getting difficult to explain. Every time I share what is happening, I end up sounding like a crazy person. I was hoping to bounce some of the details off of you to get your opinion," or "I know you have always liked my wife but there are many things I have been hesitant to share before now. Is it okay if we discuss them and you could be my grounding friend to help me process some of these issues?" might open up communication lines that prove to be quite helpful to you. Be cognizant, however, that flying monkeys are often unaware that they are working for the enemy camp. Remember the charm of a narcissist? They will charm your friends and might say something like, "I am so worried about Tracy; I don't think she is doing well. What do you think? How is she doing?" (Spying) If anyone you consider a friend says something stupid like, "It's just a divorce, get over it. Your husband is so kind and loving, I find it hard to believe these things," or "Lots of people get a divorce – move on," this is showing you that they're incapable of being supportive so stop sharing with them. Relegate them to the low bucket. If you tell your neighbor everything, you may sound crazy and after they tell two friends, you may wake up and realize you aren't invited to dinners anymore. Loose lips sink ships. Move those people to the lower bucket. They may care but you cannot trust them right now.

Lowest bucket

All you need is a simple one liner:

» "Things just didn't work out and we grew apart."
» "We have developed different interests and it was time to go our separate ways."
» "I realized that I want a different life and I am excited about my next chapter."

Be prepared for the questions:

» "What are you going to do now?" Answer – "I will figure it out." – Short, sweet, and to the point. The ball is now in your court to change the direction of the conversation and say, "Let's talk about something else," or "Tell me about that new puppy of yours!" That is all they get. It's like grey rock – just the bare bones facts.

Once you are armed with feasible scenarios, the fear regarding how a conversation could play out will be eased. You know your spouse best. Try to predict possible reactions and establish your individualized plan from there.

Chapter 7

THE DETECTIVE AWAKENS: FINDING YOUR INNER SHERLOCK

Knowing what you know now, your attention should focus on gaining a deeper knowledge of narcissistic abuse. You will learn terms like hoovering, flying monkey, smear campaign, gaslighting, and myriad of phrases that will help solve the first part of the puzzle. Until you find the words to explain what has been happening, your truth may seem unbelievable and appear crazy to others. You need to look for proof of your suspicions which will in turn corroborate the behaviors you've experienced. Once you start recognizing the patterns, along with your new narc-glossary, you can start to communicate with confidence. Bonus: your friends gain a better understanding and you move beyond the unstable status.

Time is of the essence here. You may find yourself losing sleep because you're researching all night long to identify familiar patterns. Gaining validation is one of the most important steps because without it, you can't move on. Be mindful of time spent so you can stay rested. If you have trouble sleeping, turn on a peaceful meditation channel and let your mind empty and drift off. The betrayal stories you will be exposed to will instill fear in your heart and create a vacuum of shame that you could ruminate on for hours on end, if you allow it. Honor yourself and take advantage of the self-care you deserve.

Detective training 101

The need to understand what went wrong can often manifest into an obsession as you search for answers. The action of digging, information gathering, and merging all of the clues to find what you're looking for is called "Sherlocking." Every new tip becomes a data point to help you see the big picture more clearly. During your hunt, you may innocuously override your sense of right and wrong – many people admit to doing things in this stage that they are not terribly proud of – when in fact this is all driven by your instinct to survive.

Common occurrences:
- » Hire a private investigator
- » Follow spouse to monitor their activity
- » Spy on spouse's email
- » Install a tracking device on spouse's car
- » Break into spouse's computer to search for answers
- » Break into spouse's phone to examine texts and phone log
- » Access spouse's social media
- » Stalk their social media
- » Record their spouse and (even) record the children after they return home from time spent with the spouse
- » Contact any former relationships to get a better understanding of what really happened between them
- » Research the financial truth about your marital life assets
- » Launch a campaign to let everyone know the real truth

The search for answers often leads victims into the confusing part of the journey as some find:

- » Secret second or third lives
- » Secret lovers / infidelity
- » Secret friends with whom to share their victim story of how abusive you are
- » Smear campaign(s) in full swing against you
- » Hidden money and assets – secrecy around money in the marriage is an indicative marker to look for financial abuse, hiding money, and financial control

Your spouse's dishonesty is exposed and suddenly your life as you knew it comes into full focus as one big lie. The overwhelming sense of betrayal can put the victim into a fight or flight stage of trauma which can manifest in a CPTSD[11] diagnosis. You searched for the truth, you wanted the answers, but you had no way of preparing yourself for the deception that unfolded.

Victims can move into a self-blame stage:
- » How could I have not known this was happening?
- » What is wrong with me?
- » Why wasn't I enough?
- » How can I fix this?
- » Why did I stay so long?
- » Did they ever love me?

Not everyone experiences self-blame; instead, some may move directly to the narc-blame stage, asking questions like, "How could they betray me like this?" The anger is blinding as you accept your new reality and begin to move forward with the divorce process.

This is the point of the journey, once you unearth the hidden information about your relationship and its betrayal, where the questions and answers often lead victims to land on the term narcissistic abuse. YouTube University is now in session. Throughout your quest for information, you will hopefully have stumbled upon my website[12], vid-

---

11   Complex Post-Traumatic Stress Disorder is a mental health condition where intense PTSD symptoms might coincide with other mental issues. CPTSD occurs in people who have been subjected to ongoing traumatizing experiences.

12   https://www.NarcissistAbuseSupport.com

eos[13], and blog[14]. Mine, along with those of others, provide insight into the stages of abuse, common red flags, and behaviors – behaviors that you may have seen for years, but now have the words and understanding to explain what you've experienced. Layers of subterfuge amplify as they unravel and you recognize the patterns. The new vocabulary reduces confusion, but expands emotions like anger, panic, regret, and revenge.

Data often suggests that many victims who are divorcing a narcissist have limited finances to pay a coach for guidance through this downward spiral of emotions. If this is you, (it was me), seek out a support group and talk with others who understand and can validate your experience. They can also give you helpful resources to settle the stress and anxiety. These groups are generally free or low cost and can be peer run or run by a therapist or coach. I founded and lead two groups in Colorado and in 2020, I launched my online healing groups – I have a deep understanding of the importance of finding a relatable community. Reach out through my website to learn more!

Your family and friends will not understand what you are up against. They will probably try initially but as the madness amplifies, it will become obvious that they do not have the tools to help and might eventually pull back for fear that your temporarily confusing toxicity may suck them down too. Try not to blame them. Unless you have lived it and earned a Ph.V. (V for victim educated) in narcissistic abuse, your story will always sound a bit far out.

On my website, we maintain a list of support groups[15] so you can find one in your area.

One last note about getting support: Everyone has been on an airplane and heard the flight attendant tell you, "In case of emergency, put your oxygen mask on first." *This is one of those times*. If you are worn down as you enter the battle of your life, you will make mistakes and poor decisions. Your weaknesses will be taken advantage of and you will end up with boot prints on your back. Your future and the

---

13   https://www.youtube.com/tracyamalone
14   https://narcissistabusesupport.com/blog/
15   https://narcissistabusesupport.com/book-resources/

future of your children are at stake. Get help.

The truths and falsehoods of your marriage

I know I have pointed this out on several occasions up to this point but one of the hardest truths that survivors of this type of abuse must accept is that the person they married and the person they are divorcing are two vastly different people. Once you start digging for information, what you uncover will leave you with an intense sense of betrayal. If you were the discarded, you may opt to access their phone, texts and emails, or even hire a private detective to get answers. The deeper you dig, the more dirt gets added to the pile.

Your days may be filled with reviewing bank statements, looking for things that don't make sense. Following these clues may take you somewhere that, after the fact, you wished you hadn't gone. You may find you've been financially abused, ranging from the hiding of assets to liquidation of bank accounts. A second life of infidelity may unfold as you search vigorously to unravel the truth. The discovery of secret friends, phones, and even trips, that you thought were for business, may come to light. The anger we discussed in the last chapter will be triggered. Use it to your advantage to propel you forward. Everything you find must be documented; it is important to the overall case and could help you later in the courtroom.

> **Become your own forensic analyst:** Get copies of past bank statements, capture every bank account number you have, get copies of past tax returns (you can easily get these online), and investigate your shared computer records including spreadsheets, online transactions, etc.
>
> **Lindsey Ellison,** author, narcissism expert, and breakup coach

As tempting as it will be to run to your spouse with your discoveries to question and confirm what you've learned – stop! Approaching them is a bad idea for multiple reasons:

> » You may not be emotionally strong enough for the guaranteed drama that will ensue once they realize you are on to them. By giving up your advantage, you are notifying

them to lock everything down thus blocking potential future fact-finding avenues. I am not endorsing that you spy on them, but please take heed of the risks involved if you tell them what you now know.

» You would give valuable information away that may be useful later as leverage. By giving them a heads up, you are offering them the time to craft a story, build false evidence, and turn the tables on you. This operation demands the loyalty of a spy to keep the secret until the right time presents itself.

» You risk the narcissist filing charges against you for violating their privacy.

All documents should be copied, printed, and saved in a personal cloud account known only to you. Share the evidence you found with your lawyer to ensure it is used in the best way for your case. Don't do anything illegal to obtain the information and never let them know that you have it.

Financial misconduct is highest on a judge's list of infractions followed by parenting patterns. Infidelity, in no-fault states, doesn't register as a serious offense but couple it with financial misconduct and the judge might take note. Per Wikipedia, "no-fault" simply means that a person seeking a divorce is not permitted to allege a fault-based ground (i.e., adultery, abandonment, or cruelty). If the new lover received a car or condo with marital assets, the judge could possibly equitably distribute the money by adding that amount to your portion of the settlement. Not all states are no-fault, however. South Carolina, for example, takes adultery quite seriously. I have a friend who was refused alimony due to cheating in her marriage. Be sure to get educated regarding your rights based on where you reside[16].

Another survivor had an experience that offers a good lesson: Abby's search revealed her husband, Peter, had been soliciting sex from both men and women on craigslist. She was horrified and immediately went to her doctor's office for a STD test which revealed he

---

16   To obtain guidance regarding no-fault laws in the state in which you reside, check out our website at https://narcissistabusesupport.com/book-resources/

had given her HPV. Abby was furious and desperate to let him know what she thought about him. Fortunately, she reached out to me first and I advised her to ask her lawyer if this information had any value. Abby's husband was a prominent member of the community and her lawyer knew it would be used best not as a threat, but rather as leverage to buy him their silence if he agreed to cooperate with her. Peter was aware that the shame caused would have wrecked his reputation thus forcing his agreement to negotiate. Only situations with viable evidence can wield this kind of power and only if your lawyer knows how to properly time its introduction. Abby wanted so badly to confront him for months as she struggled with the betrayal, but kept her cool and never revealed her hand. It was hard but she did it. What good is finding great evidence if it ends up being worthless when it would count the most? If he discovered that she knew his secret, he and his lawyer would have been given ample time to spin the story enough to possibly prevent it from being admitted as evidence. Since they lived in a no-fault state (they do not care if someone cheated), tapping into his pride to protect his reputation was one thing they could use to ensure Abby received a fair portion of the marital assets. Anything revealed in court in a public hearing becomes public record so they successfully utilized this as a leveraging opportunity. Moral of the story: When you find a nugget that puts your soon-to-be ex in a bad light, do not pass go and immediately ask your lawyer to decide how best to incorporate it into your case. Using it for leverage only works if they don't see it coming.

Another example would be when David discovered that his wife had lied on her tax returns. This shows her moral compass is lacking so you might automatically think it would be a good lead to follow but since this is a criminal offense, it would be better served as leverage applied with your lawyer's legal expertise.

The roles are clear: you find proof of vulnerabilities and trust your lawyer to pull the trump card at the appropriate time. Patience and maintaining your poker face are key.

There's a little-known loophole in our tax system that allows for the unwitting spouse of a tax evader to be exonerated, called the "Innocent Spouse Clause." If you are married to a person who has committed tax fraud, but you can prove that you had no knowledge of the activity, then you can use the Innocent Spouse Clause so that you are not penalized for your spouse's criminal behavior.

Guess who knows all about this clause? Narcissists. Yep, they will use this every time to claim they were the innocent victim and try to stick the marital tax debt onto you in the divorce. So if you have tax debt, you should contact the IRS and let them know that you are in a contentious divorce and are worried that your spouse will try to use this tactic. Or perhaps you are an actual innocent spouse. In that case, you should contact the IRS and request to be exonerated.

In my own divorce, we had huge tax debt. What I didn't know was that it was even bigger than I believed. You see, my husband insisted on using his long-time accountant to prepare our taxes. He owned commercial and residential real estate, and the tax structure was very complex. He assured me that I was far too incompetent to ever be able to understand the intricacies of amortization, depreciation and all of the other components of the tax laws surrounding these properties. He kept all of his documentation so disorganized that I couldn't piece it together, even though I tried. So each year at tax time, I handed over all of the tax documents and receipts from my work to him, he met with the accountant, I was presented with an inches-thick tax return to sign (we filed jointly), and off he went with it. What I didn't know was that for years, those returns were never filed.

Yes, he was meeting with the accountant, having the returns prepared, but never filing them. And I never knew.

The way I learned was that one day during our divorce, an IRS agent appeared at my door and notified me that my husband had claimed to be the innocent spouse in my reckless tax evasion scheme.

Victoria McCooey, transformation coach, creator of The Reclaim Your Power System™

Document. Document. Document.

Now is the time to organize and review everything with a fine-tooth comb. A multitude of tricks may have been going on throughout your entire marriage unbeknownst to you and this is when you need to find the evidence that they are lying, or cheating, or hiding money.

Set up a system to document and classify everything – there will be a never-ending amount of paperwork so start immediately. I had 5,000 pages. If you are not organized, it will cost you time and money in the end. If texts are being submitted as evidence, purchase apps that can download and catalog texts and voice messages. Set up a detailed spreadsheet of all the documents for quick reference later.

Next, gather all the papers that the court will require – every state has different guidelines. This is called discovery and both sides are required to produce all the requested documentation.

Log into your online bank account and print out the required statements. It may be triggering to dig through all of your accounts for these documents so take your time but do not procrastinate. If the online banking portals do not offer access to records as far back as the court requests, make an appointment with a personal banker and ask that statements be printed for you or place an order for them. Gathering these records, like tax returns, can in itself become a struggle. My ex-husband's family accountant did our taxes and he made this difficult for me. He had clearly been told to drag his feet in response to anything I requested. It was a nasty side-battle I had not planned for which necessitated my lawyer to write letters to make him produce the information. What is humorous is as hard as I fought to produce my tax returns, I can't recall if my ex ever produced his. The tax guy was on his team and he used a tactic called stonewalling, which, per Merriam-Webster means to be uncooperative, obstructive, or evasive. The withholding of documents is to be expected. When they go low, you go high to give the judge the most accurate depiction of your financial assessment.

There are situations when a lawyer must hire a forensic accountant to dig through the financial statements line-by-line to get the best accounting of where the money went. At the early stage, however, you must put that hat on and look for anything that doesn't seem right. You know your finances so who better to highlight potential discrepancies? Withdrawals or transfers of money are the first place to start. If you had separate accounts, pour over those statements with a critical eye to make sure you don't find any nonsensical $20,000 withdrawals or other suspicious activity. Focus on items that appear out of the ordinary – and surprise those who may think you don't know what you're doing or not astute enough to ask the right questions.

Follow the trail like a bloodhound. If you see a post where $10,000 was transferred to another account, jot it down, and follow the money. If you have no idea what that account is, show your lawyer. They can create a list to follow up with your soon-to-be ex's team requesting all statements be produced for any questionable accounts.

A popular ruse is to pull money out of retirement accounts, like the sleight of hand in a magic trick, to keep the money moving. Second mortgages should also be examined to be sure your ex wasn't spending that credit line inappropriately.

As technology continues to improve, so do opportunities to hide money. Cryptocurrency is another possible scheme that should not go unchecked. If they make a mistake, they might unknowingly place a withdrawal directly into a crypto exchange which is traceable. Most who are educated in cryptocurrency would be more stealth in the methodologies allowing you to only see the post of the money transferring out, thus making its destination hard to track. Find any red flags and let your lawyer follow up for an explanation of the paper trail.

Whilst studying your statements, be mindful of the types of charges. Your ex will undoubtedly inflate the figures when it comes time to determine how much money they need to live. My ex-husband had a few things on his sworn financial affidavit that didn't make any sense. One thing I've never forgotten was a huge amount earmarked for monthly rent to his parents. We demanded that he produce the statements and canceled checks for that rent. Of course, he didn't have them which dictated that line item be removed and replaced with a more reasonable rent cost for his area. Another memorable moment was when he claimed that he spent $1,000 a month on magazines. I laughed out loud as I had never, in our ten years together, seen him read a magazine. It was his responsibility to show receipts and statements for these publications and since he never did, that line item was also removed.

Filling out your discovery and sworn financial affidavit

Divorce is a full-time job, gathering the paperwork, chasing lawyers, answering requests, and following up with your narcissist's lack of compliance but what happens to a person divorcing a narcissist is nothing short of criminal. It is purely the breaking of a legal contract with a romantic history called marriage. Our family court system is not fair and just as you would imagine it to be. The courtroom feels like a factory: do the work, fight the fight, split the assets, divide the kids, gavel down, next.

One of the first tasks your lawyer will assign to you in the discovery phase is the financial affidavit. This is the form that will give the court a snapshot of your family's current economic picture. It details the budgetary factors that play a role in every marriage: how much you earn (income), how much you spend (expenses), how much you own (assets), how much you owe (liabilities/debt), etc. Signing it equates to swearing under penalty of perjury that the information is correct. So much time and money is wasted fighting over the scraps of paper but you will quickly see how cooperative your ex is going to be based on this one task. Once your spouse produces their affidavit, the two should immediately be compared for any differences. Expect the lies to flow like lava, because they will, and then dive back into the bank statements to prove that your spouse doesn't really purchase

$1,000 worth of magazines each month. Finding mistakes is not only important for the bottom line but also because their credibility with the judge will be taken down a notch when obvious discrepancies are pointed out. My ex-husband was in contempt of court repeatedly for failing to produce accurate paperwork. This pissed off the judge which enabled me to get a slightly bigger piece of the pie at the end. He said, "I am giving her more because you are not credible."

What I see most with narcissists is they have no qualms about lying on a sworn affidavit and then play dumb and ask for forgiveness once they are caught. Some believe that it is better to ask forgiveness than permission – but this would not be the case in a court of law.

One major weakness seen is how the non-narc spouse tends to overcompensate by being too careful and frugal with their numbers, not adequately planning for the future. For example, when you move out, you might be inclined to choose a less expensive apartment not knowing what future support will look like; allowing only $1,000 for rent might not be in-line with the cost of living for the area you end up in. Ask your lawyer how to handle this situation. Please do not exaggerate the numbers as your own credibility is at stake too. Your spouses' legal team can turn the table and push to declare you an un-reliable witness thus possibly winning them the judge's favor.

Allison is a survivor and her story might shed some light on this: Robert had handled all the financial aspects throughout their marriage leaving Allison little knowledge of the monthly transactions. When she obtained the joint checking statements, she saw that Robert had been slowly pulling money out of it for the past year and had amassed a separate account with over $75,000. She found the trail that prompted her lawyers to look for this undisclosed account. The judge was perturbed to hear that he had 'forgotten' about an account with $75,000. His credibility with the judge was shot.

The bottom line is, do yourself a favor and be truthful to a fault because if your ex doesn't call you out for a mistake, the judge might. They are like bloodhounds and that is not the person you want dis-trusting you at any time. You must also be practical, however, and don't short-change yourself on the backend. Honesty is always the best policy – especially in a court of law. Your word is your bond. Chances are good that you will see fireworks when your ex gets caught in his many attempts to sabotage the process.

Chapter 8

PLANNING YOUR DIVORCE

Your core mission and goals

At the beginning of a divorce, each party should identify specific goals that are kept private from the other. Your core mission and objectives will shape the negotiations and shorten the process. Sit down and do the calculations so you know where you stand and are empowered to not be pushed to accept less than you want.

If, for example, being awarded primary custody of the children is one of your goals, watch for your soon-to-be ex to start showing up to their activities as soon as the ink dries on the separation papers. The one who never attended parent teacher conferences or soccer practice, the absent parental unit who couldn't have cared less about the child's birthday party is now making a play to prove to the court that they have been misrepresented by you. This performance will naturally make your blood boil because it just isn't true. *More lies.* Your lawyer will have no answer as to how they can get away with the deceptions regarding their past involvement other than your spouse hired a good lawyer who directed them to step up and appear to be a good parent or else they could lose custody. This performance is directly related to that instruction. Judges seem to like when an absent parent shows improvements, even if it's in the 11th hour. In the eyes of our court system, children need both parents in their lives so this tactic will unfortunately have more teeth than it should. This doesn't mean you give up; now you must gather the proof that contradicts their lies.

At this point, it is critical to document everything, past and present. Create a spreadsheet to track their pre-divorce interest in the children to include dates and events. Utilize another tab on that same spreadsheet to track the missed or canceled parenting time during the divorce – all the times they didn't show up for visitation, arrived late to pick the kids up, or brought them home early. Maintain the updated data in this file; texts and email make the best proof and it will go a long way. If your ex stops communicating via text or email and calls you to cancel their time with the children, record it, if it's legal in your state. You could also send an emailed recap of the call to document it similar to this:

> "Michael, when you dropped off the kids, you mentioned that you need to cancel your next parenting time. Just so we're on the same page, I wanted to confirm that it is July 16th that you will be out of town and unable to take them. Is this correct? I need to put it on my calendar so that I can make a plan. Thank you."

This moves the verbal agreement into a paper trail, formally referred to as evidence. Any information related to dates with the children that were missed without something to back it up doesn't hold much weight. I know many may skip this step as it will seem pointless when there is no communication from the ex but don't skip it. Do it anyway! Save the email as evidence of your constant effort to communicate. The fact that they are simply not being cooperative will speak for itself. With a pattern of this type of behavior in black and white, you are creating corroboration to show the truth that is hard to dispute.

What do you want to get out of the divorce?
   » stay in marital home with kids

- » visitation/custody
- » retirement security
- » a fair alimony
- » child support that comfortably covers the needs of the children
- » peace
- » bright financial future
- » freedom
- » integrity
- » assets from the marriage – what do you really want? (make a list)
- » revenge

Consider this: what is the price for peace? You may feel like you have been at war and lost so much time already. Will fighting for specific items do more than prolong the inevitable and cost you additional money? Evaluate everything against the solid cost of tranquility.

What are some things that you could ask for but you don't really care if you get? These are called negotiation tools and are good to have in the back of your mind.

Setting short term goals lays the groundwork for the future. If you only think about after the divorce is settled, you can easily get sucked into the drama and lose track of what you need now that one home is splitting into two.

- » Who will move out?
- » Can your combined incomes cover the expense of two households?
- » Who will pay what bills: mortgage, rent, utilities, childcare, etc.?
- » Should credit cards be paid off now or later?
- » Can you still have access to the joint marital accounts?
- » Where will the children live?
- » What will visitation look like? How will the exchanges be executed safely and without drama?
- » Are there mutually agreed upon guidelines for commu-

nication with the children when they are staying with
your spouse?

> » Should the children get counseling? Who will pay?
> » Do you both agree to help the kids get through
>   the divorce?

When you begin this journey, it will take great strength and fortitude to face the unknown but you only need to find small spurts
of courage to get through each day and each new challenge. The last
thing you might think about is taking the time to write down your
intentions, but it should be the first. Without a plan, surprises will
come at you from all sides. When you set a goal to maintain integrity,
you will not only weigh each decision and choice by that standard but
you will also have a better idea what to expect from the overall event.
If your objective is to get a fair settlement, put in the work so that
accurate numbers are represented for the best possible outcome. If
your desire is to get primary custody of the kids, obtain the proof that
you are the better parent which means shining the spotlight on your
spouse's parental weaknesses. Be aware of the risks and prepare for
their propensity to fight back. Being prepared for all of the potential
obstacles is a part of understanding the goals.

In many cases, the narcissist's lawyers will suggest that your side
submit the first negotiation offer under the guise of "working with
you." I have seen this backfire nearly every time as they then see
what is important to you and can promptly begin taking those things
off the table. If you can get them to give the first offer, insight and
guidance is in your corner to help determine how to shape your
counteroffer.

How to beat a narcissist at their own game:
Clear Strategy: You've got to have a clear, strong and powerful
strategy. Be ready to go on the offensive and have your leverage
ready. Have everything you need to incentivize so that the other
side will want to come to a resolution with you. It is counter-in-
tuitive, but if you want them to come to that fair conclusion,
then you're going to have to incentivize them to do that by get-

ting leverage.

Rebecca Zung, author, nation's top 1% divorce attorney, high conflict negotiation coach

Get your temporary orders in place now!

If you are the non-income-generating spouse, the stay-at-home parent, or the one responsible for the kids until the divorce is finalized, it is imperative that the court orders your partner to begin providing temporary support so you are able to pay the bills and survive. Immediately. As I briefly touched on in Chapter 2, the narcissist will stonewall the process, delay it, and tell you that they will give you nothing. Stay calm – this is not their decision to make; beat them at their own game by getting it into the courts as soon as the legal system allows to assuage your concerns. It is merely another manipulative opportunity they take advantage of to keep you living in fear.

Ask your lawyer to get temporary orders for support in place as soon as possible, setting up the visitation schedule and financial support. This will reduce the pressure immensely as it is a major fear: how will I make it, financially? The process to get a temporary order varies in every state, but it typically starts with the official filing of the divorce with the courts. The financial affidavits would then be submitted to detail the fiscal picture showing what you will need to cover the bills as well as what assets you share as a couple. Your lawyer will ask for a temporary order hearing at which point you could be granted **or** ordered to pay temporary financial support that will last until the final order gets settled. The temporary order may also determine who stays in the house and a temporary visitation schedule. Communication recommendations are another thing you can request at this time.

Mediation vs courtrooms

Most of us have been negotiating since we had a voice. "You can use my shovel if you will loan me your bucket," or "I will trade you this baseball card for two of your Hot Wheels cars." We've negotiated for job offers, we negotiate in marriage, and we continuously negotiate with our kids. We instinctively know how to navigate each situation regardless of the outcome. We make decisions and handle the consequences.

Divorce is different due to the drag on your emotions. They will be pulled in every direction with uncertainty and fear. If you are the discarded, your world has been shattered, your power supply has one bar remaining, and you simply don't have the bandwidth for anything else. Mediation is often the next logical step in an attempt to come together, act like adults, and cleanly break apart your years together. The contrast between whom we married and who we are divorcing leaves us at a distinct disadvantage – their cruelty is bolstering their intensity, often refusing to mediate with honesty and grace.

Narcissists may be open to mediation or they may be dead set against it. Oftentimes a narcissist will agree to mediation in an effort to trick you into an early settlement if they are hiding money – proceed with extreme caution at this point. They realize that a trial will expose the bigger picture and they don't want you to know the whole truth; they want to control you one last time. The cooperative appearance of being willing to compromise is often accompanied by the subtle underlying threat that you will get nothing if you take the divorce to court. The manipulation to convince you that settling with a mediator is in your best interest is a ploy that often leaves the grey areas (loop holes) untouched for them to exploit later. A common example of this abuse would be when (and how) they may (or may not) pay you the portion you are owed from the sale of the house. The narcissist always prefers the fight. If your narcissist appears eager to go to settlement, they may play on your weaknesses by telling you that they want to save money and keep it amicable. Be forewarned: this is their Trojan horse, easily hiding assets and entering mediation without you knowing the true financial picture. Don't trust this unless you are confident that you have all records.

Many states require a mandatory mediation session designed to attempt settlement on as much as possible. This is a good opportunity to nail down the parenting questions, including the plan for the children until they turn 18, and expenses. Holiday and vacation schedules have no place in the family court – the judge will want to see that you can be civil and cooperative when they are not leading the charge. Mediation is also the place where you can get a glimpse of the cooperation level you can expect. Their lawyer's tactics will be on display as they either work with the mediator or resist every offer.

It is standard for your lawyer to be present during mediation sessions. Dependent on your situation, it could be in your best interest to not be in the same room with your soon-to-be ex, especially if you are afraid you might be more nervous with them there. This also gives you the opportunity to discuss everything with your lawyer in private, prior to making any decisions.

Mediation can be a great way to resolve your divorce: But, as the saying goes, it takes two to tango, so keep the following in mind: If you and your spouse will not negotiate in good faith, the process won't work. Don't waste your time and money mediating. Before going to mediation, write down on paper what you need in one column. Then, in another column, write down what you want. They should be different!

It's important to understand your spouse's motivation and wants and needs too: Have a reason for everything you ask for in mediation. Then, as the negotiation proceeds, you will be able to articulate intelligently to the mediator why you are asking for a, b, and c. Knowing what you need to survive versus what you may want can be key to having a successful mediation. Focus on your needs and negotiate with your wants.

When deciding whether to settle in mediation, keep in mind the alternative: Going to court? A trial? Both will cost you much more in time and money, especially if you have an attorney. If you have an attorney, it is probably a good idea to have them attend the mediation with you, but be clear regarding your expectations and what you are and are not willing to settle for. Obviously, listen to your attorney's advice and go from there.

Jason Levoy, former divorce attorney turned coach, creator of DivorceU

My ex and I were ordered to go to mandatory mediation and it turned out to be a massive waste of time and money. My husband brought his parents who sat in another room, arms crossed, saying, "She will not get anything." They collectively had no interest in settling and rejected all offers my attorney put forward. Know that if you are forced to go to mediation and your spouse will not budge, you are free to leave. You will still have to pay the mediator, but you can consciously end the perverted torture. In many ways, this is just another layer of abuse if they are not really coming to the table to accomplish anything. All the while, you are sticking around, making adjustments, hoping they will be human and do what is right. Remember that if they are being deceitful, they may not want to get the truth exposed in court so any leverage you have on them is best used in this environment to encourage them to settle.

If you are working with a mediator, you can request that he/she be the go between in your communication. This will keep conversations on topic and on the record. Many narcissists may don one of their masks at this point but if they forget that the mediator is privy to the communication they are sending you, they might allow the mask to fall and show their true self for all to see.

How to set your mediation goals

As with the divorce, setting a goal for mediation will help steer the process in the right direction. Establish a plan with your lawyer and set priorities. If your soon-to-be ex is not willing to discuss financial support or settlement of assets, maybe they would be willing to agree on the parenting pieces? Try to focus on topics that are important to you in an effort to put your mind at ease.

Since the objective of the courts is to always find a happy medium, start high in mediation and request everything on your list. Don't worry – it will be chiseled down. Remember, negotiations are about give and take but if you start off from a place of honesty and tell them what you really want, there is nowhere to go but down. If you start by negotiating with something you don't really care about, you may land at your original plan in the end and that is a win! Always have something you are willing to give up; it makes them feel like they won which could make them easier to work with going forward.

Mediation with High Conflict Folks: You know the type – smiling as they walk into the room, complimentary, saying they want very little, but within minutes they're blaming the other party, creating nothing but problems in the conference. These are really tough cases. Narcissists believe their own statements: if they say it, it must be true.

When dealing with a high conflict partner, it is easier if there are no third parties in the room except for the lawyers. As you know, narcissists love an audience. It is imperative that ground rules be set and enforced. Narcissists require options because it must be their idea, not yours.

Mediation Myths:

Mediation only adds additional time to the process and will most likely only postpone our conflicts.

False: Mediation can be scheduled more quickly than a court hearing. The same issues will arise and can be addressed in a more informal atmosphere. This allows all parties to remain calm to focus on an individualized, creative solution.

We must go to court anyway so we should not bother with mediation.

False: The bulk of family law cases are resolved outside the court by parties and counsel. The litigation process is expensive and time-consuming, promoting quicker settlements. Mediation creates an atmosphere that fosters open dialog before the expense becomes too great or the conflicts too difficult.

See you in Court – I will tell the Judge my story and get a better result.

False: People believe that if they go to court, they will "be heard." We all want to tell our story: how badly we were treated or why our position is the only fair one. Most courts, however, are unlike the "shock and awe" of television. Typically, divorce litigants walk out feeling as if they have been hit by a truck. The actual experience is rarely elation.

I already have a lawyer, so I cannot use a mediator.

False: It is common for couples to use both services. Many couples wish to avoid using attorneys and try mediation first, and mediation respects this choice. Others choose to retain counsel or meet separately with an advisory divorce lawyer to review their rights and concerns. This can be advantageous as informed people tend to make better choices.

I must hire a lawyer anyway to do all the paperwork.

Somewhat true: A mediator can draft your agreement, a Memorandum of Understanding (MOU), which can be submitted to the court along with the basic divorce forms. The court documentation will need to be prepared, but once an agreement is reached, the fees for that service are much lower. A mediator will outline alternatives for getting the necessary paperwork done, whether it be with a Legal Assistance Center or just one lawyer. Do not discount the value of getting your own legal advisor, but it may not be required.

There is no point, my spouse will never agree.

False: Eventually there will be some sort of settlement – either imposed by the Court or by the parties themselves, and most people realize this. Once the reality of the court litigation process settles in, the majority takes a few steps back and considers settlement."

Patricia Riley, former Family Lawyer turned divorce mediator

Paying for your divorce – what to expect

No one wins in divorce except the lawyers. There is nothing that keeps victims in unhappy marriages like the lack of money. If the spouse has it and controls it, it is easy to feel stuck. Many have come to me, trapped for years, with no way to pay for a divorce. Legal fees vary by location and experience, charging anywhere from $150-$600 an hour, with deposits ranging from $4,000-$15,000. And this is just to get started. When you hand over the check to hire an attorney, the moment of realization sinks into your soul... Many attorneys use a paralegal team to do much of the research and data entry so you might be able to save money by asking how much of the work will be done by them versus their team.

It is quite common to be forced to extract money from a retirement account in order to start the divorce process. Please do not make the mistake of withdrawing money without also accounting for the taxes – the IRS is not forgiving and to accrue a large debt to them on top of all the other expenses would be an unhappy discovery when the divorce finally does end. Early withdrawal fees, penalties, and interest would make this the most expensive way to fund a divorce. If you have no choice, do not add insult to injury – ensure those fees are calculated and included prior to touching the money.

Borrowing from family and friends is another common way to seed that legal bill. Many people sell personal items, like wedding rings or jewelry, to raise money for the divorce. As we discussed in Chapters 4 & 5, selling assets after you file will most likely not be looked on favorably. Before you file, it's usually safe to do. Please check with a lawyer to protect your best interests.

For those without a fund to pull from or any family to lean on, there are free services that offer guidance. Search your area for free legal advice and support but don't get your hopes up that the advice will be sufficient to go up against a narcissist in court. I do not recommend trying to represent yourself in a divorce of this nature, however I know too many who have had no choice. There are great resources available to those who have no other option; just don't do it alone. At the very least, if you can afford a divorce coach to answer your questions, you'll be better off than taking on the narcissist and his team on your own. There are also attorneys who can help build your case without actually appearing in court with you. That could be money well spent. This is a time to get creative so that you may find a way to get free. Life is too short to be miserable.

Everyone knows someone who has been through a divorce; that person can quickly tell you if their lawyer was great or horrible. I began my search by asking friends for references and almost immediately the needle was aimed directly at who I hired. Throughout my entire divorce, I had no idea what a narcissistic person was, despite the fact that I was gearing up to divorce one. I lucked out with a team that was fully equipped to understand the intricacy of my case.

Determining the complexity of your case

Prior to discussing the questions you should ask a potential lawyer, I suggest you do a little homework. It is not necessary to perform a full-on financial analysis prior to your first conversation, but I do recommend that you have the answers to the following questions at your fingertips when you do. A lawyer can get a much clearer picture of how complex your case is with this information.

1) Approximately how much money do you have in the bank? [This gives the lawyer an idea of your worth as a couple.]

2) What is your approximate debt – combined and/or individually? [If you are burdened with debt, there may be portions that will need to be disputed.]

3) What assets do you own (home(s), cars, jewelry, stocks, vacation property, rental property, artwork, etc.)? [Division of property can slow down a process as more details are added so knowing if there will be a fight for multiple properties, retirement accounts, or large assets like boats and cars will help them gauge the amount of work that will be required. The more money in different places, the more complex.]

4) Whose name are the assets in? [If you are both on everything, it makes it easier than fighting for a rental property that is solely in your spouse's name or pre-marital.]

5) What is the approximate value of these assets? [Don't stress if you don't know this yet, but if you do know, it will help the lawyer in their assessment.]

6) What assets do either of you own individually?

7) What are both of your salaries? [If you are a stay-at-home parent, don't panic. You don't need a job to get divorced, but it is important that the lawyers understand where the income is derived from as this explains your

financial picture.]

8) How many kids do you have together? How old are they? Will your ex fight for custody?

9) Do you have retirement accounts? How much is in your name? How much is in their name?

10) Have you or your spouse ever been accused of domestic violence? [I added this because if your narcissist has accused you of abuse, we know that trick may be used against you, which will add additional complications.]

11) Do either of you have any inheritance money? Was any of it comingled?

Hiring a lawyer – let's interview divorce attorneys!

A quick, albeit shady, trick that many narcissists have been known to use is to lock you out of retaining successful attorneys. If your spouse meets with an attorney before you, chances are good that no lawyer from that firm may want to meet with you due to a potential conflict of interest, even if they weren't hired.

A lawyer friend shared a trick with me that worked: A narc has an uncanny ability to look for shark (read: shady) lawyers, so I stayed one step ahead of him and researched the top (read: reputable) lawyers. This is easily done by asking friends to ask friends for recommendations, look at reviews, etc. I amassed a hot list of the best lawyers and I called them all. They had me on file and he was effectively blocked.

Strong Lawyer: You're going to want to pick a really strong lawyer and you're going to want to pick a lawyer that knows what they are doing. Make sure they know what type of person they're going to be dealing with so they can help you develop that strategy. Related to this step is making sure you pick a lawyer that you're really going to trust. And then, trust that lawyer. I say this because what your narcissist STBX[17] is going to do is try to get you to distrust your lawyer. The only reason they want your lawyer out of the picture is because then they can drive a wedge and regain control over

---

17   An acronym that refers to the person you'll soon be divorcing: Soon-To-Be-Ex.

you again. Once you pick a lawyer that you really like and you know you can trust, listen to them.

Rebecca Zung, author, nation's top 1% divorce attorney, high conflict negotiation coach

One of the most important things you can do is retain a good lawyer. You are looking for someone who has dealt with high conflict divorce; don't expect them to be narcissist experts. I also encourage you to find a lawyer who is willing to settle rather than stir the pot. Your narcissist will provide ample drama. No need for any to come from your legal team.

Categories of lawyers

SHARK LAWYER Aggressive, a fighter, and dangerous with a low bar of tactics
BARACUDA LAWYER Assertive and cunning but knows which battles to fight
TURTLE LAWYER Passive and kind but cannot fight the way you need

The Interviews

There is no point to physically go from office to office to simply ask the basic questions. You will visit the firms that make your short list later.

By phone

Phase I. Set a goal to find out if they are affordable and available. Some law firms will not speak to you until they know both you and your spouse's information to ensure there is no possible conflict of interest. You may or may not actually speak with an attorney at this point.

> » Ask if they are currently taking new clients.
> » They may ask you how you found them and if someone referred you. If someone did give you their name, share

it as it creates an immediate connection which might encourage them to keep this from being only a short pre-interview.

Face-to-face

Phase II. You have done your homework, narrowed down your list, and are ready to hire. Many firms charge for the in-person interview – be sure to ask if this is the case so that you are not taken by surprise. Lawyers, like any profession, do not like getting used for information and this is a good way for them to weed out the tire kickers. Do not assume that any interview is the lawyer you will hire. More detailed answers are necessary to solidify your trust in them. Many narcissists are in high powered jobs, like lawyers and doctors, so have your radar up and look for red flags, even if you feel like you "click." Do not let the cost of the interview be a determining factor in your decision to hire any firm. The loss of that small investment would be light years ahead of losing an entire deposit if you decide to change lawyers once the process has begun. To avoid this, slow down to feel for any genuine feelings and if there is a connection.

Meeting a lawyer for the first time is scary; the reality that the divorce is undeniable will smack you in the face on this day. You might feel apprehensive and afraid which might make it difficult to remember all that is said. If recording someone is legal in your state, ask the attorney if you can record the conversation to listen to later. Be mindful that you have not yet hired this lawyer so they might not agree to your request. If they do agree, be careful who you share the recording with to protect attorney-client privilege. You might find it helpful to bring a trusted friend or family member along, like maybe one who has confessed that they never did like your spouse once you shared your news of the divorce. Sometimes being able to discuss various points after the fact will help you realize what is the best move to make.

I have outlined some important questions, but an initial interview with any attorney is not likely to last long enough to get all of the answers you seek. Keeping your goals in mind, use them in a combination that best reflects your concerns, your circumstances, and your needs. Never hire a lawyer without meeting them first and don't feel pressured to commit to any with whom you wouldn't be 100% happy to work. Once you have met, wait a day or two and see if you feel comfortable moving forward with them. Remember, at this stage, they basically have your future in their hands.

> **Find an attorney who is not a narcissist:** How can you tell? Narcissists have little empathy for people who are victimized, especially in a marriage. If your attorney seems apathetic to your issues, and you find them defending your spouse more than supporting you, that's a red flag that they will ultimately find you pathetic and fight little on your behalf.
> **Lindsey Ellison,** author, narcissism expert, and relationship coach

Initial questions to ask potential attorneys:

1) Can you share your style of lawyering? Do you focus on offense or defense?

2) Are you a shark? Can you help me get my ex? [*This is a trick question.* If they say yes, consider ending the meeting. I do not recommend a shark lawyer. Narcissists always hire the shark slime ball lawyers who will do anything to win. If you enter into the battle with an ego-driven lawyer, the games will never stop. It's best to have an assertive lawyer who knows how to fight yet doesn't start them.]

3) Do you create a strategy for a divorce? Would we work on this together? How does it get updated as things come up? How reactive to the challenges will you be? What is the best defense? [A good answer would be that you will beat them with the truth, paper trails, and the law.]

4) How reactive would you be to the false allegations I expect from my spouse?

5) How would you know which allegations we need to fight versus those that would be more beneficial to walk

away from?

Questions about cost and fees:
1) What is the probability of getting my legal fees paid by my spouse? How often is that request granted? Under what conditions? If I am the primary earner, could I be responsible for my spouse's attorney fees? How can you protect me from that?

2) How much could my divorce cost? [When you ask this question, do so with the understanding that they cannot predict what will happen in your case. However, they should still be able to give you an informed estimate if things go well and they should also be able to breakdown average costs for the normal aspects of a divorce. Expect them to say this is an estimate, because truthfully, until they get in the ring and see what they are up against, they cannot know the true scope.]

3) What will the retainer be and how far could I expect that to go? What if the whole retainer is not used, can I get the balance refunded? What is your hourly rate and the rate for any supporting team members?

4) How often will I be billed? What is your billing policy? Do you bill differently for court time versus out of court time? At what interval do you bill? [Some are every six minutes. Verify if there is a minimum, because if they charge you for 15 minutes to just read a quick email, your bill will grow extremely fast.] Can I make payments if needed? Do you take credit cards?

5) Do you charge a "flat fee?" [Be cautious of lawyers who charge a flat fee. It may be based on only a certain number of hours; ask them if that is the case.] What if I surpass the flat fee hours? What would the new rate be? [Divorcing a high conflict narcissist is usually much more work than the flat fee lawyers anticipate so get clear understanding about this before you sign up. Cheaper is

never better. You get what you pay for. These lawyers have a tendency to push for quicker settlements and may not be good trial attorneys.]

6) (If money is a concern), Are there tasks that can be delegated to me in an effort to save money? What is the copy fee? [I think mine was .25 per sheet. In our court, we needed three copies: one for our side, one for his side, and one for the court. *My* case file books alone were 5,000 sheets and that included five years of statements, bills, and paperwork. Those 15,000 pages would have been $3,750 but I did all the work and supplied the copies to save money. I would have also been paying a paralegal $100 an hour to copy and collate them. The way we did it, the attorneys and judge could just pull out exactly what they needed to present and label each piece that was being submitted as evidence.]

7) It's all too common that people hire an attorney and then learn they are not the right fit. What type of loss could I expect in this situation? Would a refund be possible, less the time already spent? Could all the paperwork be transferred to new council?

8) What can I do to control the costs from escalating? [Look for a robust answer here with a solid strategy for keeping costs down. If they say something like: get along, settle quickly, or be reasonable to all offers, they do not have a strategy and you will be on your own watching your financial future fly away.]

9) What if my spouse runs up legal bills with unreasonable claims and accusations? Can they be held responsible for those fees?

Questions about high conflict divorce:
1) How do you define a high conflict divorce?
2) What are some tactics you are familiar with that we could expect and how would you suggest they

be handled?

Questions about their knowledge of the court system:

1) How long would you expect the divorce to take? (see state guidelines[18])

2) If I have any separate property or inheritance, are they protected?

3) My ex has hired _____. What do you know about this attorney? What can we expect? Have you ever been up against them? Did you win against them?

4) How familiar are you with the potential judges in my (or this) district? Do those judges tend to favor men or women? Do you have any concerns regarding a certain judge that we might encounter?

5) Will the courts make us go to mediation?

Questions about their team:

1) Who will be working on my case?

2) Will I have a paralegal as a point of contact? How am I billed for their time?

3) If we need investigators or forensic accountants, have you worked with any that you would recommend?

4) Will you be in the courtroom if we go to trial? Would anyone else be at our table?

Questions about communication:

1) How often will we communicate? Will it be by phone? In office? Video meetings? [If you tell them at this interview that you want to be heard and you want your emails acknowledged within a specific timeframe, you can nail down upfront if they are the right attorney for you. Many people complain that they never get timely responses from their attorney(s). This can become so frustrating that many have willingly thrown away the first $10,000 deposit to start over with another firm.]

2) Can I expect you or your paralegal to answer my

---

18   https://narcissistabusesupport.com/book-resources/

emails and calls? What is the standard response turn-around time?

Questions about personality disorders:

It is best if you do not expect an attorney to have a deep understanding of narcissistic abuse but it certainly helps if they are aware of the common tactics.

1) Are you familiar with personality disorders?
2) How do you define Narcissistic Personality Disorder (NPD)?
3) How many divorces *against* a person with NPD have you represented?
4) How were they resolved?
5) In your experience, what does winning against a narcissist look like?
6) Have you ever represented a person *with* NPD? [Most lawyers have represented someone with NPD and have seen it in action. If they say that they haven't represented someone who is narcissistic, I would question their ability to identify someone with NPD or to recognize the strategies they use.] What did you learn from representing them?
7) What do you foresee as the major obstacles for a case against a person with NPD? How would you navigate those obstacles?
8) Have you ever had a case where you needed to hire expert witnesses who were experienced in NPD? Why were they needed? How did it help your case?
9) What should I be concerned about?
10) *Bonus question #1*, if they know about personality disorders: In your experience, how successful would mediation be with someone with a personality disorder?
11) *Bonus question #2*, if they know about personality disorders: can you recommend any relevant book or information to read for insight into divorcing someone with

NPD? [To me, this is an important question because it shows that they have done their research and are willing to guide you to get some of the answers on your own. It proves the point that they are helpful and want to see you succeed. A $20 book could save you thousands of dollars by not having to ask your lawyer for the same information.]

Questions about where and how to start:
1) Should I move out of the house? Is there a risk if I do?
2) Would it be better if my spouse moved out? How long would it take to make that happen?
3) Can I use money from our joint account to pay my expenses?
4) How soon can we request that my spouse start paying support?
5) How is spousal support calculated? [If you are the possible recipient or payer, it helps to understand the formula in your state.]
6) What do I need to be concerned about regarding the children? Support? Visitation? What are the laws in our state to avoid custody battles?
7) If my spouse is abusive or has had domestic violence charges, will they get visitation with the kids?
8) What would you do first if I hired you?
   Answers to look for, if you have already been filed on by your spouse:
   1) answer the complaint and notify the court and opposing counsel that they have taken the case;
   2) arrange a hearing as soon as possible to get temporary orders to define living arrangements, child support and visitation, a communication plan, and temporary support for you, if needed.
   Answers to look for, if you haven't been filed on yet:
   1) expedite the filing with the courts to begin the process;

2) arrange a hearing for the temporary orders, as above.

Final thoughts prior to hiring an attorney:

1) Ask for references. Even if you are sold on them in that meeting, *call the references.* Read their reviews on Lawyers.com and Avvo.com. Peruse local websites like Nextdoor.com and ask your neighbors if anyone has ever used them. Get positive feedback before you write the deposit check. Ultimately, lawyers are salespeople and know how to close the deal. Never allow yourself to be rushed and always take the time to investigate their reputation.

2) Listen to your gut. If you have been in a narcissist relationship, you are probably accustomed to bad behavior. If your head is telling you that you "should" hire a particular lawyer but your gut is screaming *"Run!"* listen to your gut. It doesn't matter if that lawyer is supposed to be "the best" or whatever buzz word is on your mind. If you don't feel comfortable, *don't hire them!* What's more, if you leave a lawyer's office in tears (over and above the tears that might be expected in a situation like this) or feel like you need a shower – that is *not* a good sign!

How to confirm if an attorney understands Narcissistic Personality Disorder (NPD): A lawyer who is not privy to the machinations of a narcissist will not be able to adequately offer you legal counsel. This is particularly relevant if children are involved as narcissists are notorious for perpetrating parental alienation. During the initial meeting with a lawyer, ask about their approach with narcissistic personalities in divorce cases. A lawyer who understands NPD may suggest mediation, but only if it is highly structured and enforces firm boundaries. Clues to look for that indicate a lawyer understands NPD is that they will advise you to steer clear of any communication that could potentially be volatile. They will handle all court-related communication pertaining to the divorce. They will also encourage you to start keeping thorough records, if you haven't already, of agreements, threats, or dangerous actions made. Essentially, they will harbor no illusions about their need to barricade you to the best of their ability from the narcissist's abuse and take a proactive, but diplomatic pragmatic position.

Rev. Sheri Heller, author, Licensed Clinical Social Worker

Narc-trick: how they get you to fire your lawyer

Your spouse, without exception, will express an immediate dislike for your lawyer and attempt to fill your head with lies about them. They might say that they know someone who used that firm but fired them because all they cared about was the money. The concern will be poured on thick with the end goal to make you question your decision while they pretend to be your protector. You are being gaslit to fall back under their control. Gaslighting[19] is manipulation designed to make you doubt your reality. If you did your homework and trust your choice for representation, ignore them. They want you to go backwards and feel you should start over so that they can always be one step ahead. The goal is to drive a wedge between you and your team, cause confusion, and dominate the decision of who they will go against in the courtroom. Throughout my years in this industry, I have spoken with thousands of survivors, some of whom were duped repeatedly to fire their attorney.

Tricks of the trade: courtesy of your spouse's lawyer

The constant changing of temporary hearing, mediation, or court dates and filing cyclical motions to postpone are always the first-level attacks made by any shark lawyer. To cope with this stonewalling, think of all dates as tentative. Nerves are natural but it helps to have a set date in order to make a solid plan. When that date continually gets changed, the emotional toll can be devastating. They know this. To avoid disappointments, don't hold onto the dates with absolution.

Once court dates are announced, you might notice that your spouse's lawyer will reject certain dates just to avoid a specific judge. Some judges favor moms while others advocate for fathers' rights. Some are more lenient regarding the financial splitting of assets so

---

19   Gaslighting will be formally introduced in Chapter 9.

your spouse's lawyer, or in some cases your lawyer, might withdraw from going against a particular judge based on the challenges at hand.

Narcissistic people tend to be so entitled that they demand that their lawyer do everything they say, even if it defies court standards and rules. Most lawyers draw the line at this type of individual and won't hesitate to fire those who do not complete the paperwork and discovery, or other things ordered by the judge. Clients are important to a lawyer but protecting their own reputation ranks even higher. The consequences can be great if they show up in court breaking rules and attacking or defying the judge's orders. They can't risk jeopardizing their career so they will walk away. While this may seem detrimental to your spouse, it is actually just a delay tactic. Your ex will have no problem starting over again with another lawyer. There are plenty of fish (sharks) in the sea. The longest delay I have heard of lasted eight years – the narcissistic spouse was fired by *seven* lawyers before the divorce was eventually finalized. Be aware of this possibility.

Over-using your attorney

Divorce attorneys charge hundreds of dollars per hour. They provide advice on divorce-related issues; they are not therapists or certified financial planners and it would be in your best interest to not try to use them as such. If you wish to talk through the emotional aspect of your divorce or need career counseling or financial analysis, save your money and find experts in those fields, such as a coach or narcissist-aware therapist, vocational expert, or financial planner.

If things do get ugly where you are unable to communicate with your soon-to-be ex requiring the lawyers to handle all emails and texts, your case will get expensive extremely fast. If this is your situation, ask your lawyer to request the judge order one of the parenting apps to communicate, like I mentioned in Chapter 6. For the sake of your wallet, avoid calling your lawyer every time your spouse provokes you. Instead, lean on your coach and trusted friends – let your lawyer do the legal stuff.

Narc-trick: fake filing

A friend, who was embroiled in a caustic divorce, experienced something that was new to me. She had been educating herself on narcissistic abuse and getting ready to hire a lawyer; in fact she had visited a lawyer just that week. One day when she arrived home, her husband handed her a divorce petition written by her husband's lawyer accompanied by a letter indicating that he was willing to represent both of them to help them save money. All she had to do was sign the document and he would make sure everything was fair. Thankfully, we were having lunch that day and she mentioned it. I suggested she ask the lawyer who she was considering hiring if it was legitimate. As it turned out, the whole thing was fictitious, right down to the bogus case number. It looked very official but it wasn't real. They had even gone to the trouble to utilize Photoshop to make it look authentic. They hadn't really filed; they were trying to stop her from retaining her own representation. As sad and shocking as it was, we had a good laugh in the end. Dumbass[20]!

---

20   Refer to Chapter 4 for my Dumbass Theory.

Chapter 9

GASLIGHTING: IS IT JUST A GAME?

Gaslighting is a form of emotional abuse and psychological manipulation where the abuser influences their prey to think that they are crazy by making them question their own memory. Distorting reality so that everything they say will be an attack on the truth, it is an attempt to alter facts with lies using mind control to make victims doubt their own sensibilities and feel like they are losing their minds. This type of control happens slowly and is designed to wear the victim down to where they stop defending their authentic selves. This technique is common in narcissistic abuse relationships; most who have lived through it would swear that their narcissist enjoyed tormenting them, taking advantage of their mental confusion. They manipulate their victim to believe that they are responsible for the family falling apart, for example. Guilt, shame, and fear are catastrophic weapons designed for domination.

Gaslight, a popular movie from the 1940's, was our first introduction to this ubiquitous turn of phrase. I find it ironic that a word to describe this horrific abuse technique was coined by a movie where we saw the behavior displayed on the big screen. Typical Hollywood!

It has been established that narcissists demand control; to do this, they must weaken you. Narcissists target strong people because they are attracted to what they pretend to be. You are strong and smart, but they must appear stronger and smarter. You will need to be knocked down a notch and they are just the ones to do the job.

Notice sometime when your spouse says something you know isn't true – they will try to convince you that you are remembering it incorrectly so you will become confused and lose focus. They are weakening their prey. When you are a victim of emotional abuse and gaslighting, a slow drip of instances will begin to train you in this type of domestic torture. If you look back, you might recognize it in your relationship but had no idea that there was a name for these perplexing and contradicting conversations.

Victims of this type of abuse often wonder, "Why would anyone want to do this?" It is hard to wrap a normal brain around the reasoning but it boils down to one word: control. If they succeed, the groundwork is laid. Later, when the strategy needs to be intensified, the training is already complete. The victim has been groomed and is now ready to fall for whatever comes next.

After years of these subtle accusations, the victim will eventually stop fighting. Defending themselves is pointless and they begin to consider that they must be going crazy. They are right where the narcissist wants them: worn down with no more truth and willing to accept the brainwashing as gospel.

Gaslighting is a form of psychological abuse in which the perpetrator causes the victim to doubt their thoughts, feelings, memories, senses and sanity: Gaslighting causes victims to doubt and second-guess themselves, leaving them vulnerable to further manipulation. If it goes on long enough, victims may even come to believe that the gaslighter is the only one they can trust for their sense of reality. Prolonged gaslighting can severely damage a victim's self-confidence.

Gaslighting is a powerful tool in a narcissist's arsenal -- and

nothing invokes a narcissist to go on the attack like being reject-ed: Here are some phrases you may hear as you begin to disentangle yourself from a narcissistic partner:

"You're remembering that wrong."

"I never said that, you're making things up!"

"If you had ever loved me, you wouldn't be doing this."

"What kind of parent wants their child to grow up in a broken home?"

"You misinterpreted me."

"I don't know what you're talking about."

Divorce is the ultimate rejection in a toxic marital relationship: It says, "I know my reality, I trust myself, and I do not need you to tell me what is real." In rejecting the narcissist's false reality and reclaiming your own, you begin to slip out from under their control. Rejecting a narcissist can trigger an intense wave of gaslighting as they attempt to regain control of the story. Protect yourself from manipulation and confusion by keeping careful notes of any con-versations you have with your narcissist. Capturing screenshots of text or email conversations can be a helpful point of reference if the narcissist denies their words. And checking in with trusted loved ones who can validate your experiences can be an excellent antidote to the poison of gaslighting. Remember that your experiences, like your thoughts and feelings, are valid. You do not need your narcis-sist to validate them in order for them to be real.

Amy Marlow-MaCoy, author, Licensed Professional Counselor

How gaslighting is used in divorce

There are many gaslighting tactics included in this insidious clas-sification:

Future faking

If the narcissist is not the initiator of the divorce, they will make su-perficial promises to undergo counseling, of future plans, or anything deemed necessary by the victim to lure them back under their spell.

Judges, lawyers, and court processes
In a courtroom setting, the goal of the pathological lying narcissist will be to repeat their lies so frequently that even their own lawyers believe them. Flowing like water, the lies stem from the narcissists inability to feel guilt and their lack of empathy.

Endless motions
Most narcissists refuse your requests for paperwork; even the court ordered variety is ignored until the very last minute. They make motion after motion, demanding documentation from you while they never produce anything. Accusing you of not providing full disclosure introduces doubt which prompts you to double check yourself and worry that you are not in compliance, when it is them not following instructions all along. Gaslighting by motion is done to increase your legal fees, create drama and frustration, and control your reaction.

Kindness
If the narcissist pretends to want to settle amicably, telling you that you don't need lawyers and there is no need to fight, they are trying to "kill you with kindness." This adds confusion as it tends to contradict their past actions.

Hide and seek 101
In a divorce of this nature, items will undoubtedly "go missing" – from financial records to expensive art or collectibles. You might "mis-place" jewelry and berate yourself as they accuse you of losing something so expensive. They have now planted a seed to make you believe that you are forgetful or careless. The truth may really be that they hid or sold the asset, but because of your "memory problems," they blame you and deflect any suspicion in their direction.

Case #1: Michelle and Tony were married for years. From the beginning of their relationship, Michelle noticed that she was getting more absentminded about the little things. She still ran her business flawlessly and everything seemed normal, except for the time she spent at home. She was always losing her keys or her favorite earrings wouldn't make it back into the jewelry box. At first, she wrote it off to that extra glass of wine or being tired from the stress at work. Forgetting something at home was a consequence of an overworked brain and she was happy that she had no issues at work. One day when Michelle and Tony were running late to an event, the car keys went missing again. Tony used this opportunity to tell her she was losing her mind; he even jokingly accused her of having Alzheimer's. By using humor to soften the dig at her memory, he was able to refrain from starting a fight by making her laugh. He would ride in on his white horse to help her look for the missing item, appearing as the savior and good guy.

The missing keys were never found in the same place twice. At first, it was a simple location change: where she normally left them on the table by the garage door shifted to the kitchen counter by the phone. That seemed like a natural mistake, despite her concern as she had no memory of leaving them there. As the gaslighting progressed, the key's locations became downright strange and unexpected. At first, Michelle defended herself, "I always leave my keys on the table by the garage door. I didn't move them to the bedroom; I have never done that!" Michelle was at a loss.

One day, Tony found the keys in the pocket of a coat that she had not worn in months. This forced the gaslighting to be ramped up to cover his own mistake of putting the keys in the wrong coat pocket. He insisted she had worn the coat just the other day and made snide comments about how she couldn't remember something so simple. He was convincing. Was she losing her mind? After all, the keys in the pocket were proof that she had worn the coat.

Years later she started to see the pattern: an item goes missing and Tony is always there to be the hero, saving her from her own memory issues. This covert technique instilled the possibility; his goal was to create uncertainty so she would question her own mental acuity.

Manufactured jealousy

Narcissists are experts when it comes to emotions which can be surprising considering they are known for not having any of their own. They are able to create situations where you doubt what you saw or thought. You may feel that they don't trust you but when you speak up, they accuse you of being the jealous one.

Secrets you were forced to keep

The truth is always a fear for a narcissist and they will do whatever it takes to keep the behaviors that their victims endured a secret. If you question something, you will be told that what you saw or heard wasn't true, blatantly denying the facts and skeletons of your marriage and divorce.

You are to blame

Narcissists love to deflect accountability. They will do whatever it takes to turn the children against you by blaming you for the demise of the marriage and the subsequent breakup of the family. You will be held responsible for wasting all of the family money because you want the divorce.

Using sex as a weapon

To most of us, sex is the sharing of the most vulnerable part of us and we don't give it away easily or without trust. In the beginning of the love bombing stage, the sex is revealed to be amazing and consistent. Later, in the devalue stage, the frequency wanes and it will be your fault that they lost interest. "There is something wrong with you" is the narrative during this time. Once the divorce is set in motion, the lack of intimacy will be used to explain the failure of the marriage: your failure. This distracts from the truth that they have found a new upgraded supply and want nothing more to do with you. They can't tell the world the truth, so you are, once again, to blame.

Lies with a purpose to confuse and control

Lies about events or conversations are a fail-safe technique to make a victim doubt their reality. Have you ever had a conversation with your spouse where they claim they told you that their parents were coming for the holidays, but you have no memory of it? Or when they told you they were going out with their friends on Saturday, but you have zero recollection? Often, they are downright lying about dialogue that simply never occurred.

Narcissists train their victims with these types of fabrications by calling you stupid or uncaring when you don't remember. They first attack your memory and then compound it with a secondary degrading comment that attacks your sanity.

The criticisms might sound like, "Why can't you remember things that we talk about? Am I that unimportant to you?" or "Am I so inconsequential that you choose to not listen when I speak? How do you expect us to communicate better when you clearly don't care about me?" Imagine how it would feel to be told that you do not care about them because you don't recall a conversation. You might already know. It tears out your heart and all victims promise to remember things better in the future. This is surrendering to their dominance to keep the peace and stop the attacks.

The language of gaslighting:
- » "If you weren't such a bad husband, I wouldn't have cheated."
- » "No one agrees with you. You are the only one who thinks that I am a bad person."
- » "You will get nothing if you divorce me! I will ruin you."
- » "If you divorce me, I will turn the kids against you and you will never see them again."
- » "You never made any money so without me, you will be homeless."

(Case #1, cont.): Michelle was repeatedly told by Tony that she was losing her mind which thrust her into a hypervigilant mode, determined to pay closer attention to where she left the keys. She had learned the gaslight eggshell dance and lived in perpetual fear of where the keys might show up next or how Tony would react if they went missing again. She had lost her will to argue because her words were always met with anger and blame, smothered in his heroic performances. He already had additional gaslighting in the works because she had proven to be a star student in the hide and seek technique. He knew he could control her.

Case #2: Beth and her husband, Mike, were married for 26 years. He worked an office job and she stayed home to raise their two kids. Their entire marriage, Beth had been gaslighted to believe that they were poor and one step away from losing everything. He controlled every penny and would not allow her to work. He manipulated her by making her return any groceries over his pre-determined $50 limit, yet there were things that puzzled her, like when he would buy something expensive on a whim. If she spoke up, she was torn down, and punished in passive-aggressive ways that made life unbearable. His efforts to hide the money they actually had required him to make her believe that they were about to lose the house or the car. She lived in a constant state of fear. It wasn't until the divorce that she found out they were millionaires. She is much better off without him.

The weaponry of gaslighting in a divorce
Finances within a marriage are typically where the narcissist's control is unparalleled. In this generation, stay-at-home dads have become the new norm. Of course, stay-at-home moms are obviously still prevalent but I am intentionally trying to include the dads because they get abused too. The one with the higher income tends to keep their job and oftentimes that higher earner is the narcissist. In a perfect world, that career surrendering parent who has stepped up to do their part for the family would be as revered as the parent who continues to work outside the home. By their selflessness, the kids are kept with a loving parent rather than in daycare where they would be destined to spend the majority of their days if both parents worked traditionally.

The worth of a stay-at-home parent varies all over the world, but according to a 2020 report on salary.com, a stay-at-home parent in the USA is valued at $143,102 a year.

I have spoken with hundreds of stay-at-home parents who were not the breadwinner and most had the same story: they were told they were not entitled to anything because they did not work. This gaslighting technique is utilized to brainwash them to think that the work they do to support the family has no merit. The fear that they will get nothing financially freezes them to stay in a toxic relationship. While every state and country has different guidelines as to how community property is split, in general the courts endeavor to divide marital assets 50/50. So, telling the stay-at-home parent that they will get nothing if they ever leave the narcissist often keeps them trapped in a marriage needlessly. Divorcing a narcissist often becomes financial abuse because the court system is ultimately used as a weapon.

Case #3: Carol is one of those victims. She financed her husband's medical school by working two jobs and when he finally reached his goal, she willingly gave up her career to start a family. From the moment they met in college, that was the agreement.

A wrench was thrown into their plan, however, when they had a special needs child who required Carol's attention past the age when he would normally have started school. There were doctor visits, tests, and therapy that needed Carol's coordination and it became her full-time job. Carol and Dave were married for 30 years before he decided to start dating his assistant and want a divorce. Dave threatened Carol with no settlement if she told the truth about his affair. The years of emotional abuse to convince her that she had no worth, no claim to their home or property, and no rights to any of the money that he had saved for their retirement left her feeling hopeless. She had not worked for thirty years and she was convinced that his threats were credible.

Their divorce was not an easy one; fighting a narcissist who has money when you think you have none is never simple. The entitlement comes on strong because the narcissist feels the money is all theirs. Dave had drilled into her head that her work had no value for so long, she believed him. Why would he let go of anything? Carol had stopped arguing because when she spoke up, a vicious fight ensued that she never won. In her attempt to keep the peace, she lost herself entirely.

Dave's gaslighting kept Carol prisoner for 30 years. He had someone to care for their child (babysitter/nurse), someone to cook and do all the housework (maid), and someone to help him keep the respectable mask of a perfect family that he could use to convince others that he was normal. Despite his intention to gaslight her to expect nothing in the divorce, Carol walked away with half of the mortgage-free house that had increased nicely in value. She received half of all the assets, retirement, and due to the state laws where they resided, after 25 years she was entitled to alimony for the rest of her life. Her greatest wish was for me to tell her story so that others have hope after this type of brain-crippling abuse.

Anyone who has lived in this environment understands that it was designed solely to put fear in their heart. It was to control you to stay and be whatever they needed, or as we now know it, supply. *Learn your rights.* Every state is different so exhaust Google or talk to a lawyer before you get trapped, and then abandoned, after thirty years of servitude.

Distorted alternate reality

When you are divorcing a narcissist, the lies told in marriage get escalated into a distorted alternate reality, better known as false allegations. A lie is usually simple, "You are a bad mom," or "You stole money," but these get blown up into an unabridged, detailed nightmare. Where most of us tend to follow the belief system of less is more, narcissists think the more details they give, the more believable it is. The courtroom becomes a circus and they are the star of the show jumping through the rings of fire as they desperately try to keep from getting burned.

Case #4: During my divorce, I was accused of forging a change to our prenuptial agreement. A few days before our wedding, I was told that my soon-to-be in-laws had drawn up a document that I was expected to sign no later than the day before the ceremony. I now realize that it was coercive control to set this roadblock in front of me, when I was focused on all things wedding, and with no opportunity to really understand what it meant. My fiancé eased my concerns assuring me it was just a formality and it would mean nothing because we were marrying for life. He agreed that it seemed silly but it was important that we please his parents, especially since the wedding was at their house the next day.

I was given a small window to have my lawyer approve it. Once she did, we would sign in front of her and another lawyer in her firm who would act as my soon-to-be husband's advocate since his attorney was based in New York. My mind was in a million places; the wedding was the next day and there was so much to be done. As he and I sat together, holding hands, she reviewed it and found a line written in, surrounded by legalese, that I would have never seen on my own. The line was an important one: I would waive any rights to spousal support in the event of dissolution.

My lawyer, who was based in Connecticut where we lived, told us that it was against the law in our state to waive spousal support rights in a prenuptial agreement so with his lawyer's approval as well as my fiancé's acknowledgement, it was crossed out. I can still hear his words as he squeezed my hand tightly, "Tomorrow I marry the girl of my dreams. I will always take care of her, no matter what." We signed on the dotted line, accepted our two copies, and left without a backward glance. His copy was put in his parents' safe and we put the other copy in our safe deposit box. I never dreamed I would need to look at it again.

In court, they manufactured an elaborate plot against me, exasperated that I had crossed-out the line in question on our legal document on my own; I was forced to defend myself against forgery charges. My Colorado-based lawyers, where I now resided, subpoenaed my lawyer from Connecticut to testify in my defense. I was lucky that her memory was good – she remembered us and his words as he agreed to cross off that detail. He and his family had an original copy, but they denied it. Had they produced the real document, their story would have been moot. It hurt to be accused of something I did not do by someone I thought loved me, and that disempowered me. The goal of them creating this detailed rouse was to break me emotionally and financially and fly under the law to deny me any support. They did their damnedest to make me look like I was only ever interested in his money which was imperative in order to protect his finances.

Throughout your divorce, if you are painted as an evil character in the story, you too will reflexively go on the defensive. This is the ridiculous part about family court; it feels like Perry Mason without the innocent until proven guilty part. Every claim like mine that is flung around a courtroom is just another attempt to manipulate what the judge thinks about you. They will keep throwing hateful accusations up against a wall just to see what sticks.

Always be conscious of what you know their goal to be. In my case, it was to establish that "Tracy crossed off a prenup line," and not pay me support. This was critical because if they were able to prove that I altered the paperwork, then they would have won the right to call me a gold digger for the six remaining hearings. Do you see why it's so important to defend the truth? In the scheme of things, this was a battle that definitely needed to be fought. He had an uphill battle ahead of him as I was prepared to fight until my dying breath.

First, the onus was on him to lay out his case that I was only interested in his money. Then, they ordered me to have my career and potential earning power proven. All of this in an attempt to convince the judge that I couldn't be trusted and that I was really just looking for a sugar daddy.

If this sounds like your situation – maybe your spouse is fighting to not pay more money in child support – you'll need to categorize every lie as part of the plan to achieve their goal. They'll need to discredit you as a parent and prove that you can make more money than you do. They will have to show the court that they did not have the time before to prioritize the children, but they are now changing their lives in order to play a more active role. The positive is that the burden is on them to make their case, whatever it is.

Lies will be told throughout that denigrate you and while they may hurt, now is the time to carefully pick your battles. Keep a close eye on the bottom line because fighting every small infraction could destroy your financial future. No matter how much you need to prove to the world that what's being said isn't true, it isn't worth fighting if it will not matter to the judge. Don't bring a knife to a gun fight.

The best advice I can give is be prepared. Gaslighting is intended to paint you as something that you are not. The pain will be compounded because the person you loved, the one you thought would love you forever, is now smearing you in open court. Many victims of abuse struggle with authority so having this all play out in front of a judge will cut even deeper. See a coach or therapist to learn how to handle the confusing pain and let your lawyer decide what requires your attention.

Differing memories

There are three sides to every story: your truth, their truth, and *the* truth. I heard this statement at a party when I was going through my divorce and it really hit home: we all see things differently. If we watch a tennis match, or go to a concert, or a Broadway show, each of us will remember things differently dependent on where our mind was at any given time or which character held our focus. Did we watch the crowd during the set point or the winner as she victoriously jumped over the net? Perspective.

At first, they appear to be kind to help you find the keys. Over time, they will slip in the occasional dig about your forgetfulness and may even express concern for your failing memory. To the victim, this does its intended job of making them feel like the abuser cares and then takes on self-blame and even responsibility for losing the keys.

To the victim, gaslighting is a slow unconscious loss of reality. To the abuser, it is the slow misdirection of truth to gain control over the victim. Any attempts to call the abuser out on their lies are often met with snarky comments that are a secondary form of gaslighting. The intent is to intentionally not answer specific concerns and instead, turn them around – doubling down to make the victim feel like they are losing their mind.

The first line of attack is projection – insisting that you are crazy, insensitive, jealous, insecure, or an ingrate with no sense of humor. If you are told repeatedly that you are overreacting, you will begin to wonder if you are. It seems reasonable to speak up in your own defense but when this is met with additional derogatory comments, it becomes another instance that you find yourself walking on eggshells. You have learned to predict their reaction and it simply is not worth the energy that would be expended. And with this goes another crumb of your soul.

Goals of gaslighting

To better understand why narcissists gaslight, we must break down their goals. Depending on what they want to accomplish, different desires will see different things. For example, in a courtroom, it would be important to discredit you in front of the judge. Whether touting you as a bad parent or as a leech trying to suck their bank account dry, they will always claim that you are the irresponsible one, the crazy one, or the one who can't be trusted. If you are lucky, you will recognize their motive so that you can put your emotions aside and block out the pain they are trying to inflict. The beauty of this is that you can be prepared and allow yourself to only focus on what is most important – coming out the other side with your finances, family, and sanity intact.

Goal: they do not want to pay as much child support
What can you expect with a goal like that? Your spouse might try to prove that you can make enough money to support the kids or, conversely, that they do not make enough to offer adequate assistance. Some have been so dedicated to their narrative that they go to the extreme of quitting their job. They may petition to get more parenting time just to reduce the amount they owe. Faced with the threat of them spending more time with the kids, you might feel compelled to give up the child support battle in favor of their not getting more parenting time. This is one of those situations where you must pick what is most important. You lose one but win another.

Goal: to take the kids away from you
Continuing to be cast in a bad light as a crazy and neglectful parent, accusations like sexual assault, being raised in a crazy household, and lacking a solid support system will be fodder for the courts to weigh. In the narcissist's efforts, they will turn the children against you by poisoning their little minds, gaslighting them to see things differently than they remember. The children are told warped illusions of things you never did, a divide is built, and they become fearful of the "normal" parent. To be brainwashed with lies that tap into your deepest fears would make it easy to pick a side without knowing the truth. The repeated patterns of the lies are what make them powerful.

Sub-tactics: To prove they are the better parent and deserve the majority of parental time. This tactic usually means that their plan is to build a case against you of what they perceive to be errors in parental judgement all the while promoting a false narrative of their own deep involvement with the children. They gaslight you by sending confusing emails which prompts your defensive and angry behavior. These emails will be used to show that you are crazy and not a safe option for the kids.

Narcissists are infamous for breaking all the rules when it comes to turning children against the other parent. Covert methods are used, often implementing a reward system to buy the child's love so they can gang up on the other spouse (i.e., mom is being mean and won't let them go to Hawaii with dad). This tactic probably wouldn't make it into the courtroom, but in your kitchen, you must defend yourself from your own kids. If you feel your relationship with your children slipping through your fingers, you will be weakened for battle. Mission accomplished.

Some comments that your narcissist may make categorized in the gaslighting arena:

Goal: to make you question your reality
"It didn't happen that way. You are crazy/you have mental health issues/you need help." or "You know I am only kidding when I said that. Why can't you have a better sense of humor?"

Goal: to implant a narrative that will ultimately stop you from speaking up when they are flirting or acting improper.
"You are just insecure and jealous. It is embarrassing when you act this way."

Goal: to confuse you and question your memory
"I never said that! or "You never remember what I really said. You don't listen when I speak!" or "Why can't you see you have a memory issue?"

Goal: to make you think you are not entitled to feel emotions
"You are too sensitive. Stop overreacting."

Goal: to make you think that you nag when the reality is they never answer your questions, forcing you to repeatedly ask the same thing
"Why do you hold onto everything? Can't you just let it go?" or "How

many times are you going to ask me the same question?"

Goal: to shut down the discussion of a particular topic
"Why do you keep bringing this up?" or "Why do you obsess about this?"

Goal: to shift blame and make you doubt yourself
"You are the problem here, not me." or "This is the first time I ever cheated and it's all your fault." or "If you had just (fill in the blank), then I wouldn't have had to cheat!"

Goal: to deny what you know to be true in order to make you think you're crazy
"I never said (or did) that. You are imagining things."

Goal: to have you live in fear of losing your children
"I am going to prove to everyone what a terrible dad you are. You will never see these kids."

Goal: to make you fear you will have no money or not have enough money to start over
"You are not entitled to any of my money. I will see that you end up with nothing."

Gaslighting is mind control with a specific purpose. Hearing other's stories might spur an ah-ha moment to help the puzzle pieces fall into place. While the following story was not something that occurred during a divorce, it does help show how gaslighting can be present over time, like a slow drip. The fact of the matter is, you were always strong enough to stand on your own but gaslighting, by definition, is designed to create uncertainty in your mind. Know your facts and erase the gaslit recordings because *they were never true.*

Slow drip: gang gaslighting – the case of the missing scarves
Jeff lived with his parents in their large ancestral home. In order to keep him close and under their control, they customized the basement into his private man-cave apartment. Ann had been dating Jeff for six months and spent many weekends there including a fun-filled long weekend which was planned for the Fourth of July. Ann packed all of her favorite clothes; when she arrived, Jeff's mother compli-

mented Ann's fancy designer scarf and asked to try it on. Ann shared that she had brought two scarves from this designer and ran downstairs to get the second. Jeff's mother fussed with the one around her neck and openly admired the other. Dinner was served and Ann uncomfortably watched Jeff's mom eat with her $2,000 scarf around her neck like a napkin. After dinner, her scarf was returned and Jeff and Ann retired downstairs for the night. Ann was very conscientious of her belongings and proceeded to carefully wrap her expensive scarves in tissue paper, leaving them flat-folded on the coffee table.

The next morning, the scarves were gone. Jeff and Ann looked everywhere: behind the sofa, they moved the cushions and they both thoroughly combed the entire space with no luck. Jeff then suggested that they ask his mom and dad if they had any idea as to what happened to the scarves.

They went upstairs to the kitchen and asked Jeff's parents if they had any insight. His mother spoke first and said, "What scarves? You weren't wearing a scarf when you arrived here last night. Are you okay? Did you drink too much? You probably thought you brought the scarves with you; clearly you did not." Then she turned to Jeff's father who backed up his wife and confirmed that he also hadn't seen any scarves. Desperate to not feel like she was losing her mind, Ann turned to Jeff who looked at his mom and dad and proceeded to follow their lead. "Come to think of it honey, I don't remember the scarves either." The good news was that Ann had healthy boundaries and decided it was best if she did not stay the remainder of the weekend. She packed her things and left.

Jeff, predictably, texted her incessantly, suggesting that she look at her place because the scarves were not at his house. His hoovering by text was overwhelming so she agreed to meet him for lunch three days later. She told him to bring the scarves or $4,000 to cover their cost. To put this into context, Jeff's family had plenty of money. They did not need the scarves for any reason other than entitlement. She had something that Jeff's mom wanted.

Jeff arrived at lunch with nothing but his impish grin, under the assumption that it would do the trick as it always had. Ann was angry and determined to get off the ride. Once again, she demanded her scarves or the money. She would not be able to replace them as one was out of production (a collector's item) and the other was a gift from her grandmother but she was not willing to let them get away with this. Unable to blind Ann with his charm, Jeff got angry and called her a gold digger. He claimed that she was just like all the other women in his life and only wanted him for his money. The irony was Ann was wealthier than he was and did not need his money.

A week later, upon the threat and deadline to go to the police, the scarves were mailed to Ann's mom with a scathing letter expressing their disappointment in how Ann represented herself.

The gang gaslighting was evident from the moment Ann walked into that kitchen with the intention to manipulate her by all following the same story line. Tribal gaslighting is when others jump on the bandwagon and gaslight as a group.

Ann dodged a bullet by recognizing how evil the family was before it was too late. She escaped but still struggles with the knowledge that there are really parents who are so sociopathic that they would steal from their son's girlfriend. The coordinated effort by the entire family shows their malevolent tendencies.

Extended plot: my story of gang gaslighting – the case of the Home Depot dollars

My husband had been carefully saving his American Express points for years. As newlyweds with our first home purchase behind us, we chose to utilize enough points to order $1,300 in Home Depot gift cards, where we found ourselves to spend a great deal of time and money. When they arrived in a FedEx envelope, he put it on his bedside table where it stayed mixed in with an ever-growing stack of papers. A few months later, we decided to utilize one of the cards but they were nowhere to be found. The search for the Home Depot dollars began. He blamed me and said I must have thrown them out but I knew I had not seen them since he originally opened the envelope.

For the next ten years, those missing Home Depot cards were the bane of my existence. It became a running family joke and I was taunted mercilessly for my "bad memory." He would make jabbing comments every now and again, reminding me to not forget where things were hidden, always pouring other instances of my "forgetfulness" into the Home Depot dollars bucket. I spent years defending myself all the while being callously reminded to keep an eye out for the cards each time we moved to a new house. "Maybe you will find them this time," he would say. As intended, his hurtful criticisms kept me on hyper alert, hoping that maybe I *would* find them. It never occurred to me to fight back and turn the tables on him since he was the one who accepted them from FedEx. Eventually I acquiesced and accepted being the butt of the jokes and in so doing surrendered to the madness of the lie.

Had I known then what I know now about gaslighting, I would have looked harder for the facts. I should have stopped playing their game and searching for those gift cards – they were long gone. I was the organized one in that relationship and that is my truth.

These days, I tend to reflect on past situations and the possible solutions to them and I see many little signs. I remember his parents had been upset that he took over 130,000 points to buy the gift cards in the first place. Then a few weeks later, they were no longer angry. Did he give the gift cards to them? Did he exchange the cards for something else that they wanted? I will never know but when I review the tape in my mind, I am now conscious of seemingly inconsequential looks they would give each other when it was brought up. The glances they thought went unnoticed, the looks that prove they knew more about it than I did.

Gaslighting by email – the case of the Hawaii vacation

Narcissists are covert and everything is calculated. Gaslighting by email is real.

> *"Tina, you said I could take the kids to Hawaii for spring break so I made reservations. We leave on Friday the 15th and return on the 24th. Thanks, Robert"*

The reality was Tina had never told Robert that he could take the kids anywhere; it had never even been discussed. This, however, became his reality and he would swear on the kids' lives that Tina had agreed prior to his purchase of the tickets.

Robert was allowed to play the victim while Tina became the bad guy who changed her mind and denied the children their exotic vacation with their father. "Kids, I bought tickets to take you to Hawaii because I want to give you the world, but Mommy said no because she is mean and doesn't love you."

You can bet that the offending email would be introduced in court to show the judge that Tina is not trustworthy. If the judge is presented with evidence that games are being played, credibility is lost. The most important factor now is for Robert to produce the proof that there ever was a discussion where Tina gave her permission; his team will undoubtedly insist that she agreed in person so there is nothing in writing. For your protection, make sure all discussions are always documented via email to maintain a paper trail – in this case, Tina should have explained that she never gave him permission and that he is not authorized to take the kids anywhere unless he formally puts it in writing. That email would be the necessary counterproof to rebut his claims. It is imperative that any communication that might end up in court be kept emotion-free so there is no opportunity to show instability. Keep it simple, "Robert, I did not authorize you to take the kids on spring break. If that is your desire, have your lawyer send my lawyer a note so it can be formally addressed." It's best to end it on a hopeful note, despite the fact that there is no intention of approving it. This response will still not make him happy but at least it might prevent an escalation.

Be the one who demands everything in writing from the beginning. If he does not answer you, send another email outlining that you have not given permission for any activities with the children. If lawyers are involved, be sure to cc your lawyer on all important disputes. Your efforts for open, documented communication can now be used as proof that you had been clear from the beginning when you requested a response.

Gaslighting with proof and evidence – the college loan story
During my divorce, I was accused of forging federal student loan papers for my college-bound son. My second ex-husband was not his father but he helped raise him for ten of his eighteen years. My ex's family lived a more than comfortable life and they repeatedly insisted that they would pay for his college education. This was not something I expected or wanted but they were so insistent that I gave up trying to fight it. They were confident that my son was going to be successful so they felt it critical that he learn to hobnob with the right kind of people and establish connections that he could utilize for the rest of his life.

Every time I tried to save money for my son's education, I was met with resistance from my husband and forced to listen to his parents repeat their promise. They drilled the importance of an Ivy League school into his head and would even go so far as to say that if he didn't work hard enough to be accepted into one, they wouldn't foot the bill for another.

When it came down to which schools he applied to and the application process, their hands were in the mix. I thought a particular mid-level school was lovely but it was quickly shot down; they controlled everything and vetoed several that he expressed an interest in. Ultimately, they settled on a school in DC with an annual price tag of $62,000 purely based on its status. It was "good enough" for them. When the acceptance letter came in the mail, we had a family meeting and with their insistence that the tuition was covered, my son accepted the offer.

My parents had set money aside for my son when he was born. By the time he was ready to begin his freshman year, it had grown to over $30,000 so that was used to cover the cost of his first semester at this prestigious college. As per the school's deadline, we paid for the first semester immediately and then began the process to secure financing for the second half of the year.

The plan we developed as a family was that my in-laws would pay off the second semester in installments, but we needed to create a paper trail. Securing the loan was completed with all four of us on the phone: I would relay the questions from the online application to the group and together we filled it out. Should both my husband and I be on the loan? Since my husband made the bulk of our money, it was quickly decided that only my husband's name should be listed. Should we defer the payments until my son was done with his first semester? No, it would be fully paid off in three months so no deferment would be needed. My husband was approved for the loan and the university was notified; my son was welcomed back for the second semester.

The loan was solidified approximately six months before my son was leaving for college and prior to being told via telephone that my husband wanted a divorce.

We were in divorce court most of that fall when the loan payment got applied to the Spring semester. That was when the shit hit the fan. During the trial, my soon-to-be ex stood in unity with his parents to deny that our phone call to collectively fill out the application ever took place. They insisted that I applied for the student loan in my husband's name without his knowledge and accused me of internet fraud and forgery. This is when I realized that they had been gaslighting my son and me for years regarding their intention to pay for his education.

Fortunately, I had a long thread of emails between me, my husband, and his family which included an email sent from his parents after the call in question, complimenting me for doing such a good job. In the end, armed with the documentation that I produced, the judge declined their forgery claims. My ex was ordered to pay back the $30,000 loan and I thought I was exonerated.

Sadly, the story didn't end there. A few months after the divorce was over, I found a police detective's card on my door with a note to call him. I learned that my ex-husband had filed criminal forgery charges against me and I needed to provide any evidence I had that showed the contrary, including the judge's decision that I had not forged the college loan application. Within a few hours, the bogus charge was dropped. Phew, I dodged another bullet.

I would like to say that was the end of the drama but narcissists will go to any lengths to hurt you – especially when they feel as if an injustice has been served. Like clockwork, my ex contacted the federal government and accused me on the federal level of forgery and identity fraud. Again, I had to send all the paperwork from the trial and the judge's decision, as well as the local police's decision of my innocence, to the federal government. It took nearly five months before my name was cleared of all wrongdoing. While these allegations were proven false in a courtroom, publicly questioning and damaging my integrity was the win they ultimately wanted.

Why do they lie so much? The false allegations

"Narcissists lie and deny even when there is no reason to lie."
– Tracy A. Malone

The more narcissists are trying to hide, the more distractions they deploy. False allegations will generate constant work for the lawyers while creating the potential of financial damage that will keep their victims frozen in fear. A narcissist demands loyalty and demands secrets be kept, just like throughout the life of the marriage.

No matter what words come out of a narcissistic person's mouth, *always* believe their behavior. Love doesn't demean, dismiss, discount, or degrade you through words or actions.
Rhoberta Shaler, "The Relationship Help Doctor," host of the Podcast, Save Your Sanity: Help for Toxic Relationships

False allegations are a common tactic in a courtroom setting
The lying displayed in a courtroom involves the fabrication of stories with the intent to defame someone's character. These can be enormously destructive because the purpose is to sway the judge to rule against the opposing party. It is also called libel and/or slander. Libel is written defamation and slander is spoken. This is a fine line – some will merely voice their opinion, like "she is a bad mother," or "he is a bad father," for whatever reason – typically nothing earth shattering. Judges can usually see thru these false allegations for what they really are: a difference in parenting styles and a contentious parting of

the ways. Once you are labeled a crook in court, however, you will feel tainted and driven to restore your reputation.

In divorce, judges are accustomed to back and forth he-said, she-said rhetoric. When a narcissist cranks up the juice to full blown lies, it becomes more difficult for a judge to sort out the truth from fiction. Any false allegations made in a courtroom setting become part of the court document, despite the fact that no opportunity is provided to disprove them. The fact is, unless the lies directly affect a child, any attempts to clear your name will fall on deaf ears. It will not stop the victim from trying, though. It is against human nature to listen to inaccuracies being levied against you or someone you love without taking a swat at defense. Every bone in our body yearns for the truth to be known.

The basic lie

If you were to open a dictionary, you will find the term lie defined as an intentional false statement, or misinformation, a pretext, or half-truth, a fabrication of reality, deception, or fable, or a myth. In a courtroom setting, however, it is called perjury which under federal law is classified as a felony. Narcissists will build on those meanings and amplify them, hell-bent to cripple their victim. It's heartless and cruel yet there generally is no recourse.

A "little white lie" to a simple question is harmless: "Honey, does my butt look big in these jeans?" "No dear, you look perfect." While possibly superficially hurtful, it would not damage someone. A lie from a child such as, "Mommy, I finished all my homework. Can I watch TV now?" is not horrible in the overall scheme of things, although you would want to ensure it does not become an on-going habit.

Narcissists use a similar semi-truth strategy when they craft lies against their spouse. Mixing in a small piece of sincerity makes the lies more believable and hurts their victim deeper because of the truth in it. Often the bits of interjected honesty were deep secrets that they had promised to protect.

GASLIGHTING: IS IT JUST A GAME?

"When a narcissist says he doesn't lie, he is lying."
– Tracy A. Malone

Pathological liars

By definition, narcissists are pathological liars. Per the online Cambridge Dictionary, pathological simply means unreasonable or unable to control part of his or her behavior. We have all told a fib at least once in our life, intentionally or unintentionally, but when a narcissist lies, they are consciously building an alternate reality. This act is habitual to a point that they become unaware of where a lie stops and the truth starts. If a lie is repeated enough, they become convinced and therefore, are justified. Pathological liars lie endlessly, regardless of whether or not a lie is warranted. During your marriage, you undoubtedly recognized thousands of little lies, not realizing that they actually amassed to something much larger. These become glaringly obvious once it becomes clear that they never stop making things up.

Smear campaigns

A smear campaign is a calculated effort to destroy a victim by spreading lies about them to the people they know, love, and trust. They are one step up from simple pathological lies (if pathological lies can be simple?!) when they begin to spread the falsehoods. As is now clear, these are not just little lies but rather wild made-up stories filled with shady details that contain only a dash of truth. Isolation is the goal, fostering a sense of abandonment during this difficult time when support is crucial.

The audience for a successful future smear campaign would have been cultivated for years. I often use the example of a herd of antelopes. The lion doesn't go for the strongest in the herd; instead they seek out the weakest due to its vulnerability and ease to catch. You don't have to be the fastest – just don't be the slowest. The friends who blindly believe the narcissist's lies are either currently under their charming spell or the seeds were planted years before the divorce was even filed. Your friends and family have long been under surveillance to determine how close they are to you or to see if they may hold some small resentment that could be exploited later. They have been unknowingly groomed by your narcissistic spouse that may have started with something as simple as a harmless joke about you at the dinner table. The narcissist watches closely to see who laughs and who immediately defends you. Many families have inside jokes about each other and the narcissist will pounce on these so they can further abuse you publicly with this same joke at a later time. It sounds innocent because of the context of the family dynamic but it's diabolical and mean spirited in its true intention.

Your friends who like to gossip will be targeted first, knowing that they will be easy to charm and cultivate as trusted comrades. When the time comes to dribble out the smear campaign, they will become the flying monkeys to do the narcissist's bidding and spread the lies about you. The lies will always start with a little nibblet of truth to encourage the person to listen, blossoming into a full on blatant fallacy. Key people in your life will be chosen next: family and church members or even neighbors who are convenient to include in the terror. Only those who are firmly in the victims corner will walk away unscathed and incredulous at the attempt on their friend's reputation.

Your narcissist might push the narrative that you are a drug addict or alcoholic. Years before the divorce, you were out with friends having a good time. The wine was flowing and, when you got up to go to the bathroom, the narcissist spoke up to all who would listen that they were genuinely concerned about your drinking and wished you would get help. As time goes on, they build on that storyline, next sharing that sometimes you drink so much that you are unable to properly care for the children. Expect the story to change for each group of friends. For example, one group might be told that "you are an alcoholic," while another group will hear that "you are a child abuser." The singular goal is to create havoc for you, causing emotional stress, and creating unsafe places for you to find support. These lies form the foundation of a potentially harmful coup d'etat.

Allegations of cheating are also standard fodder during a divorce. In many courts in the USA, there is a no-fault law[21] which means

---

21   https://narcissistabusesupport.com/book-resources/

regardless of whether one of the parties cheated during the marriage, it will not be taken into account for the final decision. If you are not cheating, however, this claim will cut to the core and prompt the need for redemption. Rules will be bent and rest assured that the innocent coffee you had with a friend will be twisted into claims of infidelity. With this said, if they throw a cheating accusation at you, do yourself a favor and start looking closer at them as that is always a good indication that they may be doing that very thing. Expect this to become their sensational cover story to share with all who will listen post-divorce.

I recently learned from an inside source that my ex-husband divorced me "after he walked in on me having sex with another man in our bed." While this is ridiculous and categorically untrue, we must examine the logic, or the lack there of, of this fabrication. It would not be possible for him to introduce himself to someone and say that he cheated on his wife for years, *but* he *could* become the victim of that very same horrible backstory. His new supply would (she did) pity him once he elaborated about all of the terrible abuse he had to endure at the hands of me, the cheater. This also set her up into another phase: triangulation. This succinctly pitted her against me by driving a wedge where there wasn't one before, discouraging her from ever reaching out to me. After all, I cheated and lied; in her eyes, I am a horrible person. Why would she ever reach out to me? Fun fact: she did reach out to me after they broke up and we became fast friends, having a common enemy about whom to share war stories. We remain close to this day.

Lies fall easily off a narcissistic person's lips because they have no empathy for the havoc they will create in the victim's life. They are entitled to lie and hold the delusion close like the gospel. There is no scientific proof that they actually believe in their alternate reality but they sure live in it comfortably.

» The goal is to become the victim and hero
» The goal is to isolate the victim by triangulating them
with your friends and family

In a perfect world, we would never feel the need to convince our friends and family that lies being spread about us aren't true. A real friend would simply know they are not authentic and stand up for you. Ideally, a genuine friend will immediately share what they've been told to give you a leg up against the onslaught. If they have already been triangulated and taken over to the dark side, you may never get them back. At some point in your recovery after the divorce, it may be necessary to clean your house of all toxic people left behind. Ask yourself, "Why would I want to have someone in my life that I cannot trust?" The same guidelines should be followed for toxic family members.

This will be gut-wrenching; it's a backstabbing betrayal mixed with a boatload of abandonment. You will go through the standard emotions that correspond similarly with what you might feel after a death: denial, anger, depression, and then sadness at the loss of someone you called friend or family. If you are currently embroiled in your divorce, it is best, for now, to just let them go. You need your mind and body to be in top emotional strength. The key is to not waste your time or energy feeding the lies. Honor yourself and sort through the debris at a later date.

It may appear easy for me to say that you should not waste your time and emotional energy on these lies, especially if you are knee deep in the vortex, but it isn't easy at all. With that said, I have lived it so I know it to be true. I promise that one day it will be less painful. One day, maybe after the divorce, you'll be able to separate the crazy from the bizarre and dilute it all down to see the sick reasoning behind their drive to ruin you.

With the help of hundreds of support group members who will share some of their outrageously scandalous stories, you might find it unchallenging to see the reasons why the lies perpetrated against you were chosen. Narcissists have a memory like an elephant and when it comes to things that happened throughout your marriage that they can negatively spin, they never forget. Remember when I mentioned that just because the divorce ends, it doesn't mean the attacks against you will stop? You cannot control what they say; you can only control how you let their words affect you.

Once the divorce is over, even though you may continue to be haunted by their actions, the narcissist will quickly find a new supply so that they can continue to get their needs met. You should accept the fact that you will be painted as one or a combination of the following:

» Alcoholic
» Drug addict
» Mental disorder diagnosis
» Child abuser
» Thief
» Liar
» Cheater

There are many reasons why a narcissist might launch a smear campaign against you at this point, but the bottom line is, they can't play the victim to their new supply unless there is a villain in their story. You are that villain.

Common smears told to friends and family:

» You are cruel and treat them terribly. (victim card)
» You prevent them from seeing friends, family and/or the kids. (isolation victim card)
» You turned the children against them or you physically or sexually abused the children. (they are the better parent victim card)
» You refuse to be intimate with them. (withholding sex victim card)
» You make all the decisions because you are so controlling. (control victim card)
» You deny them access to their own money and control the household money by keeping them limited to an allowance. (financial abuse victim card)
» You are physical with them. (physical abuse victim card)
» You cheat on them [and most likely they will say they walked in on you with someone else]. (adultery victim card)
» You are not affectionate and are withdrawn and distant;

despite their attempts to be physically attentive, you deny them. (emotional abuse victim card)

» You call them horrible names and berate them daily, often in public. (verbal abuse victim card)

» You question their every move, always demand to know where they are, and consistently deny them the opportunity to do what and see who they want. (victim of a controlling partner victim card)

» They will claim that they tried everything to make this marriage work, but you were never willing to do your part. (martyr victim card)

» They gave you everything and this is how you repaid them. (martyr victim card)

These are almost always a direct reflection of what they are doing or have done. The deflection tactic is comparable to them holding up a mirrored shield to divert the attention from their behaviors. They believe this to be their superpower and that they are entitled to tell these tales because you are evil and must be destroyed.

Despite the fact that I had solid evidence of my husband's affair and produced it as part of our court case, he doubled down and fabricated a detailed story of my infidelity. An added bonus for him was that he got a victim card point because it was "his friend" that I "cheated" with. This accusation never made it to court because it simply didn't happen but that didn't stop him spreading it on thick to any of my friends and family who would listen. The desired damage was done as he sullied my reputation and cost me people I had called friends. His goal was achieved. In retrospect, I came out the winner – he did the work for me to flesh out the people I really did not need in my life anyway.

You are the crazy one: a smear campaign
Goal: To discredit you. In a defensive haste, telling truthful stories about them makes you that much more likely to not be believed. It can easily sound like sour grapes. For them, going down this road sets up future stories which will allow them to head in any direction. If

they want the kids, for example, calling you crazy will plant a seed of doubt with a judge. Understanding their goals will help you see why they choose the types of arguments that they do.

Script: They plant seeds of concern about your behaviors to your friends and family. It becomes more believable because it always comes from a place of "concern for you." The narcissist gets to wear the dutiful spouse mask that they just want you to get help. This drip of distress is often started long before the divorce, seemingly in the back of their mind all along. What it might have looked like: You were on the way over to see friends and the narcissist started a fight. When you got to the party, you were not laughing and joking, still upset from the argument. Then, behind your back, they tell your friends that you are moody, and they're afraid that you may be suffering from depression or have a personality disorder.

A bi-polar label is a popular buzz word as are borderline and histrionic. I don't hear narcissists calling their spouses narcissists often; they usually bypass that and go for the gold: a psychopath. In the courtroom the script will vary based on their goals.

Being categorized as the unhealthy one is baffling to the victim. While you have been living day-to-day with Jekyll and Hyde, it feels surreal to have this madness turned around on you. Being forced to listen to these lies in court seems so unfair but if they accused you first, you must exercise caution. Any attempts to convince the court that these are actually the things that they did could take the shape of revenge and damage your credibility in the end. The harder you try to point out their behaviors, the crazier you will eventually look. Mission accomplished.

You are financially irresponsible: smears
Goal: To show that you are the fiscally irresponsible one. This sets you up to have every financial decision questioned including how much you are requesting for support.

Script: Whether or not you are the primary provider, attempts may be made to show the court a case study of your spending habits by producing false documentation. By producing receipts for joint purchases or even things they bought, accusations that you flagrantly spend money are viable. Remember that there is typically a nugget of truth in smear campaigns: the dishwasher broke so you ordered a new one while your spouse was at work, but that part of the story will be purposely left out, painting you as a money waster. Joint credit card balances will also be attributed to your excessive spending habits.

Common goals for narcissistic-driven smear campaigns:

- » To win!
- » To mess with your head
- » To make you defend yourself to the point that you end up looking crazy
- » To portray you as the evil one
- » To paint themselves as the victim
- » To hurt you by turning people against you and isolating you from your support system
- » To con the judge to vote in their favor (i.e., money, assets)
- » To run up your legal bill
- » To get the kids

Plan for the lies
You know your soon-to-be ex best. Write down anything they might accuse you of and have a solid approach mapped out that you could produce to show the truth.

The lies won't stop
Understanding up front that the lies will not stop is the gift that keeps on giving because you know what to expect and have the opportunity to learn coping skills that will help you manage them accordingly.

Lies the narcissists tell
A narcissist will tell different lies about the same thing to different people. This can stir up turbulence for all involved. They thrive on the chaos this creates.

To discern the motivation behind the narcissist's actions helps make them hurt us less. Understanding the strategy in their minds depersonalizes the falsities and protects our emotional resilience to deal with the ensuing pain they create. Once you learn how to process the fabrications, you will have the advantage to be able to decode the deception and assimilate the reasoning behind them.

SurTHRIVER smear campaign stories:

Case study #1: *Amber's post-divorce lie that circulated through her social circle: "I am Italian and I lived in the Bronx with my parents when he met me. We were so poor that I couldn't even afford a wedding dress."*

Apparently unbeknownst to her ex, Amber is Irish. Her sons' father was Italian, but she is not. I believe saying that she is Italian made her less "Hampton perfect" in his eyes, unlike the new girlfriend.

Amber was born in the Bronx, but had not been back since she was seven and hadn't lived with her parents for nearly 40 years. That little snippet of truth mixed with the meat of the story somehow added to its credibility. To say that she still lived there when he met her was designed to put her into a different (in his eyes, possibly lower) class than the new supply, elevating her status. It was used to put his new supply on a pedestal – they were in the love bombing stage. In fact, Amber's parents were wealthy, lived on the water, had a yacht at the yacht club, and several summer homes. His attempt was designed to show that she was dependent on him and that he saved her, making him a rescuer of "the poor" – the hero. Maybe it was also a test for his new supply to see if he could generalize ethnic slurs and if she would agree with his bigotry?

Amber's interpretation of why he may have used "this lie": Amber's ex's new girlfriend was fed Amber's sons' last name, probably to throw her off Amber's internet trail.

Case study #2: *Cassandra's narcissists lie, post-divorce: "He said that he never loved me but fell in love with my daughter, who was a toddler at the time. He told people that I beat my little girl, emotionally abused her and only fed her chicken nuggets. According to him, he only married me to save my daughter. From me."*

Cassandra's daughter, "the toddler," who he professed to love so much, was not a toddler at all. She was eight when they married.

Calling her a toddler was a message to his new supply that he loved young children. She wanted kids and he repeatedly claimed, using Cassandra's child as a cover, that he loved them as well. In fact, he was both physically and verbally abusive to Cassandra's daughter throughout their time together.

At first, Cassandra's reaction was "It's impossible that he didn't love me! I would have known!!" However, the more she thought about it, the more she believed it was probably true. Narcissists are not capable of loving anyone besides themselves; they only use people for supply. Cassandra felt that he *acted* like he loved her and anyone who knew them as a couple would confirm that they were very happy together. That is what she believed, too, until he asked for the divorce.

Case study #3: *Ralph's lie to the courts during the divorce: "I single-handedly built and ran the business that Julie (his soon-to-be ex) and I owned together."*

Ralph and Julie were married for 23 years and they successfully owned a business together. In reality, Julie ran the business while Ralph only pretended to be in charge – he was rarely off the golf course long enough to bother with any work. During their divorce, Ralph started to show up at the office to appear more involved. His end game was, of course, to get a bigger piece of the pie in the division of assets. When Julie produced the proof that Ralph was more of a figurehead than a worker, a narcissistic injury occurred because the truth was made public, exposing his mask. The divorce escalated as he devised lies about Julie to discredit her and the integrity of the business. In this case, Ralph discrediting Julie in this manner ended up hurting the business beyond repair. This is a perfect example of how a wounded narcissist will lash out against the truth despite the possible damage it could do to his co-owned business. He was blinded by his rage.

Case study #4: *Three years post-divorce, damaging lies are still being spread about Abigail: "My husband called his attorney to notify him that I had put a hit out on his life."*

Narcissists have a hard time going away and will endlessly stir the legal pot. If, in fact, he had felt his life was in danger, why didn't he call the police? Why call his lawyer with instructions to contact her lawyer? His angle had always been to discredit her and promote himself to victim. There was no hitman but by projecting this lie, he was able to criminalize Abigail, cost her more legal fees, keep her fearful that she would never be free of him, control her emotions, and garner sympathy for himself from others. He had existing felony domestic violence and cruelty to children charges and by accusing her of this, he could devalue the truth in the charges against himself by making her into the criminal. Even though she had medical documentation to prove she had been hit in the face and had ribs broken, he used a smoke and mirrors ploy. He could not accept the charges against him so he falsely accused her, and in his mind, he was exonerated.

The lies fabricated during divorce feel like poison slowly seeping into your blood. Listening to the delusional tales creates a wound that tarnishes your soul. Your heart fills with rage and the narcissist inches up a leg, damaging you to the point where it's harder to fight, harder to defend yourself and remain sane, harder to do the work needed for the divorce, and harder to parent the children that may be in your care. If you are constantly playing defense, it becomes harder for you to speak up and tell the truth about them. Your fury is giving them supply because they see they can still control you.

Every lie they tell has a reason. Find the reason and acknowledge the truth to loosen the stranglehold that they have over you. This manufactured reality has no bearing on your case so do not feel threatened. They are merely lobbing softballs at the judge while attacking your character to wear you down. "Letting go" is the only cure. This does not mean that you condone or agree with their lies. This is *for you*. It only suggests that you are done allowing them to steal another moment – you have had enough, reached your limit, and demand your life back in order to move on. We are not gifted with the ability to change yesterday but we *are able* to change every day going forward. The secret to accomplishing this comes down to a choice: when the memories float to the top of the havoc they have wrecked on you, stop and realize that you are holding onto something that you cannot change. Make the choice right then to let it go. Choose peace over the poison and take back your life.

Exercise #3: Recognize and cast out the lies

In order to take advantage of the benefit of preparation, make a list of any potential lies that you might hear throughout the divorce. Identify and document any proof that shows each are not true. For example, if it's announced that you are a bad parent, showcase what demonstrates that you are a great parent. Find people who are willing to share the positive things that they know about you as a parent. Ask if they would be willing to chronicle their experiences – add these to your binder where you are accumulating all your information to have at a moment's notice. Write down examples of your spouse's less than stellar skills in this area to keep close in case it comes up. They don't expect you to have pre-planned for an ambush and they certainly do not expect you to be a step ahead of them. They intend to catch you off guard by attacking your greatest strengths so you will be distraught, curl up in a ball, and not fight back. Don't let that happen. Show them the fighter that you really are.

Defending your honor can be expensive. My divorce cost me $100,000 and when it was all said and done, I walked away in debt. If I could do it over, I would turn the other cheek from many of the false allegations that I felt the need to defend myself against – they were meaningless in the end and only cost me money. Looking back, I see that I had been so weakened by the extent of the evil that was cast upon me, I was unnecessarily driven to disprove his lies. In recovery, I had to learn why I sought approval and validation from anyone other than myself. I lost friends; as sad as it was to grieve the losses, I feel blessed to be able to know now, without a shadow of a doubt, who is genuinely in my corner. Keep those friends and forget the others. This lesson is what I hope everyone who reads this book can understand and accept.

Chapter 10

THE TRICKS TO EXPECT

If you have ever seen the movie Groundhog Day, you may relate to the main character who is forced to relive the same day, situations, and scenarios over and over again. A relentless barrage of tricks will be hurled rapid-fire at the victim of a narcissistic divorce to wear them down. They will be forced to repeat steps, resubmit paperwork, and constantly backtrack to produce new evidence, all the while thinking, "I have done this before."

Obstruction

Ignoring court orders repeatedly is an obstruction tactic that will buy time, but will ultimately upset the judge. The narcissist will procrastinate and do whatever it takes to slow down the process including not handing in any required paperwork until the last minute. The victim may even be blamed for these delays (i.e., they can't get access to statements) with the mindset being to run up the expenses whenever and wherever possible.

Projecting

In an attempt to cover up their shortcomings, the victim will be made the focus. While the narcissist regularly delays providing any paperwork, their lawyers will go thru the victim's documents with a fine-tooth comb to create focus elsewhere (i.e., a missing [blank] page from the American Express bill).

Diversion

Any trick that gets used in divorce should always be considered a diversion. Each time a new tactic comes into play, think "What are they trying to hide?" Look hard at the timing. Distractions buy time and get the attention off of them and their actions. The harder they push, the more they are likely trying to hide.

Stonewalling

Narcissistic people thrive on conflict and have a desire for control. By stonewalling, they refuse to answer requests, creating delays that can be emotionally charged. The lack of cooperation slows down the process which ultimately drives the costs up for the victim.

File motion after motion

False allegations must now be defended against, incurring additional charges for the lawyer and their team.

Tricks they play:

They will try to win at all costs: They are going to try to make you look as bad as possible, no matter how ridiculous it seems. Everything you say, do, or even the way you breathe, is going to be twisted and manipulated in whatever way possible.

They will try to get the best of you: It's going to look like they're trying to win at all costs, but what they're actually trying to do is manipulate you at all costs. Just remember now that you are stepping out of their world, you don't have any more value for them. They want to hurt you before you hurt them.

They will use the court system as their sword: They're going to file as many motions as possible, litigate as much as possible and make you spend as much money as possible. Overall, they just want to make your life miserable by dragging you through the court system.

They will try to obstruct you from everything: They're not going to provide the discovery that they're supposed to. They're just going to make you work for everything. As part of that, you're going to end up having to file motions to compel and again, you're going to be running up your attorney's fees. They'll even have court orders and they're not going to obey them.

Rebecca Zung, author, nation's top 1% divorce attorney, high conflict negotiation coach

General list of survivor-submitted narc tricks:
- » Ruin your credit
- » Steal your credit
- » Steal your money
- » Hide money and assets
- » Control every penny you spend while they spend freely
- » Quit their jobs or refuse to work
- » Prevent you from working
- » Refuse to pay their share of expenses
- » Take your social security or benefits
- » Refuse to make you a beneficiary of their life insurance
- » Refuse to disclose all marital assets
- » Trick victims to sign over property and assets
- » Refuse to allow you or the children medical care
- » Lie about debt and liabilities
- » Lie about income to get you to pay a greater share
- » Break the law by not paying taxes, dragging you down with them
- » Stop paying the mortgage causing the loss of dwelling
- » Take out credit cards in the kids' names
- » Sell the kids' things (from bonds to Xboxes)
- » Steal kids' money (i.e., empty college funds)
- » Refuse to pay child support
- » Refuse to pay alimony
- » Refuse to pay medical and other expenses laid out in the decree
- » Produce files that are incomplete or cannot be opened

> » Hack into your computer and phone
> » Shift the blame to distract from their behaviors
> » Change parameters once agreements are made

SurTHRIVER stories: Using the children as a weapon

Situation: Before my ex filed for divorce and moved out, we agreed to remain amicable and support each other, including a 50/50 custody split. Later, I found out he was building a case against me to get sole custody of the kids because he didn't want to pay child support. He threatened custody evaluation which would have drug out the process an additional six months. He didn't get sole custody but I was forced to settle to finally close the door and end the war.

Lesson: You will face many choices to either end the drama or continue fighting; weigh them all with your long-term goals in mind.

Situation: We were "coached" and agreed on how we would tell our daughter about our divorce and even planned to answer any questions she might have together. After we told her, my husband immediately broke our arrangement: he jumped up from the table and offered to drive her to a friend's house. He took a detour to continue the discussion without me. He knew I wouldn't say anything because I wouldn't want to create a scene in front of our child. I was totally duped and he made me look like the bad parent. The alienation started that night.

Lesson: Narcissists break agreements. The person you thought they were isn't real and when it comes to divorce, they will break every promise to make you look like the bad guy. Never let down your guard.

Situation: Once I filed for divorce, my ex asked our adult daughter to go camping with his new girlfriend and her kids. They all drank heavily and encouraged our daughter to drink with them despite the fact that she was an alcoholic and had been focusing on her sobriety. The pressure caused her to relapse. It was his sick way of bonding with her and they became drinking buddies, drinking together every day. I became the bad guy because I tried to get her help; he shut her out of my life for five months.

Lesson: Expect no limits when the battle begins. A healthy parent would not encourage a child struggling with sobriety to drink. Normal parenting guidelines do not apply.

Situation: Not one person in his family or any of our friends has spoken to me or our daughter since I filed for divorce.

Lesson: Prepare to lose family and friends during a split and plan accordingly.

Situation: My wife worked on the kids from the moment I moved out of the house. She tried to turn them against me with hateful lies about things that had happened in the past. She told them hero stories about how she had to protect them from me and made them fearful of even coming to my house. Every visitation became a warzone as my kids resisted our relationship. The courts didn't care.

Lesson: Always keep dialog free and open with children during a divorce, making sure that they know they can ask any questions with no fear of anger or other recourse. Chances are good the parent feeding the lies will not have the same offer.

Situation: My wife had discussions with our children about my supposed mental illness. She taught them to be afraid of me. She was reading books to our children teaching them how to deal with an unstable parent.

Lesson: Document this type of behavior and get your kids into counseling.

Situation: I found out that my wife was practicing emergency drills with the children in case I became violent. She was making false allegations about me to all of our friends and neighbors and I was treated like a child molester. I was able to prove that she was lying, but the damage was done. I lost many people I thought were my friends.

Lesson: Understand and accept up front that some people who you believe to be your friends will not be there for you when the dust settles.

Situation: Despite the judge and therapists instructing my wife not to communicate through the children, she did it anyway. The kids began to resent her for it but if they spoke up and tried to set boundaries, they were called names and punished. She created the resentment in them but took *me* back to court for parental alienation.

Lesson: If you have a volatile spouse, be sure to keep the communication open with your children so they never feel that anything done is their fault. Their mental health is of the upmost importance.

Situation: He used the children to manipulate me. My ex acted like "Disney Daddy" and, by faking concern for me, tricked them into telling him what I was doing. The children were used as spies for rewards like phones and money.

Lesson: Ground your children in real life experiences. They will learn that this fun and loving mask does not align with reality and the behaviors exhibited are never consistent.

Situation: When we were newly separated, my husband decided to take our two boys on a vacation. I was given papers to sign which allowed him to take them out of the country. I was told they were going to France even though the papers didn't specify a location. When I pointed this out, he said it was the standard paperwork and embarrassed me in front of the boys, pressuring me to sign. He kidnapped our children for three months. I got little help from the police because we were still married, he was their dad, and I had signed that damned paper. To get them back wasn't easy since we didn't know where they were going or ultimately where they ended up. I was forced to hire private investigators and international attorneys to get my children returned to me. I couldn't sleep or eat and developed PTSD, worried to death over my boys. Nothing happened to him in the end because I signed that release.

Lesson: Always trust your gut – if you are asked to do anything that doesn't feel right, ask a professional that you trust. It will save you a great deal of heartache, time, and money in the end.

Crossing a dangerous line – the criminal element

I hated writing this section because I knew it would accentuate everyone's deepest fears. I also knew, however, that it would be irresponsible of me to write a book on the tricks narcissistic people play during a divorce and not include it. It highlights the additional damage that can be done if one jumps too quickly into a new relationship without sufficiently managing emotions, *learning* from their past experiences, and healing. It is critical to take the time to understand what went wrong and why.

We have already established that when a narcissist gets angry, the anger will quickly turn into rage, and that rage brings about the need for revenge, no matter the cost. My son's college loan story in Chapter 9 was meant to highlight how my ex was so incredibly upset when the judge deemed him the financially responsible party that he continued to harass me for years. That court order, which added insult to injury compounded by the fact that he would have to spend money, led him to go above the judge's head to the police and eventually the federal government in his quest to accuse me of fraud. He was hell-bent on having me imprisoned even though he recognized without a shadow of a doubt that the judge's decision was made because of the evidence I was able to provide. He couldn't accept losing. He lost because I had the proof that he was lying.

I shared this drama because, after the fact, I realized how learning about narcissistic abuse saved me from carrying my shame with me beyond that point. I feel extremely fortunate that I survived my terrible divorce without the words or understanding of what exactly was happening and why. Some days I look back and wonder if it was sheer luck. My inner fortitude to keep digging and keep studying enabled me to learn what I needed to persevere.

After my divorce, several friends felt I needed to "get back out there" so they introduced me to their "sweet friend." He, too, had been through an acrimonious uncoupling and felt we could help each other get our grooves back. I dated that man for over two years and while I knew he was not *the one*, he provided me good practice to learn how to socialize again. He appeared safe and kind at first but over time, his lack of responsibility and dependability started to show me that he couldn't be trusted. I broke up with him many times but his charm and hoovering always sucked me back in. Even though I lowered my bar for what I could expect from him, I later discovered that his behaviors were textbook narcissistic personality disorder (NPD).

I was at his house one day when he made a comment about a mutual friend that caused a light bulb to go off in my head. I had never been jealous or suspicious yet something he said jolted my intuition radar. I asked him if he was cheating with her at which time he furiously stood up and screamed, "I will not tell you who I am sleeping with and I will not tell her who I am sleeping with or either of you who I am sleeping with!" Up to this point, I had yet to question his behavior so this felt like divine intervention. He answered the question with more honesty than I had realistically ever seen from him; I packed up my stuff and left, in tears. Over the next few months, he would knock on my door, buy me flowers, leave notes on my car, and call or text frequently. "He wanted to explain." Through it all, he never asked how I was doing. His only concern was how he could dig himself out of this hole while keeping me on the hook as his chief babysitter.

A few months had passed when I heard a sermon at church on forgiveness. I made up my mind at that moment that I would forgive him. I didn't want him back but I wanted to heal and get closure; I was unaware of the dangers associated with trying to get closure with a narcissist. That same day, with the memory vivid of our mutual friends sharing that they didn't know which one of us to invite to parties because "we" were so weird, I decided to pull the trigger. I needed to put my mind at ease. I knocked on his door and his son, who I had babysat for, hugged me and we chatted until my ex got home. When he realized that I was there, he opened the door and ordered me into the garage.

Without preamble and clearly annoyed by my unannounced visit, he asked why I was there. After months of him banging on my door, I informed him that I was ready to talk. The conversation went nothing like I had planned – he baited me, yelled, and kept calling me crazy. I had never seen him lose his temper and was shocked. I didn't even know how to recognize baiting until after this day.

What had *I* done to be called crazy? I began to get scared and the tears started to fall. I was there to forgive *him* for sleeping with whom I referred to as "door number two" but *I* was the one who had done something wrong?? The whole conversation was baffling and lasted about six minutes. As I approached my car to leave, he callously pointed out "door number three," his "Australian Facebook stalker" who he claimed not to know, sitting in his car. She had haunted our relationship for years. I said, "I don't want you back, but if she is your new girlfriend and she is going to the party next week, I should meet her so it's not weird." I leaned in and waved at her while he tried to block me from getting too close. He picked up his phone, threatened to call the police, and asked me to leave for the first time. I got into my car with the 911 operator on speaker, backed out of the driveway, and floored the gas pedal. I think that was the angriest I have ever felt. Since he had called the police while I was there, I decided it might be in my best interest to go to my local police station and ask for their advice. I didn't get the closure of forgiving him because I was under attack.

My local police department connected me to his police precinct who informed me that he had filed a trespassing charge against me and that I needed to make a statement in person. When I asked the officer if I needed to bring a lawyer, he said, "That is up to you ma'am." I felt all of the blood rush from my body when I realized I could be in real trouble. A few hours later, two officers showed up on my front porch with an arrest warrant.

They escorted me into my house so that I could change my clothes. I was then handcuffed and unceremoniously pushed into the back of their cruiser. Through my tears, I asked why I was being arrested; that was when I found out that there were three charges against me: trespassing, reckless endangerment (because of how I sped off when I left – he said he was afraid for his life), and domestic violence (DV). Apparently, there's a law in Colorado that states if someone calls the police against someone they've been in an intimate relationship with, it automatically becomes a DV charge. I didn't know much about this at the time, but I knew I hadn't touched him or even raised my voice so I was really confused.

Who was this man who was putting me through this legal hell? How could a man I had loved for over two years do this to me? I found myself in jail, crying, my wrists shackled and chains around my waist, connected to a literal chain of offenders – we were all in line to see the judge. I felt like I was in a movie, watching the other criminals in their different colored jumpsuits waiting to be heard. I was released 24 hours later and informed that I would need a criminal attorney to fight these charges.

Two weeks went by when my new lawyer notified me that this man had recorded[22] our conversation in his garage and because of it, the DA was adding an additional charge to my case: menacing. That charge indicated that I went there with the intent to hurt him! I rushed to my lawyer's office to listen to the recording. No surprise, it was heavily edited! Half of the conversation was missing; important parts about his son, and door number two, and his ex-wife were gone! No wonder it took him so long to mention it to the police. I told my lawyer about the missing sections and asked if that would be considered tampering with evidence. I discovered that he turned out to be a bigger narcissistic dumbass than the ex-boyfriend when he said, "You are not the victim here. You are the perpetrator and have no rights." I crumbled to the floor in defeat.

It became my mission to find an expert who could prove that there were parts missing in the recording. I did not know the law but I felt confident that he was breaking it by falsifying evidence with the singular intention to add more charges to my case. I shared it with my music minister and church neighbor to see if they knew of anyone who had the proper equipment that could confirm that the recording had cuts in it. The church music team quickly identified where the cuts were in the audio file but we knew they would not hold any clout in the eyes of the law. I was directed to a couple of audio professors at two colleges who graciously adopted the project to help me. They had their students run reports that pointed out exactly where the cuts in the audio were. The interesting part of the analysis was the line, "Tracy, I want you to leave." The students overlaid the sound wave patterns and concluded that he injected the same line *seven times*. In a model that could have been lifted straight from CSI, they explained how the waves of that sentence could never be exactly the same; these

---

22   Check my resources page to learn the parameters of recording a conversation in your state at
     https://narcissistabusesupport.com/book-resources/

seven were all identical. He had lied on the police report when he said that he asked me to leave seven times. He was literally constructing his own proof.

Armed with my new evidence, I confidently presented it to the police who shot me down by saying that I had made it all up and that because I had paid the universities, which I hadn't, they would write anything I asked them to. To appease me, the officer said he would ask my ex if he had altered the recordings. Really? Not unexpectedly, the officer came back and said that my ex claimed that he didn't alter them so they were adding the extra menacing charge to my file. The only chance I had to prove my ex's recording was a fake would have been to have the actual unedited version as well which could have sent him to jail for tampering with evidence. "Guilty until proven innocent" once again rang in my head along with the echo of my lawyer telling me that I had no rights. I was a mother and a business owner with employees and dozens of clients, how could this be? My lawyer informed me that for $30,000, we could fight it. I didn't have $30,000. I had no choice but to plea to one of the lesser class two charges. That was my $10,000 option.

A restraining order was placed on me which actually turned out to be a gift – I was forced to go no contact which allowed me the opportunity I needed to heal. I had to go to six months of domestic violence classes, I was on probation for 18 months, I was required to engage in 70 hours of community service, and I now had a record. And, if you are not aware, each class I took and every visit with my probation officer came with fees attached so the entire ordeal turned out to be a very expensive learning experience. The worst part, though, was when I was forced to appeal to the judge in order to leave the state so that I could attend my son's college graduation. Yup, the graduation from the school I worked so hard to pay for on my own after the divorce and the college loan fiasco. The thought that, because of this man's lies and despite having my hotel room booked for over a year, I might not see my son graduate was unforgiveable. Thankfully, the judge granted my travel papers and it was a beautiful celebration.

As a side note, a few months later I learned the truth about that driveway encounter. The girl in the car was not his "new" girlfriend; rather, they had been actively dating for two of *my* two and a half years. That was why it was so important to him that we didn't meet. She and I have since become friends, with the common disgust of a single human, and even traveled together on our joint bucket list trip to Italy.

The support I have received since I came out about my arrest on YouTube has been staggering. Hundreds of other survivors from all over the world have reached out to tell me their heart-wrenching stories. They always leave the true victim to pick up the pieces; the aftereffects and trust issues that develop after experiences like these can be overwhelming. Here are a few short ones:

Sabrina: Baby daddy was not paying for diapers as the court had ordered him to so Sabrina was surprised when he called to tell her that he had bought some. With the baby in tow, she went inside his house when he invited her in and as she reached for the diapers, he suddenly smashed his own face into the wall. He called 911; she was arrested, jailed for assault, and lost her baby for a year.

Shelly: Shelly was arrested for spitting at her soon-to-be ex's car. He promised her a check; when she got there, there was no check. Furious and revolted at her continued naivety, she spit at his vehicle in disgust and went to jail for it.

Cindy: Cindy was trying to gain the courage to finally divorce her abusive husband. They had moved into separate residences but would occasionally get together as he pretended to want to work it out. She had slept at his place the night before and when she got to work, she realized that she had left her computer charger on his table. She knocked when she arrived at this house but then saw another woman through the window! She got angry and banged on the door. He called the police and she was taken to jail.

Stephanie: Stephanie's first incarceration occurred during the divorce when her husband lied that she was violent. Once released, she realized that he had completely emptied their house: her clothes, the food, and all of their furniture was gone. At 72 years old, Stephanie was forced to live on a hardwood floor for the next few months. In the end, her husband had her sent to jail seven times.

Scott: Scott was married to his partner but began suspecting things were changing. He followed his husband to a bar and witnessed him kissing another man. The argument escalated quickly. Scott's husband called the police and falsely accused Scott of hitting him. Scott went to jail.

Leslie: Leslie was a great mom and she loved her kids to the moon and back. During her divorce, she was ordered out of the house and forced to stay with her parents. One day, Leslie stopped by to give gifts to the kids but her husband called the police instead and had her arrested for trespassing.

Natalie: One day, John got home after Natalie had already fallen asleep. She awoke to him screaming at the end of the bed, "Don't hit me, stop hitting me!" He then ran into the bathroom, slammed the door, and called the police. Natalie had no idea what was happening. Come to find out, he had recorded the audio and submitted it to the police. She went to jail.

I lead support groups and at most meetings, there are typically between three and five people who have been arrested because of their narcissists. Their lives were shattered into tiny pieces with three little numbers: 9-1-1. This is where I see the greatest lack of empathy shown by the spouse they happily slept beside. The narcissist's need to win will override any feelings they pretended to have for you. You have become the enemy and their guns are locked and loaded.

In reality, only a small percentage of narcissists have their partners arrested but those who do are extremely malignant and dangerous. The stories of false arrests certainly cry out for police and legal system reform but until that day comes, protect yourself.

Soul-crushing shame accompanies being arrested by the person who promised to love you till death do you part. It rocks your world like a nuclear bomb, taking you down to a place where you are rendered completely numb. Please get support to avoid any lasting effects. Share your feelings with trusted friends or a therapist so you can see clearly how the shame should be theirs, not yours. When I decided to tell my story, I had already let go of the shame. Shame only holds the power you give it. When you are ready, talk about it. Don't blame yourself. Recognize that this is them still trying to control your emotions and future. It's been many years now and I am able to joke that I'm a criminal. I can either hide that it happened and allow myself to feel badly or I can own it and let the shame go. I choose freedom because I accept that I can't change the past or his decision to be an asshole. But I can change today, this moment, and every moment from this point on. His hateful actions will not define me.

Games that they play

These surTHRIVERS have seen every trick in the book:

Having you committed #1 – my soon-to-be ex had me involuntary committed to hospital under the guise that I was suicidal. Once committed and silenced, he filed a domestic violence charge against me as well so I was unable to return to our home. – Jessica

Having you committed #2 – he had me committed which prompted the court to give my daughters to him because I was deemed dangerous. The legal battle to get them back lasted for years. Eventually, I was allowed supervised visitation that cost me $200 each time I saw my girls. This tactic ruined my career, lost me my girls for three years and constructed a wall between us that I have not been able to repair. – Abigail

Having you committed #3 – he had me arrested and institutionalized. While I was in the hospital fighting to get out, our house was being cleared out. When I returned, I had no kids, no furniture, and all my clothes were gone. Even my medicine was removed. – Jennifer

Planting evidence – my ex-wife planted cocaine in my car and then called the police. I had never even seen cocaine before. I was arrested at work and forced to hire a criminal attorney. My character was maligned and the judge presiding over our divorce battle seemed to weigh this against me even though the case was still pending. – John

False criminal charges #1 – prior to our divorce, he threatened my life. He grabbed my arm so hard that he left a bruise and screamed "I'm going to kill you!" over and over. I was so afraid that I slept behind a locked door in the guest room that night. The next morning, the police woke me and said he had reported that I had threatened his life. I was arrested and forced to defend myself. This coincidentally landed as a defense in the divorce in an attempt to get more custody. – Becky

False criminal charges #2 – she had me arrested for abusing the children. I would never do that; I am a great father and she knew it. She was jealous of our close bond. I had to prove my innocence and it wasted time, damaged my reputation, and hurt my relationship with my kids. Narcissists target your strengths in a smear campaign. They have been married to you, so they know your weaknesses and your strengths – they will use them against you in the divorce process. – Richard

Parental false allegation – my husband stole my two boys from me. He lied in court by saying that I punched them in the face when they were four years old and also maliciously claimed that I let them play with knives. The court awarded him custody which opened them up to his emotional abuse for years. One is now in prison due to the after-effects of his father's abuse. – Allison

False abuse charges #1 – he faked abuse and opened a DFS (Division of Family Services) case against me. I spent tens of thousands of dollars to fight the charges, which were eventually dropped due to lack of evidence. But not before I spent my entire retirement savings. – Colleen

False abuse charges #2 – he threw himself at my vehicle and then called the police to tell them that I had tried to run him over. – Savannah

False abuse charges #3 – he would phone the police and say I was hurting him. He did it so often that they finally told him to stop. Then he would phone the police and say I was hurting the kids. They had to come out each time to ensure the kids were safe because they didn't know us or know what to believe. At first, they took it very seriously and I thought they might take my kids, but after 100+ times, I knew they believed me. – Maya

Unwarranted restraining order – I asked her to show me her phone to prove she wasn't having an affair. She looked at me like a deer in headlights and stormed out of the house. When I went to look for her, she blew it out of proportion and claimed I was stalking her. She managed to get a restraining order against me which gave her the opportunity to move her new boyfriend into my house with our kids. To this day, her boyfriend believes I am the dirty animal she told him I was. – Alejandro

Fake police charges – my husband hated my family and didn't want them to visit for Easter. He made a false report to the police and had me arrested. I spent Good Friday thru Easter night in the worst jail in California. I had a clean record, not even a parking ticket, but because the Department of Justice background check system was offline during the holiday weekend, I could not be released on bond until I was cleared. Three months later, the judge threw the book at him when he admitted he had lied. – Isabella

Projection claim of abuse – during our divorce, I unveiled my soon-to-be ex's domestic violence that I had hid throughout our entire marriage. I had lived in fear because he had me convinced that if I ever told anyone, his career would be over and we would be homeless. Once I exposed him in the courtroom, he tried to turn the tables, become the victim and paint me as the abuser. Fortunately, I had the photos to prove my version was true. – Mia

The distraction – when our daughter's car was vandalized, my ex-husband had both me and our daughter investigated for insurance fraud. – Nancy

Ruining your credit – I owned my house before we got married. We lived in it for over twenty years. Just before he asked me for the divorce, he conned me into signing papers that he claimed was for a second mortgage. In actuality, he was putting the title of the house in his name. At the divorce, he was granted rights to stay in the house with the kids until they graduated high school a few years later. My home would then be sold and I was supposed to get the proceeds. He was ordered to pay the mortgage but did not. I fought endlessly with him in court to no avail. My house was foreclosed on and I walked away with no house and ruined credit. – Camillia

Turning off the utilities – on a cold winter night, I got home from work to discover that he had all our utilities turned off (they were in his name): power, heat, gas, cable and the alarm system. He planned this on a Friday night knowing I would not be able to get the services turned back on until Monday. I lost time at work on Monday so that I could get everything hooked back up. Lesson: if you can put the utilities in your name as soon as they leave, do this. – Carol

Freezing you out – Bob was moving out of the house in the dead of winter in Montana and I left for the day to give him space. His boxes were already packed and I knew what he was taking so I felt like I could trust him. When I returned home, I realized he had taken the thermostat off the wall. It was 30 degrees and I had two small babies in a house with no way to turn on the heat. My lawyers fought this in court and he was ordered to pay for the new one to be installed. In retrospect, I should have asked a friend or family member to go to the house while he packed up to monitor him. – Victoria

Garage wars – Upon moving out of the home we had shared, Alex cut the wires that opened the garage door. If I had followed my gut and not allowed him to be alone in the house, he would not have been able to do this. – Alice

False tax reporting allegations – my ex-wife reported me to the IRS and lied that I had withheld information on my tax returns. I am not sure what innocent until proven guilty is because my life became a living hell for over a year. I lost a ridiculous amount of time and money over that lie, yet there was no consequence for her lying to a federal agency. – George

Burning down the house – the judge ordered my husband to move out of the house and leave me there with our three kids, two dogs, and one horse. Within a week of him leaving, when I was out at one of the kid's events, my neighbor called to tell me that our house was on fire. The investigation pointed to arson and eventually proved he was responsible. He is now in jail. His narcissistic rage pushed him to do something I never would have thought possible. I saw no warning signs and he had never been violent before. I thank God that we weren't home and the animals were all outside in the barn. – Anne

Running up your credit – my wife opened eight credit cards in my name and ran up $100,000 in debt. We are still going through the divorce process so I don't know how it will work out yet but my lawyer said we can use it as leverage to get her to back away from the fight altogether or we can press criminal charges. – Ted

The tricks that affect your job or career:

Trying to stop you from working – she started causing drama each morning to make me late for work and then she would show up at my place of employment and create a scene there. I lost my job because of the "crazy." – Peter

Serving papers at work – my ex had me served at work. It was a dramatic event because my ex told the police that I was dangerous and she was afraid for her life so in addition to a sheriff, police escorted that sheriff. This forced me to not only defend myself and lose friends but I almost got fired as well. – Martin

Courtroom tricks:

Stonewalling #1 – my husband never produced a single piece of discovery and was charged with contempt of court at each of our hearings. In the end, he brought only four pages. The judge was so frustrated that he let him get away with it. – Sabrina

Stonewalling #2 – I was denied access to our taxes by our accountant simply because my ex paid for them. Dozens of motions to get them to comply went unanswered. Eventually the judge ordered the accountant to give me copies. It was such a waste of my money to fight to get something I had every right to. The irony is while it was his family accountant and he had the access, he never supplied his tax returns and instead blamed it all on me. – Linda

Creating false legal work – she insisted on adding an outside inheritance lawyer to include a four-page "inheritance clause" (I have a rich uncle; I was told it would be one paragraph). This is something that would never be allowed in court yet I got stuck paying additional legal fees for it. – Daniel

I am too weak to work – my ex-husband was in great shape and always super healthy. During the divorce, he claimed that he was extremely sick, walked into court with a cane, and went on reduced hours at work. This trick backfired on him because the judge based our alimony on my husband's potential, not on his fake cane-walking performance in court. – Debbie

Courthouse rattle – in the courthouse, she stated that I accosted her in the hallway during a break. – Samuel

Stealing all the paperwork #1 – the first lawyer I saw (and wish I had retained) warned me up front to make copies of whatever financial statements I could find (our taxes, his salary, banking, investments, the mortgage, etc.). He warned that they would all go missing the second I asked for the divorce, and that's exactly what happened. As expected, they "disappeared" the morning of the meeting while I drove our son to school. Thankfully, I hid a second set in a suitcase in the garage until I was ready so I was able to produce them at the meeting "on his behalf." Ha! – Kris

Stealing all the paperwork #2 – she took every single piece of financial information out of the house and refused to allow me access for my attorney. – Lawrence

Protect yourself from financial tricks:

Tricking you into holding debt – from the start of our relationship, my ex talked me into using my credit cards for our joint purchases – vacations, date nights, clothes, household goods, etc. He was cavalier about it and said it "only made sense" for him to just use his cards for business. When we divorced, he convinced the judge to dump 90% of all our personal credit card debt onto me claiming that it was all my debt (since the cards were in my name) and that his cards were his responsibility. – Catherine

Hiding money – he hid money in the Cayman Islands. When we presented them in court, he said he no longer had those accounts. Even though I had all the statements, because the accounts were international and he denied having them, the judge did not admit them as evidence. He walked away with a free and clear five million dollars. – Sydney

Tricking you out of your house – upon deciding we'd break up, he told me that he would take the main house and I had to move into the converted garage. His logic was that since he made more money than I did, he was entitled to the big house. I was so brow-beaten by then, confused and emotionally battered, I gave in, even though it was 100% my assets that had bought the house. When we met, I owned two properties; he had an old SUV and no money in the bank. It took me three years of fighting to finally get him out of my house. If I knew then what I know now, and had already "channeled my inner Wonder Woman," I would have stood up to him and said, "No. My money bought this house. You move. I'm staying." – Jennifer

Mileage scam – airline miles and credit card points are things that must be divided upon divorce. My wife and I were negotiating how to split them up when the court decided for us: each gets half. It's in the decree; no one knew that she had already cashed in all the miles. My only recourse would have been to take her back to court to fight that she was in contempt but that made no financial sense. She had moved all the miles and points at the very beginning of our negotiations and just pretended the entire time. I want to warn people to pay attention to these small details. – Justin

Damaging your credit – my husband intentionally damaged my credit. He started making his court-ordered payments on our joint credit card late, thereby hurting my credit. Also, each time he was late, I'd have to ask my lawyer to email him and threaten to take him to court for breaking the court order. My ex knew this cost me money. His response to the lawyer was always apologetic as if he'd just forgotten, but we all knew better. – Payton

Changing their job – my wife of 40 years started working part-time until the divorce was finalized. She then changed jobs and has worked full-time ever since. The part-time hours meant she couldn't give me any financial help. – Frank

Quitting their job – during my divorce, my husband got fired from his high paying job. He then claimed he could not afford his own lawyer, much less the temporary support he was ordered to pay me. We were living 2,000 miles apart at that time; I had moved and all of our mail followed me. I started to receive DSW bucks in the mail.

I am unsure of the purchases required to get rewards, but coupons were coming in every few days. What was he buying that gave him these kinds of rewards? He was using our joint reward account so I created an online profile to track his spending habits. He was buying thousands of dollars in shoes! I printed out all of the pages which showed a picture of the shoe, the size, and the price. I wish I could have captured the look on his face when we presented these to the judge! He was ordered immediately to pay me the six months of back support he claimed he was too poor to pay. This is a perfect example of the helpful information you can find by following the clues. – Tracy A. Malone

Commission scam – my wife sold high-end cars and had always done very well. During our divorce, she wrote her sales in someone else's name so it looked like she wasn't making any money. She claimed the divorce was too stressful for her to be on her "A game." This reduction in her income doubled the support I had to pay her – and she continued her stellar selling after the divorce was final. – Victor

Co-mingling money – when my mom passed, I got an inheritance which I deposited into our joint account. Three days later, my wife asked for a divorce. Because I had put the money into our account, it was considered joint assets and she got half. Her black widow tactics of waiting till the money arrived was cruel even by legal standards. – Harry

Opening credit cards in spouse's name – my soon-to-be ex opened new credit cards in my name and proceeded to run them all up to their limits. I was left with the debt in the divorce. He lied in court when I accused him of this and said that I opened the cards and gave them to him to buy things we needed. Lesson learned: I now monitor my credit and get alerts if any new activity occurs. – Madison

Canceling credit cards and closing bank accounts – all my credit cards were canceled and our joint bank accounts closed leaving me with no access to any of my own money. I was afraid that once the accounts were closed, it would be a costly nightmare to obtain all the required statements from the banks. I was correct. Since he refused to pay me any support during the divorce process, I was forced to move back in with my mother at the age of 42. – Molly

Getting your name off the mortgage – in our final negotiations, it was agreed that my husband could keep the house for one year. After the year, he would sell it and give me my half of the proceeds. We decided not to take my name off the mortgage or title as long as he made the payments on time. During that year, my husband took out a $100,000 credit line for improvements which placed a lien against the property. Since I was not on those loans, I never saw the paperwork. When it came time to sell, I lost money because the second mortgage had to be paid out of the proceeds. – Laureen

Loading the credit cards – during our divorce and after quitting his job, my ex showed up in court with a credit card receipt that showed a $20,000 payment to his lawyer. We had no joint credit card debt, which I had made sure of throughout our marriage. My lawyer feared that this charge could be considered joint debt and I might end up responsible for half of it. To counter, my lawyer insisted we put $20,000 on my card. My husband pulled the same $20,000 trick a second time so I again followed legal advice and agreed to charge another $20,000 on my card. Assured by my lawyer that my husband would end up paying my legal fees, I was not worried. In the end, my husband was not ordered to pay my legal fees and I was stuck with $40,000 on my credit card. – MaryEllen

Stealing equity – my ex took out a $107,000 cash loan against my house that I had owned free and clear. It took over two years, several court dates, and thousands in lawyer bills, but I finally got the money back. – Josie

Bank account scam – when we first started dating, my (then) boy-friend said he needed a special account that his ex-wife wouldn't be able to track. He asked me to open one in my name and give him the debit card; he would give me money directly each month to fund the account. I loved him and opened the account. My friends took off my blinders by explaining the dangers and I immediately closed the account. He became enraged at my insensitivity when he really "needed my help." I was so trained to see the good in people; I felt guilty and I opened it up again. He didn't respect my boundaries and

I allowed it. I was so afraid of him but I married him anyway. His behavior never changed. This is just a snapshot of the financial abuse I endured. – Katie

Falsifying financials – at the first meeting with our lawyers, my ex came up with the "ratio" (income-debts-expenses) that ended up being used throughout our entire five-year divorce battle. No lawyer or judge would change it to the correct amounts despite having evidence of the false facts that my ex had so beautifully displayed on a professional looking spreadsheet. That initial calculated move cost me thousands and thousands of dollars and even negatively impacted the retirement monies I was awarded. Narcs are very skilled at falsifying financials to benefit them. My suggestion would be to not let something that seems unimportant in the beginning see the light of day. All the details need to be 100% accurate from day 1 to ensure they won't haunt you later. – Lillian

Asking for tax returns – a friend told me that I could request my spouse's tax returns for every year after the divorce so I made sure it was included in the decree until he met his alimony obligation. I was surprised to know that if his income went up over the next ten years, then I could go back to court and get my alimony reevaluated and adjusted. – Evelyn

Secure your own financial planner – when I first went through my divorce four years ago, we settled in mediation and I pretty much took the first deal I was offered. After fighting for the alimony he was ordered to pay for the last two years, I have been embattled in a legal nightmare that never seems to end. What I realize now is how vital it would have been to have brought a financial planner onto my team in the first round. I have one now and the financial security that I gained in knowing they are reviewing all his paperwork helps me sleep at night. I had no one to advocate for me from the onset so this is an empowering game changer. – Shannon

Get a forensic accountant to review their financials no matter what they say or report. I separated from my ex long before the internet. I was pregnant with my son. I did not expect that he would completely distort his financial information, fail to provide tax returns, and refuse to give my attorney any income information.

The judge awarded me $30 a week in child support. It was such a paltry sum, he didn't bother to pay it and it would have cost me more in lawyers' fees to go after him than it was worth. The fact that he'd kidnapped two children by a prior marriage, and disappeared to Argentina, also motivated me to adopt a "let sleeping dogs lie" mentality. Subjecting my son to the nightmare of kidnapping was not worth the risk. His father simply disappeared without a trace.

Seventeen years later, when my son seemed worldly enough to withstand his father's manipulation, I went after him to recover his ongoing debt. The back child support would help to pay college expenses. My attorney convinced me that he could keep us in court for months. My son wanted to go to college and raising him without child support had put a huge dent in my finances. I accepted the measly amount that had accrued.

Ultimately, once the internet enabled me to investigate his lifestyle, I found that he owned the apartment his mother was living in. He had claimed he was unemployed, homeless, and sleeping on her couch. He was, in fact, living and working with the publisher for Elvis Presley who owned a 50% share in his music and also owned approximately 75% of the music coming out of Nashville. He had become the trustee for her foundation. All that time he claimed he was a pauper, he lived with her in a 22 room mansion on 5th Avenue and was globe-hopping in grand style with no regard or care for his son. Had I hired a forensic accountant when I pursued back child support, the judge could have considered his lifestyle to determine reimbursement.

Joyce Short, author, Founder of the Consent Awareness Network

Dumbass tricks:

Tracking your moves – after he moved out, I started to notice messages on my phone marked as read even though I knew that I hadn't seen them. Emails that I saved would disappear. He was tracking every move I made via my phone and computer. Before you start to see any odd behaviors on electronic emails, texts, or even Facebook messages, block them and turn off any shared iCloud accounts. They often can continue to access everything especially if you are still on the same phone plan. – Carol

Canceling the insurance – my children and I were taken off the family insurance plan and I was never told. It was months later when my daughter got sick that I discovered we had no insurance. My lawyer had assured me that once we filed, my husband would be required by law to continue our coverage until a decision was made later in the process. We had to make a motion and pay more money but he was ordered to put us back on the policy. He faced no consequences for his actions. I want people to be aware that they should double check any joint policies frequently to avoid any unnecessary issues. – Sophia

Appealing the rulings – after our divorce was finalized and orders were put in place, I began to sleep better. No sooner was the ink dry on our decree when I got the papers that my wife was appealing to overturn the decisions. I had spent over $50,000 to get the orders the first time and now she was firing up another battle. We had our day in court and the higher court threw out most of her disputes, but I was still forced to spend more money that I didn't have. It was discouraging to see that this type of legal abuse was allowed. – Thomas

Keeping the Airbnb rent – we have jointly owned rental properties. During the divorce process, he kept all of the rent and wouldn't give me my half. We had to fight for it in court and while I ended up getting my portion, I lost quite a bit of it in the fight. – Beth

Isolation – prior to filing for divorce, my husband convinced me to move out of the country, leaving my family and support system behind. When he filed a short time later, I was isolated and trapped in a foreign land, fighting for my financial life and to keep a roof over my head. – Nicole

Destroying memories to emotionally wound you – my husband deleted all of our family photos from the computers and backup devices. He tried to erase our entire life! This was very stressful – I lost memories of my son's first baseball game, his only violin recital, and his first day with braces. I didn't understand why he would do this. I learned after the fact that he and his family did not want me to have any pictures of their family home so instead of just deleting those, they deleted everything and pretended like they didn't understand why I was upset. Since he had always kept pictures on his personal computer, the judge ordered him to make copies for me. The last day I ever saw him was our final day in court when he brought a portable drive and told the judge that all of the photos were all on it. When I got home, I discovered there was nothing on that drive at all. After the divorce was over, I had a company recover all the photos from the original hard drive and put him behind me forever. – Carolyn

Criminal poisoning – I began to get extremely sick and no doctor could figure out why. I suffered for years with unexplained neurological symptoms until, as a last resort, I was tested for poison. My wife had been poisoning me for years. – Russell

Ridiculous tricks to create drama and legal fees – she told my lawyer that there is no proof that we were ever married. Obviously, I had proof but I still had to pay my lawyer to answer this claim. – Patricia

Parent of the year – during the divorce, my husband went to church every week, joined the PTA, and donated quite a bit of his time and money to fake the image of the All-American Dad. In eleven years of marriage, he never went to church or volunteered. – Elaine

Sabotaging the process – he would only agree to divorce me if we used the "Collaborative Divorce" process which kept us out of court. He was smart; a lawyer with rich friends, he knew what he was doing. He showed up to the first meeting with our "financial neutral" (an accountant) without any of the requested financial documents and just sat there, obviously hoping to see me squirm. After months of these unproductive meetings, we eventually came to an agreement. I understand a typical divorce agreement to be approximately 20 pages; ours, through the collaborative divorce process, was 80 pages. This was a miserable failure with my narcissist. – Julie

Delay tactic #1 – her expensive lawyer "didn't tell her" it was court day. Apparently, she was waiting for her lawyer at his office, so court was delayed an hour while we waited for her arrival at the courthouse. I incurred $500 in legal fees for the unexpected delay. – Gary

Delay tactic #2 – my ex's lawyer sent me the hearing confirmation with the wrong courthouse listed. I waited there. By the time I got in touch with my lawyer and learned I was in the wrong place, the judge was upset that I was late and we were forced to delay for six weeks. When the email with the incorrect information was presented at the next hearing, my ex's lawyer said, "Sorry, it was a mistake." – Rhonda

How to cope with and move through the extra helping of abuse that will come at you during the separation-divorce: It is important to recognize that you are still being actively abused during the separation-divorce process. Your abuser will appear calm and collected while methodically planning his every hurtful move. It's extremely easy to play directly into his hands, to want to defend yourself, and get the courts to hear your truth. But no matter how loud you shout or how hard you fight, you won't be heard. Now is the time to put your energy into healing activities and self-care routines. Write your experiences and emotions freely in your journal. Establish positive, healthy habits. Putting your energy into healing during the stressful court process will lay the foundation for your new life post-divorce.

Don't expect to be believed in court: My ex admitted to me that he had been lying, manipulating, and having an affair. The admission came prior to the night he tried to kill me with police photos of my bruises. I had lots of evidence and because I was telling the truth, I naively expected that the court system would believe me. I quickly learned that emotional abuse really didn't matter to the judge and was quite surprised to discover the photos of my bruises around my neck were given only a moment's consideration by the judge. I was shocked when my abuser walked away with only a "stern" warning simply because it was his first offense and the judge felt that my "emotional abuse" story reflected an unhealthy relationship -- no more, no less.

How to avoid revictimization by the court system: Sadly, there is no magical solution to a broken legal system. On some days, you will feel the court and divorce process is as abusive and traumatizing as your relationship was. You will feel revictimized, lost, and without a voice. To minimize the negative emotions and feelings brought on by the court system, have a fabulous support system in place with a great friend, family member, therapist, coach, or clergy who will listen to you, hear you, validate your experience, and remind you that it isn't your fault.

Susan Ball, author, abuse recovery coach

Financial abuse – the deception

As with other forms of abuse, financial abuse can begin subtly and progress over time. It may be stealth initially as the narcissist feels you out to assess your willingness to trust them with money. The "simple" act of divorcing a narcissist can easily turn into financial abuse as well due to the uneducated and inexperienced courts of our legal system.

A common misconception about victims of financial abuse is that the victim blindly handed over the control of their money. This mistaken belief does additional damage from people who judge the victim's financial strength; by the mere fact that an abuser rigidly controlled them, they are victims. Banks are the biggest offender of this judgment, often not extending credit options to the victims because of history caused by the abuser. They were in fact preyed upon by a wolf in sheep's clothing, a smooth talker, a charmer, a chameleon, and in many cases, someone who sold them empty promises of a brighter future. What the narcissist doesn't tell these unsuspecting targets is how they will be used, in most cases abused, and devalued and discarded being left penniless, homeless, and struggling for their bare necessities.

There are a few ways these initial testing tactics appear:
  » They invite you to lunch and then say they don't have any money.
     Test: will you step up and pay? Do you have financial boundaries or are you willing to put others needs before your own?
  » They drop not so subtle hints about how they really want something but can't afford it.

Test: this is to gauge your empathy to see if you will buy the item for them.

» They offer to split the check.
Test: are you willing to pay the total or will you split the ticket?

» If you are new to living with them, household duties will be established.
Test: they may offer to take control of the bills, beginning the slow drip of control.

» They suggest that you combine accounts or ask you to co-sign on a loan.
Test: They tell their victim story of how their ex ruined their credit and ask to be added to your account to hide from that person.

One thing an abuser can do is guilt you into giving up your power. To prove your devotion to them, you might think, "I should give them what they want, then they will love me," or "I will do the exact opposite of their crazy ex to help them feel bonded and secure."

Whether subtle or overt, there are common methods that abusers use to gain financial control over their partner. These include:

» Forbidding the victim to work.
» Sabotaging work or employment opportunities by stalking or harassing the victim at the workplace.
» Causing the victim to lose their job by physically battering prior to important meetings or interviews.
» Forbidding the victim from attending job training or advancement opportunities.
» Refusing to work or contribute to the family income.
» Controlling how the money is spent.
» Not allowing the victim access to bank accounts.
» Withholding money or giving "an allowance."
» Not including the victim in investment or banking decisions.
» Running up large amounts of debt on joint accounts.

- » Withholding funds for the victim or children to obtain basic needs such as food and medicine.
- » Hiding assets.
- » Stealing the victim's identity, property, or inheritance.
- » Forcing the victim to work in a family business without pay.
- » Refusing to pay bills and ruining the victim's credit.
- » Forcing the victim to turn over public benefits or threatening to turn in the victim for "cheating or misusing benefits."
- » Forcing the victim to write bad checks or file fraudulent tax returns.
- » Forging joint tax returns.
- » Filing false insurance claims.
- » Refusing to pay or evading child support.

As targets, we trusted our abusers and were horribly conned. This often leads victims to feel powerless.

Case #5: Alice had been a stay-at-home mom to the couple's three children. Her days, like most stay-at-home parents, were filed with shuffling kids to sports, lessons, and play dates, mixed with the thousands of things that need to be done every day to maintain a household. She was an active part of the children's lives and she made sure that her kids knew they had at least one parent that they could always count on to be there.

This role wasn't one Alice just came upon; it was what was discussed and planned with her husband when they got married. Alice had been an executive prior to marriage but they both wanted the kids to be raised by them rather than a nanny. She willingly gave up her career while her husband took every opportunity to complain about money. He also started controlling it: his money, his rules. He got the final say on all of Alice and the children's activities.

As their relationship started to break down, her husband sent constant reminders to Alice that she would get nothing if she tried to leave him. She began to believe his threats because she wasn't the working parent, she didn't think she had any rights to the money or assets, and even if she did muster the courage to leave this abusive relationship, she would walk away with nothing.

This is not how the court systems work! Assets are primarily divided by a judge with guidance to make things even. Most US states have alimony laws and despite Alice's non-working status for 25 years, she was entitled to and granted alimony for half of the years they were married. Even though her ex had her convinced that his retirement was his alone and she would not get "one dime," she ended up with half of everything. The fear of being left destitute has kept men and women alike from understanding their rights. Every state has slightly different laws so please check with a lawyer as to what yours are. Don't be controlled by financial threats.

Financial tricks – taking from the mouths of babes
Financial entitlement – of all the low-down, dirty tricks a narcissistic person can pull, stealing from your kids is by far the most painful. Who could do this?

Some things that survivors have experienced:
- » Cashed out the children's bonds
- » Closed the children's (college) savings accounts and disappeared with the money
- » Sold children's electronics
- » Sold the children's cars, bikes, and toys
- » Opened credit cards in their children's names
- » Opened lines of credit in their children's names
- » Ran up hundreds of thousands of dollars in debt in their children's names
- » Sold the children's social security numbers
- » Canceled credit cards on children's activities (like soccer or summer camp)
- » Took the payment for public services from children
- » Stopped paying for college, school, activities, and sports
- » Cashed checks for college and keep the money rather than pay for the semester (thus having the child kicked out of school)

Financial tricks – 401k: the fight for your future

As we age, our retirement savings becomes a volatile weapon in divorce. In one way or another, we have all earned it and it can sometimes feel like a fight to the death to get what you deserve to protect your financial future.

Case #6: Michelle had always been the saver in the household. She and her husband, Paul, made the same salary and most expenses were shared equally. Paul had expensive toys, like fancy cars, and he enjoyed golfing trips around the country with his pals. They always joked about how they were a perfect match – he liked to spend while she balanced him out with her frugality. Seemingly perfect until someone wanted a divorce.

For twelve years, Michelle turned a blind eye to Paul's cheating and wild spending habits because she knew that if she divorced him, she would lose half of everything she had so carefully saved. The house would be split, but knowing what a lazy, cheating spender he was, in order to be kept in a manor he was a customized to, she firmly believed that he would most certainly fight for half of her retirement money.

This is a classic case of how a 401k can hold someone hostage in a relationship that has run its course – it kept Michelle stuck for an extra twelve years. Looking back, she sees how backwards her thinking was; twelve years ago, her 401k was half of what it is today. Now he stands to get half of $500,000. If fear hadn't gripped her, she wouldn't have lost so much time living with an abusive disrespectful person, and she would have been in the hole for only $125,000 rather than $250,000.

Financial tips when divorcing a narcissist: As soon as they become aware that you are filing for divorce, your narcissistic partner is likely to drain bank accounts, hide financial assets, remove or destroy financial records and evidence of abuse or infidelity, cancel health and life insurance policies, remove personal property, overpay income taxes to claim a refund after the divorce is final, delay billing customers, fail to pay bills, recklessly spend marital assets or run up debts, bounce checks, or fail to pay child support or alimony.

Some steps that you can take to protect yourself include the following:

Move half the cash in joint bank accounts to an account in your own name before you let your spouse know you plan to leave.

Order a credit report often during and after the divorce.

Obtain a credit card in your own name before you file for divorce. Freeze joint credit cards, and close out joint credit cards with a zero balance right after you file for divorce.

Request insurance companies to let you know of any late payments or nonpayment of premiums.

Give instructions to banks and investment firms that a divorce is pending and approval from both of you is now legally required for any changes or withdrawals.

Rosemary Lombardy, author, financial advisor

Chapter 11

NARC-PROOF YOUR DIVORCE DECREE

The hues of grey in a divorce decree: DANGER!

While we know narcissists live in a black and white world, I believe that when it comes to divorce, they play the grey areas of a decree to their advantage – the grey area being the fine line between what is allowed versus what is not. Standard legal language that has been written into decrees for years includes loopholes that a narcissist will test and abuse. This stems from them believing that rules do not apply to them. Their objective is to painfully twist everything so you will eventually give in and stop fighting. Narc-proofing a divorce decree will not be easy simply because the more guidelines or restrictions you ask for, the more push back you will endure. While this drama over details may incur extra-legal dollars up front, the cost will pale in comparison to going back to court later. Ultimately, you could save thousands of dollars if you plan for the grey and prevent subsequent exploitation. For the best protection, ensure that your narc-proof decree is solid and written to include penalties for non-compliance.

Lawyers and judges may not see the urgency in creating consequences to orders in decrees because, in their eyes, they are legally binding. If you haven't already, you will see how hostile divorce can be so do your best to think these details through while you are in the process of defining the rest of your life. Your future and that of your children can easily be derailed if you don't make every effort to get all of your ideas into the original decree.

Examine everything that is written in the decree and ask yourself, "What if they don't do this?" What if they don't pay you the money per the court order in 60 days? What if they don't put the house on the market as ordered? What if the 401K or pension doesn't get transferred into your name? I can tell you what will happen: more court, more drama, more legal fees, and more stress!

If you are divorcing a narcissist and your decree has any area where they must comply with something specific (i.e., make payments to you), do yourself justice and include a consequence. Assume that they won't pay on time or sell the house as they were instructed. Whatever your particular circumstances may involve, be sure it is covered completely with the expectation that it will need to be addressed in the future. I have spoken with many survivors who have been subject to legal abuse for years after their divorce due to a failure of sufficient narc-proofing in the original document.

While you may be exposed to various tricks that continue long after the divorce is finalized, remember that it's always about control. Think of the decree as a "boundary document" – the legal rules you are both obligated to follow post-divorce. It makes no difference whether or not you have children or if you're only separating assets. Narcissists will go to great lengths to make your life a living hell so *anything* that can be put in writing up front will do nothing but benefit you in the end. Knowing your rights will put an end to the gaslighting and stop the fear in its tracks. As I have mentioned previously, I have compiled a comprehensive collection of guidelines by state[23] on my website. Start there to understand what your state recommends and build in the necessary protection in the event (and the probability) that they

---

23   https://narcissistabusesupport.com/book-resources/

will not comply.

Most people would presume to follow the law as it is written; it is common that what become the grey areas seemed clear enough in the beginning. You take for granted that your ex will obey the law as this is a boundary most would never consider pushing but you should never assume that a narcissistic person will see or do things the same way as you, even if it's written in black and white. I will go out on a limb and say *especially* if it is written in black and white: that equates to a challenge and they are *always* up for a challenge. This is why it is critical that the way a decree is written must be iron clad from the start. Pick your battles, have things in your proposal that you are willing to negotiate on, and know which things are most important. An example of this may be different parenting styles — perhaps you believe the kids should not own a cellphone until they are a certain age or have limited access to TV daily. While watching endless TV seems like a ridiculous waste of time, the children are not in danger. Placing limits on social media, internet, gaming, TV, and friend time or establishing curfews, chores, and diet and exercise routines are variations that are not typically determined by a judge unless they endanger the child. These could simply be adjustments that you and your children must make. Hold fast to your rules and accept the fact that your ex will go against everything you are trying to teach. If homework is not a priority when they are at their home, it will be the kids who suffer. As hard as it may be to watch your straight A student fail their first class, make it into a teaching opportunity. Show them that despite homework rules not being enforced, it's ultimately your child's responsibility to keep up their own grades. It's a hard lesson but this is also your child's journey and they must learn to advocate and take responsibility for themselves. A judge will be concerned about what is in the best interest of the children on matters that physically put them at risk but for the majority of instances, their stock answer will almost always be "it wasn't defined in the original decree." Do yourself a favor and do it!

Defending the grey areas of a divorce decree after-the-fact is expensive as well as emotionally taxing on the family. Being dragged backwards to fight a second time for something that was already granted by a court is something I have experienced personally and it is a fresh type of hell that I wouldn't wish on my worst enemy.

A contempt of court battle: an example

Elizabeth and her husband, Eddie, owned several rental properties at the time of their divorce. Eddie was given sixty days to put two of the properties on the market so the assets could be split and he was ordered to have Elizabeth's name removed from the remaining properties. The order seemed clear and reasonable and they both signed the decree, which is a legal contract. By the time I met Elizabeth two years later, her ex-husband had not followed through with any of the orders and had also not paid her any equalization payments despite all of her legal attempts to collect.

What should happen since he didn't sell the properties or remove her name from the other deeds as instructed? Nothing was written in the decree to protect Elizabeth. Eddie made no effort to sell the properties and stopped responding to Elizabeth's lawyer's calls for answers. Two years later, she was forced to begin another legal battle.

Elizabeth invited me to be a spectator at the "contempt of court" day to experience in living color what her lawyer indicated would be a "shit-show." Her lawyer was prepared with three thick binders, one for the judge and one for both sides, carefully collated with each evidence page individually marked in another effort to force Eddie to respect the decree instructions. The prep for this trial alone surpassed $30,000 as her lawyer filed motion after motion in an effort to get Eddie to comply. Eddie owed Elizabeth quite a bit of money at this point.

Eddie lived out of state and decided to represent himself. It's never easy to see your ex after a divorce and going back to court after years of fighting was not going to be a good day to see him again. When the judge came in and Eddie had still not shown up, Elizabeth's lawyer asked how the judge would like to proceed. Irritated, the judge suggested she call one of her other cases first to give Eddie a bit more time.

Twenty-five minutes later, Elizabeth's disheveled ex strolled in carrying a laptop and a few pieces of paper. He took his seat, opened his laptop, and proceeded to request a continuance because he wasn't ready. I enjoyed watching the judge's reaction just as much as Elizabeth and her lawyer. The judge, however, was not happy and refused him any additional time. In the judge's eyes, that was a tough pill to swallow after she was kept waiting all morning. The hearing began.

Eddie had the floor first and proceeded to ask Elizabeth one ridiculous question after another that only highlighted just how ill-prepared he was; he had not made copies of the few papers he brought with him and the exhibits he was trying to present were unlabeled. The judge offered him exhibit stickers along with instructions on what needed to be done but her patience had already worn thin. She decided to hear yet another case while Eddie properly labeled his papers. With Elizabeth back on the stand, Eddie continued to instigate arguments while the judge reprimanded him repeatedly. It was the shit-show I was promised.

When Elizabeth's lawyer finally took control, she did an amazing job. The evidence Elizabeth had produced was based on her access to Eddie's checking statements. Her lawyer was able to prove that Eddie had loaned two people $20,000 each – the money he was to have paid Elizabeth. She also had evidence that he was collecting ten percent interest on this money. The only documentation Eddie brought was a Zillow printout to show that the homes were finally on the market; it also foolishly showed that he had only put them on the market two weeks earlier. The last piece of the puzzle that tipped the balance in Elizabeth's favor (and drew on the importance of her access to his statements) was that he had taken his girlfriend on a $4,000 cruise the month before. This revealed that he had the money but chose to spend it in ways other than fulfilling his obligation to Elizabeth.

Despite Eddie's insistence that he hadn't had any luck getting the rental properties refinanced, he was ordered to get Elizabeth's name off the properties within thirty days – no excuses. He was also ordered to pay the outstanding equalization payment within the same time frame and if both things weren't done, he would be seeing the inside of a jail cell until she was paid in full. Elizabeth's lawyer asked for her legal fees to be paid as well as interest on the money since Eddie had been making money on it by not paying her. It was clear in the judge's answer that she wanted to grant Elizabeth these requests but her hands were tied since they were not stipulated in the original decree. Unfortunately, she wasn't entitled to anything additional.

Taking measures upfront to pad your decree with any possibilities you think might possibly occur while you already have a lawyer retained will save money in the long run. As with any negotiations with a narcissist, don't expect them to like it or not fight it. It's your choice as to when you fight or when you pay. To get any specifics into the official decree, your lawyer may need to show the judge how your ex is a potential flight risk for payment and then ask to be granted these additional guidelines.

The secret sauces: protections to add to your decree

In the next sections, I have gathered grey area ideas for consideration and planning purposes. Many of these would not need to be spelled out in this detail if you are not divorcing a narcissist so most lawyers wouldn't know or be prepared to incorporate this added protection. It is your responsibility to speak up and demand this language be negotiated or it will never end up in your decree.

CYA – protect yourself!

Since going to court with Elizabeth, and with the help of an attorney, I developed a paragraph that I promised in the introduction that I would share with you – the 'what if they don't comply' clause (WITDC). From experience, I know that if it had been added to the original decree, all of Elizabeth's additional pain and suffering and financial bleeding could have been avoided. The beauty of this one brief paragraph is that it also covers them in the extremely unlikely case that you don't comply. It's fair for both sides and there is little reason that you wouldn't be able to get it added. Ask your attorney to request a clause similar to this to be written in legal guidelines for your court system:

> **Attorney Fees:** *The Parties shall each be responsible for their own attorney fees and costs necessary to finalize this Separation Agreement, the Affidavit of Decree, and the Decree of Dissolution. If either Party must seek legal assistance to enforce the terms of this Separation Agreement, the Party who is in non-compliance shall be responsible for the reasonable attorney fees and costs incurred by the non-breaching Party.*

Note to tell your lawyer: "The protection I am asking for is based on past behaviors and expected patterns." If your spouse has a history of failing to comply with temporary orders, gather the examples for your lawyer to justify the need to the judge. Real life precedents are the best proof of future actions. Request the specifics in your clause, including that they are to pay your legal fees if they do not comply, if you must return to court to seek enforcement. Your spouse can fight it but you will absolutely not get it if you don't try.

Life insurance – if your spouse is ordered to pay alimony, ask that they also be required to carry life insurance during the alimony obligation period. While this may seem morbid, it ensures that you will get paid in the event that they pass away unexpectedly. Request that it be written in the decree that you are to be given proof of the current insurance at least once a year.

Reverse life insurance – I had a 60-year-old client who was concerned that if she died, the financial obligation that her husband was under would dissolve. The money he was to pay was all she had to leave her adult children so her lawyer wrote in a clause that the alimony would be paid to her estate until its ending day if anything should happen to her. The other side agreed.

Grey areas to consider
The hundreds of data points that you could lay out will be overwhelming to a judge. If you go to a mediator, these seemingly small details can be ironed out and, as a bonus, save you money by not

having them settled through the court system. The following topics to consider grey areas represent situations that have happened to others.

Selling your home sweet home

There are many things to consider when selling a home post-divorce. A big factor is when it will go on the market. Often, the judge establishes the timeframe, 30-60 days, for example. Ask your lawyer to be overly specific, even utilizing an exact date when possible. This way, you have a concrete action plan if they would be non-compliant in the allotted time. Identifying that they are 47 days in contempt is much stronger than leaving it open to the vague 30-60 day interpretation: When did the counting start? Did it start when you signed or when they got their copy? You get the picture. Assume that anything that could possibly go wrong will if left to their devices.

What happens if the house is not put on the market by the specified date? Would they be in contempt of court? Yes! What then? You must go back to court and spend more money. What if you had the foresight to have penalties already in place and the security of knowing that they would be required to pay your legal fees if they didn't comply? It's comforting to be covered from the very beginning.

Who chooses the realtor? Do you both have to agree? How many times would they be allowed to veto a realtor choice? Who pays for the real estate photographer? Would the home need to be staged professionally because one of you moved out and now it doesn't show well? Who pays for that? What fee would the realtor get? It is important that whoever the realtor is, both sides be notified when potential buyers would be viewing the home. If the narcissistic spouse picks the realtor, they will start by smearing you so the realtor may become unhelpful when you need information. Try to build a relationship with the realtor so you are in the loop. Cut out the middleman, reduce your stress, and demand equal communication for showings, offers, or other concerns. You cannot expect the communication from your soon-to-be ex. Ultimately, the contract for selling the house is a commitment; you own half, so you get to make the rules too. Get everything built into the contract upfront to protect yourself.

Who decides how much to list the house for? Who pays the appraisal and listing fees? While it is understood that your realtor will do comparisons and offer guidelines for the sale price, narcissists are famous for their difficulty and entitlement. In this case, they will feel it's their prerogative to demand the highest amount in that recommended range and often won't agree to compromise. The risk here is that if you try to sell the house at the higher price, what will it take for them to agree when it needs to be lowered? The time to negotiate on that timeline is before you sign the papers with the realtor. It would be best to acknowledge that the realtor is the expert and consent based on their judgement.

Could you both agree on the lowest price you would accept for the home? What would be the criteria for lowering the price? Map out these details. Many times, I've seen where the narcissistic spouse refuses to approve lowering the sale price to market level. They feel they are entitled to more and the bonus of driving you crazy is a great supply. This trick slows down the process and can leave you without the cash you may need.

What if your soon-to-be ex refuses to allow the house to be shown when the realtor calls? What if they don't ensure the house is clean for showings? Keep a spreadsheet that tracks the times they denied the realtor access to show the home or other negative interaction. Get written confirmations from your realtor in the event you end up in court fighting the process.

Once an offer is made and an inspection determines repairs are needed, whose responsibility are they? Who decides what company to hire to do the work? Can you ask for three proposals and jointly decide? Should a timeline be established for a contractor to be selected and if they don't comply, can you alone hire the organization to complete the repairs? Their angle to block every contractor you suggest is liable to put the offer on the house in jeopardy.

A SurTHRIVER Story: Carol's husband refused every contractor proposal because he perceived them as somehow being aligned with her. Since the necessary work was not completed as the agreement stipulated, the sale fell through. They were then forced to have a judge approve the contractor which slowed down the process by six months.

What recourse do you have if your soon-to-be ex refuses to remove their belongings (i.e., a car, gym equipment, or tools) once the house has sold? I have seen narcissistic spouses do this very thing. Is it your responsibility to pay your movers to move their effects in order for the house to close? The burden falls on the spouse living in the house who must try to get rid of the pieces and then risk being sued for disposing of their contentious spouse's property. As with every step to this point, document all communications (and copy your lawyer) regarding your ex's belongings and your efforts to get them collected. Protect yourself!

Who pays for the professional cleaning prior to the final walk-through on closing day? This might seem petty but if you are financially drained from the divorce, you may not have the $500 to spend.

How will the profits from the home sale be distributed? If the home is in both of your names, the check will be payable to both of you and will require both signatures in order to be deposited. Into whose account should the check be deposited? If you do not trust your narcissistic partner, ask if one of the lawyers can place it into an escrow account to be distributed. Or perhaps the title company would be willing to issue two checks. Think of every possibility and try to cover yourself but it would be best to have this decision made and approved up front. How soon would the money be disbursed once it clears? What if they don't give you the money? Could it be written into the decree that interest be paid to you? Get it in writing.

MY SurTHRIVER Story: My husband had already moved back east when we sold our home. To distance himself further, he elected to skip the closing altogether and gave his divorce lawyer his power of attorney. They made it extremely clear from the beginning that I would not be allowed to claim the $50,000 proceeds check, going so far as to threaten police action if I tried. For my own sense of safety, I felt compelled to bring a friend to the closing for protection against their aggressive threats and then his lawyer didn't even show up. I had to call my attorney, at my expense, and ask him to contact my husband's attorney to find out what was going on. We sat across the table from the new owners for over an hour, unable to sign the papers. My lawyer finally called back and stated that his realtor had signed a power of attorney and, unbeknownst to him, they wanted him to sign my husband's name. Once finalized, my lawyer was instructed to email a photo of the check in his safe to confirm that it was out of my control. My ex was successful at his last-minute intimidation tactic that put additional fear and confusion in my heart as well as forcing me to pay several hours of unnecessary lawyer fees – another way to financially control me.

What if your spouse plans to buy you out? When will you get your money? Other assets may need to be liquidated for them to be able to pay you. How quickly they move to sell those might be yet another grey area they could exploit.

To recap, the decree is a legal contract co-signed with someone who has proven themselves untrustworthy. By laying out as many details as possible in advance, you are saving yourself that many headaches later. For each step, include specific dates where possible. Knowing up front that legal action may be your only alternative for satisfaction, include your legal fees to be paid by them in the case anything ends up back in court due to their negligence or delays.

Other assets
Do you have rental properties? Do you own a business together? Share any retirement accounts or investments? All the same precautions should go into the decree with dates, penalties, and applicable legal fees if they do not comply with the outlined agreements.

Rental properties
If they are collecting rent and not paying you your portion during the divorce process, ensure your lawyer is aware so that they can go after what is yours. If they tell you that you have no right to any portion of the collected rent, chances are good it is not true. Always defer issues like this to your team to handle.

Business evaluation
If a business is co-owned, finances may be creatively massaged and the business undervalued in an attempt to walk away with more mon-

ey. A non-partisan forensic accountant should be retained to give an accurate appraisal of the business' worth.

401K, retirement, and pensions

A recurring mistake I see in divorce situations involving younger people is the decision to give the marital home to the spouse to live in with the kids in exchange for keeping their 401k plan. A house is a liquid asset that can be sold at any time. If you are not the proper age, a 401k is basically untouchable or will be laden with high penalties if you need to liquidate it to live on. Depending on how your account is set up, you might not only be taxed but also potentially incur early withdrawal penalties. Be sure to explore your options fully prior to settling on investments as your sole source of income.

If you need to liquidate investments from a brokerage account, keep in mind that you may get hit with long-term capital gains taxes that could be as much as 20%. Consider the cost as part of the equalization. Why should they get their half while you are stuck with a 20% fee? Do the research to understand penalties and costs before you agree, and make sure you are not losing extra money because it wasn't calculated appropriately.

Difficulties may arise when dividing pension plans or other retirement accounts that state and local governments often have for teachers, firefighters, police, and government workers. The splitting of these assets may be complicated and take substantial time and knowledge. Basically, a pension is a salary and while guidelines for each can vary, the benefit is typically until *the holder* dies; most do not include continuing to pay the spouse after death. If this is one of the pieces of your settlement, be aware that if your spouse dies, you may have just lost that money. Life insurance may be a good solution. Add into the decree that life insurance must be maintained so that, in the event of their death, you would still get compensated.

Social Security

If you have been married for at least ten years, Social Security benefits may be available that should not be left on the table. You might be entitled to half of your spouse's social security payments once they retire *or* 100% of your own benefits. Specific conditions must be met such as you never remarried and are over 60 years old. Ask your attorney to determine your rights and add this detail into the decree or you may find yourself walking away without this benefit. This assistance is typically additional to any settlement so remain vigilant and don't let them remove other items to include this in the decree.

Inheritance and divorce

In most states, inheritances are considered separate property and usually not subject to be part of a divorce settlement. However, if the inheritance has already been co-mingled, it is deemed marital property. For example, if it is re-invested back into the house by remodeling, that would be considered co-mingled and it cannot be claimed individually – it goes into the marital pool. Simply depositing inheritance money into a joint account also immediately labels it co-mingled regardless of it still being in savings and accessible. If the inherited money is the narcissist's, you can expect them to fight tooth and nail to get it back at the negotiation table. Financial intimidation regarding inheritance laws is a common form of abuse; ask your lawyer to explain the rules in your state or country so you do not waste time or money fighting for something you are not likely to get.

Alimony protection tip

Horror stories abound about deadbeat dads/moms who refuse to pay per the judge's order and the battles that ensue. Most states have a family court system payment option: by demanding they pay your alimony and/or child support through the family court system, you will be privy to an extra layer of protection to ensure you get your money on time, every time. If they are to pay you on the first of the month, your ex must make the payment to the court system a few weeks in advance in order for the disbursement to be sent directly to you from the court system. If your ex does not comply, then the state goes after them; they can garnish their wages, take their tax refund, and much more. It's them against the state at that point which takes you out of the equation to fight again with lawyers and courts. There are plenty of deadbeat parents currently in jail – the family court system has that power. Ask your lawyer to demand this as an option to protect your alimony and/or child support.

Payment of debt

If your spouse is ordered to pay any debt for you, it is advisable to have them pay you directly rather than the creditors. Abusers like to ruin credit; it gives them control and supply to make your life a living hell. You can count on them to not pay on time and/or missing a few months here and there. They will have excuses ready every single time. Do you really want to have to keep monthly tabs on their actions as they relate to YOUR credit? Of course you don't. They know you won't be able to drag them back to court each time so they will test and abuse this far too often.

Parenting plans within the decree

The most heart-wrenching aspect of divorcing a narcissist is how it affects the kids, directly and indirectly. Helplessly watching them be used as pawns is painful and the lack of willingness to negotiate simple parenting guidelines for their protection is disconcerting for all involved. Narcissists put on the good parent mask in public while, in the background, they begrudge you adequate child support and try every trick in the book to get that support payment lowered. The contrast between this fake persona and the real parent who does not want to pay their fair share is infuriating.

The biggest mistakes in the grey areas of parenting plans are the decisions that were made based on the children's ages at the time the plan was written. When the child is in preschool, you have decisions to consider based on the child at that stage of their life. As children age, their needs will change; the accommodations you make today must be well thought out for the future teenager playing sports and traveling to competitions and camps. Do your research for the future costs; protecting your children's financial future means planning and forward-thinking. If the children's needs are frozen in time in the de-cree, you will find yourself back in court often, spending $20,000 with every fight. Talk to friends with different aged children for financial strategy advice; planning ahead will save you money in the long run.

Plan out the parenting schedule for the entire year ahead of time: This will save you a lot of drama and arguments over who gets the kids for holidays. Typically, alternating holidays works well. For example, if you get the kids on winter break this year, your spouse gets winter break next year.

Jason Levoy, former divorce attorney turned coach, creator of DivorceU

The traveling papers and children's passports

If your family has ever traveled out of the country, your children may already have passports. One major determination would be who will keep them in their possession. A fear many parents in high conflict divorce cases have is the potential for kidnapping, especially if your ex is from another country. If a spouse has the money, the means, and direct access to the passports, they become a threat. In cases with multiple children, arrangements can be made where each parent holds onto one passport until the other needs it for traveling. Don't get a false sense of security that they won't still try something. If the risk is present and you are worried, you can also request an attorney's office safeguard them.

If you are planning a vacation, depending on the age of the children and what is involved in your decree, you may be required to obtain a permission slip from the other parent first – perhaps it might be needed for a flight but not a short drive into a neighboring state. Whatever makes you feel the most secure. The grey area of this permission slip is whether your decree stipulates a deadline of when the notice must be given for travel and when the permission slip must be returned. Give yourself plenty of wiggle room: I have heard horror stories from many survivors that the narc-parent refused to hand over the passport causing trips to be canceled. What would you do then? Take them back to court to recover the expenses of a trip? That would be your only recourse and often the cost of court outweighs a $5,000 ruined vacation. Even with consequences set in the decree for this type of situation, you still may not see less bad behavior.

Visitation

Many circumstances must be considered as you set the visitation schedule for basic visitation, holidays, and vacations factoring in exceptions and make-up times. Fast forward to the needs of a teenager involved in activities that require obligations of their time. Flexibility and what is in the best interest of the child should be obvious. For example, if the required event falls on your ex's weekend, make it clear that they are responsible for making the transportation arrangements for it. If it is an event that you also plan to attend, make it clear that either parent can attend but the child must go home with the parent assigned to that weekend. While it may be easier if your ex didn't show up on your weekend, for any reason, it is ultimately what's in the best interest of the child. By always being fair to both sides when writing the parenting agreement, you have a better chance of a seamless settlement.

The creation of standard holiday and vacation calendars is critical with the typical rotation for major holidays set at alternate years. The grey area that must be plainly defined is when the holiday begins and ends. Mother's Day and Father's Day can be hard if you don't have the kids on your designated day. You can try to negotiate these independent of your parenting time with the understanding that if you pick up an extra day, your ex might want to make it up another time. Clearly define that they can celebrate with the kids on their holiday too which may make them more likely to agree. Negotiate and detail all specificities of visitation times as well as special cases like this in the original decree or be prepared to fight it later.

A SurTHRIVER Story: Allison created a holiday schedule that would be viable until the kids were 18 but failed to define start or end times for the visits. Taking advantage of this, her husband picked up the kids on Christmas Eve but refused to bring them back since no end time was delineated. His "assumption" was that he got the kids for the entire holiday vacation so he combined this holiday with his next legitimate weekend and kept the kids for ten days. He walked the grey line to torture Allison. Once she saw this pattern of behavior, she immediately petitioned the courts to specify the start and end dates going forward.

When drawing up a visitation schedule, allow for the "what ifs" that may develop in your child's life. If your spouse wasn't the primary caregiver, they may not be comfortable caring for a sick kid and very often will insist that the child gets picked up in this situation. What will your policy be for that? As with everything else, document any instances like this throughout the separation as well as post-divorce in case you ever need any evidence of their bad parenting skills. As they grow, the kid's needs change and both parents should be willing to bend in the best interest of the child. We know narcissists do not play well with others so try to think of every scenario and plan accordingly.

Pickup and drop off procedures for the children

Depending on how high conflict your ex becomes, the pickup and drop off experience can be traumatic for all involved. In extreme cases, parents can plan to exchange the children at police stations or visitation centers, or wherever neutral parties are present to supervise.

Set your rules and boundaries early: Will you allow your ex to come inside the house? Should they call from the driveway? What rules must you both follow for the sake of the children? These may seem superficial and overkill for a decree, but if they don't comply, you can build a case against them much more easily. Your lawyer might suggest that these steps are overly controlling but they are basic protection that could save both you and the children years of drama in the end. If expected behaviors are written equally offering protection to both sides, you stand a better chance of getting them approved into the law of the decree. Once there, you have legal standing if it becomes necessary.

Sole decision-making

Be prepared upfront: sole decision-making rights are always the hardest thing to get from a judge and usually the most common warzone in a decree. Notify your lawyer if this is your goal as most courts have specific criteria that must show your ex to be an unfit parent. Proven physical abuse, sexual abuse, or the parent having been diagnosed with a mental illness or violent tendencies might be among the things that could sway the decision in your favor. Since narcissistic personality disorder is a personality disorder rather than a mental illness, this is not a slam dunk. Professionals might need to get involved to prove your point. It won't be easy so expect a battle. While each state in the USA has different guidelines, once granted this right, you may still be required to be transparent with your ex about information regarding major decisions, like health care and education choices. If it is your ex who is petitioning for sole decision-making rights, be sure that your decree spells out that you are entitled to know the choices and decisions made for your kids even if you aren't involved in making them. Always keep the WITDC[24] guidelines in mind.

Legal decision-making considerations

"Legal decision-making" is the legal right and responsibility to make all nonemergency legal decisions for your child which may include education, health, religious, and personal care. There are three different ways this can be ordered: joint legal decision-making, joint legal decision-making with one parent having final say, and sole legal decision-making.

Discuss these options with your lawyer and get recommendations based on how it relates to your case. If you agree to joint custody but the two of you cannot agree, you will find yourself back in court. Laying out as many topics that you can agree on will drastically reduce the post-divorce legal abuse.

Medical decisions

Defining who is responsible for medical decisions can be left to the primary parent, but not always. The need for control always makes its way into a family dynamic when children are in need of medical care. It's not uncommon for the narcissistic parent to deny the dentist's suggestion of braces or block a child from getting counseling simply because they don't think there is anything wrong. Who decides these things and what if you can't agree? Where it can get sticky is if the narcissistic parent is responsible to pay for medical and has equal weight in all decisions. They might dig in their heels and hold you

---

24   Refer to the CYA section at the beginning of Chapter 11.

hostage with that added layer of power. If you have one of these narcissists, your request will likely be seen as a ploy to get more money rather than the simple fact that your kid needs help.

Vaccines

If one or both of you are against vaccines, be sure to add that detail into the parenting plan. If your ex never agreed with your anti-vax beliefs, joint decision rights give them permission to march your kid into a doctor and get any and all vaccines they haven't had up to that point and there will be nothing you can do about it. There have been cases where parents end up in court to fight about each individual vaccine. With any luck, having it in writing could help avoid this expensive mess. If vaccines are a joint decision that might be a future issue, what would stop the narcissistic parent from taking the kids to get the vaccines and then play stupid after the fact? Is there a contempt charge? Only if it's in the decree but even then, the damage would already be done.

Vision and dental care

Who pays for glasses, contacts, exams, dental visits, braces, and uncovered copays? How often should the child be examined? Who is responsible for making the appointments and doing the leg-work to ensure that the children receive proper care? Who keeps the insurance documents and is financially responsible for anything beyond a copay? Going back to court or picking up the tab yourself will be the only option if it's not carefully spelled out in the original decree.

Emergency care or surgery

What constitutes an emergency? How will the other parent be notified? How quickly? If your kid was at the other parent's house and had a raging fever all weekend, would you want to know? If your kid was taken to the urgent care after falling off a balance beam, would you want to know today or Sunday when she arrives home with a broken bone? Define the boundaries and guidelines for any emergency care. If you will be communicating through an app like Our Family Wizard or Talking Parents, can you break the rule in the case of a hospital emergency? Remember this goes both ways so if you want them to call you, you must be willing to do the same. Blocking emergency information about your child can set a bad precedent that can backfire on you if the kids get hurt when they are not with you.

Education and college

Preschool, religious school, private school, public school, technical school, college – who pays? Did you know that most courts cannot make one parent help the other pay for a child's education unless it is already an agreement in their decree? What are the limits or guidelines? Transportation to private school? Uniforms? Computers or other learning tools? Have this discussion up front and plan for your child's future. I know a lady whose wealthy ex agreed to pay for their kids' higher education but the costs associated were never defined. If one agrees to pick up the tab or split the expenses, define the limitations or you could get taken to the cleaners. Colleges are crazy expensive and it's not just the tuition; consider creating a budget – application fees – test costs – tuition – housing – food – books – supplies – clothes – activities – transportation – school tutoring... the list can be endless. My son joined a fraternity which incurred thousands of dollars more than I had originally anticipated. Plan for any and all possibilities.

If you don't have a savings plan for your child's higher education, incorporate student loans into the negotiation process. Would your ex agree to be responsible for paying off those loans? If they won't agree to the entire tuition, maybe you could add a clause that they will assume a portion of the debt your children will incur. Anyone can apply for student loans – the parents and the children – and there may also be grants available. The financial aid office of any institution should be able to direct you where to find these. In order for my son to be approved for the grants from the school he attended, he was required to apply and take on federal loans of approximately $6,000 a year in his name. If your ex won't pay tuition, would they pay for travel or housing or food? Knowing what to ask for and solidifying a settlement on matters of education in advance will save you one battle later in life. Don't forget to set the dates that money is due to the schools; you do not want your child to find out tuition hasn't been paid at the beginning of the semester. Document each time you send them an invoice as well as any reminders because covering your butt is always important. They can easily blame you for not telling them the tuition bill was due. If things get contentious, send all correspondence by registered mail so they must sign for them to add an additional layer of documentation. What if they don't pay? Include legal fees to their responsibility in the decree if they do not comply with any detail that they signed off on.

Setting limits and defining expectations: an example

Melissa and Mike had plenty of assets and despite his narcissistic ways, he did want to care for his two kids, including their college educations. The decree stated that Mike would pay for college; a simple line that gave Melissa security to know the girls would be taken care of. A few years later, their first daughter was accepted into Brown University but when the confirmation came with the price tag attached, Mike balked. He claimed he had only budgeted for a state school, not a $60,000 a year school. The battle began. They went to court because it was not clearly defined in the original decree specifying a budget or Mike's intention. Melissa spent $20,000 for the judge to decline her request for Mike to pay the bill and, in the end, they split the cost of Brown.

Phones: the modern battle

How old should the child be before owning a phone? Who will pay for it? Who will have the phone on their plan? Note that if the narcissistic parent holds the keys to the child's cellphone account, they are afforded the opportunity to spy on the texts and calls from you. If they give you the money directly and you maintain the phone contract, you will have fewer issues. One parent can block the calls from the other parent's phone as soon as the kids arrive and unblock it as they leave. In some high conflict divorce situations, the children can be ordered to keep their phone on them 24/7 in case they are in danger or need help. If you don't share your children's cell phone passwords with your ex, they can't take the phones to screenshot all the texts between you. If it's not in the decree, it's not enforceable.

Cars and transportation

How old will the child be before being allowed to drive? Who will pay for driving school or lessons? Who is responsible for getting the child a car? Is there a set maximum for that parent or for each of you to share? Who is responsible for the car insurance? At what age is it okay for the child to drive themselves to the other parent's house? When one parent takes on the responsibility to buy the child a car but without any guidelines for cost expectations, that parent has the autonomy to refuse to buy anything that the other parent may suggest. These battles can go around and around without the proper details and protection in place.

Sports, clubs, activities, school trips, and camps

Who decides which activities the kids can participate in? Is there a budget per child? Are sleep-away camps acceptable? Religious camps or retreats? Can they be co-ed? Is there an approval process for them to agree to the camp of your choice? What happens to parenting time if it coincides with time the child is enrolled in a camp? We all want the best for our children, but as they get older, the cost of their activities increase dramatically. The cost for soccer in fourth grade is not the same as when they are selected for a high school varsity or traveling team. Similarly, the cost of camps for a six-year-old is not the same as a camp for a fifteen-year-old. Do the research now and plan for inflation if it's down the road.

Children as tax deductions

Claiming the children as dependents on tax returns is usually something that is rotated annually. Creative situations can be devised by splitting the children with each parent taking half as deductions so both sides may benefit every year. At the time of this book's writing in 2021, stimulus checks per child occurred which is unprecedented.

Pre-planning and strategizing accordingly is fiscally responsible and will likely save you money in the long run.

Relocation

Often there are clauses that limit how far the primary parent can move the children away from the other, such as not beyond 50 miles. I saw a mom battle her ex for approval for four miles beyond their pre-determined limit. The child's father tried to block her and her new husband's move which prompted her to take him back to court and rewrite her visitation agreement. While the judge allowed her move, she did end up spending $15,000 to make it happen; the bright side was that she took that opportunity to modify the parenting plan to adapt for the age-appropriate changes of their child that were not accounted for originally.

My lesson from experience: relocation via divorce decree

When I divorced my son's father, we didn't have a written relocation clause which had seemed unnecessary at the time. I had never lived beyond the ten-mile radius of where I grew up and had no expectations that I ever would.

Life often hands us things expectedly: I didn't plan on meeting the man who would become my new husband nor did I ever imagine leaving the safe confines of my hometown. I was love bombed with all the relationship-rushing tactics and expeditiously married him. Within a year, he got a job 2,000 miles away; it all happened so quickly. We had never discussed moving but it was sold to me as the new beginning for our family. Since there was no relocation clause in the divorce decree with my son's father, we were forced back to court to redefine the parenting plan. My son's father had been accustomed to having our son every other weekend and one weekday night so his parenting time had to be addressed. The judge approved our move from Connecticut to Colorado with modifications. The conditions were absurd but my new husband wanted his new job and his new life so badly that he agreed to all the financial obligations in the updated relocation decree. In hindsight, I understand the isolation tactics at work, to keep me from my support system and my son from his dad so that my new husband would become the one my son relied on.

We were allowed to move with the following conditions: my son was to fly to Connecticut every other weekend, at my expense, but because he was under 18, his father insisted that he not travel alone. I was required to stay in Connecticut every other weekend as well so that I could then fly with my eight-year-old son back to Colorado. On the opposite weekends, my son's father would fly to Colorado, his airfare, rental car, and hotel all financed by us. After fronting the cost to get these new parameters in place, my son's dad pulled the plug on this expensive and tiring process after only six weeks. He traveled to Colorado twice and said it was too much work. We continued to pay for my son to go to his dads for Thanksgiving and vacations because we knew we had dodged a major bullet.

Before you judge me, realize that my second husband made good money and it was he who insisted that we take this new deal. I objected to the arrangement but he assured me that the financial aspect was not a problem. My rationale behind sharing this story is to show the importance of a solid relocation clause. However, never forget that the clause can go both ways – if they move, you may end up with the responsibility of arranging any necessary kidlet transportation to your ex.

The introduction: when do the children meet the new supply?

Being a fortune teller would be an extremely helpful ability when planning for any future possibilities that might arise. For example, the discussion should be had regarding when is it okay for either of you to introduce the kids to any prospective mates. Since narcissists tend to move on very quickly, a colossal frustration is that they have a propensity to introduce the kids to their new supply too soon. This is especially difficult if the kids haven't yet come to terms with the divorce and are feeling sadness, grief, or loss. Often, they hastily blow through multiple new liaisons causing the kids to feel less loved and more abandoned each time. To avoid the drama, set up guidelines for both of you to follow; since this also pertains to your dating partners, it can be an easy win. Consider the children's ages and how sensitive they are to the separation and new living arrangements when establishing the rules.

Communication

If the goal is to successfully co-parent children, communication is probably one of the most important aspects of your parenting plan. Narcissists will abuse the terms in every way imaginable with the sole purpose of driving you insane. You can expect varying ends of the spectrum from constant vile texts, emails, and messages to radio silence – complete incommunicado. From the outside looking in, the silent treatment may appear to be a less painful experience but it is frustrating and can limit your parenting decisions when you need answers. Conversely, the flood of text messages and abuse by technology leaves victims worn out and fearful of their own buzzing phone as they prepare for more attacks. Most survivors wonder, "How can this harassment be allowed?"

Search out any and all undefined grey areas and situations that could backfire before you sign a decree. Make sure your lawyer is willing to fight for this specialized protection – it is their job to show the judge why detail of this variety is critical in your particular case. The cray-cray and narcissism will show itself given half a chance.

The question you must implant in your mind is: What if they don't comply (WITDC)? Never lose sight of making preparations to cover any situation that may arise.

The narcissist won't play by the rules -- and maybe you shouldn't either: Narcissists, antisocials, and psychopaths are experts at manipulating the "gray area" between complying with the law and breaking it. You may want to do the same. If aggressive action will help you recover your money, protect your kids, save your house, whatever -- well, sometimes it's better to ask forgiveness than permission.
Donna Andersen, author, founder of Lovefraud Continuing Education

Chapter 12

THE COURTROOM DRAMA

Marriage starts out as fantasy and romance sprinkled with a commitment to love each other til death do you part. You get consumed inside a bubble of picking napkin colors and designing the cake with dreams about the future of children, a white picket fence, and a minivan in the driveway. The one thing that never crosses our minds during this love bombing phase is that getting married is a legally binding contract and divorce is the dissolution of that bond. Be clear: when the fairy tale ends, it comes to a screeching halt and that's when the legal woes begin. Overlooked by our heart's involvement at the onset, even though it didn't feel like a business deal, it was.

Now, a judge or magistrate will hear your case and decide your fate; a complete stranger will split your assets and determine how much time you will be allotted to spend with your children. You suddenly wish that you had thought of the fancy wedding invitations more like a contract than an uncomplicated love commitment from the beginning. Family court is not about honesty, fairness, or justice. Along with everything else, you must now learn to protect yourself from the financial and legal abuses that will result from a contentious high conflict divorce.

Contrary to what you've seen on TV shows like *Perry Mason* and *Law and Order*, "innocent until proven guilty" simply doesn't apply in divorce. Envision a combination of a Jerry Springer episode mixed with the movie *War of the Roses*; this mashup is much more accurate.

Everything up to this point has been the roller coaster ascending; the descent begins with courtroom drama where it accelerates so fast, the g-force presses you tight against the seat, you gasp for air, and everything goes dark. Suddenly you're falling, your heart is racing, and you can't stop screaming, "When will this end?" As the fall slows to a sudden jerk to the left, you realize that the ride has only just left the platform. We call this divorce.

Roller coasters do end but you need to be strong and prepare well. This ride will impact your life, your children's lives, and your financial security forever.

Grieve the life you thought you would have, grieve the illusion of the person you thought that they were, and grieve the death of a dream. Take the time you need in order to move forward without reservation. You will get through this and you will emerge stronger and happier, so have faith. Healing begins with being able to make peace with the things you cannot change; you cannot change someone with a personality disorder. I am *not* suggesting that you accept their behavior because it is never okay to allow yourself to be treated badly. Surrender to the fact that no matter how hard you try, you can't love them into being better. Narcissists can't love anyone other than themselves. They can pretend to love you, but only until they move on to their next supply.

Treating the narcissist as if they were a reasonable and normal human being includes these errors:

Telling the narcissist in advance that you are filing for divorce, so the narcissist runs out and files first. This is a mistake because who files first generally has the advantage; anything filed in response is a defensive move and you are coming from behind. This happens because a victim has a deep-seated belief that if they are nice enough and communicative enough, then the narcissist is somehow required to play fair in return. Nothing can be further from the truth.

Going outside of custody court orders to bargain with the narcissist. I can't tell you how many of my clients think that if they give up their court-ordered rights to holidays, etc. with their children, then surely the narcissist will give them favors in return when they need them. Again, this never works. You simply cannot go outside of the decree or temporary orders -- they are your best friend. Lean on them. Learn from them. People who are in "normal" divorces can make exceptions to the orders -- someone divorcing a narcissist can't. Do not ask for favors and do not give them.

Arguing with the narcissist during proceedings (or at any time). They thrive on upsetting you and drawing you into a debate -- the truth is not important to them. You are not obligated to answer them at any time -- that's what attorneys are for. If they violate the decree or temporary orders regarding custody, simply copy and paste the appropriate section from the court document into an email (preferably through the Wizard system[25], so documentation is appropriately recorded) and send to them without comment. Don't respond to any replies -- instead, forward them to your attorney.

Debbie Tudor, author, Licensed Professional Counselor-Supervisor and Life Coach

Court information you need to know

Preparing for court

When it is time, your lawyer will request the required financial paperwork from you. Your narcissist, however, will undoubtedly slow-play providing his portion, stonewalling the court, and constantly delaying his submission. Excuses will be exhausted from "It's your fault because our accountant won't call me back" to "The dog ate my homework." It's extremely easy to get angry at the entire process. You were able to

---

25   Communication apps such as Our Family Wizard or Talking Parents

submit your information on time so how can they get away with do-ing nothing? I personally dealt with this scenario and it was exasper-ating. By the time he was on his last leg with the judge, he submitted enough just to get by, using the same tired excuse that I had blocked his access to our joint bank accounts. The judge eventually got so fed up that my husband's credibility was completely shredded. It would have never occurred to me to not produce what was required by the court system but for them it was by design; his lawyer chose to walk a very dangerous line.

Negotiating

Negotiation is an art form. Some are very slick: "He could sell un-derwear to a nudist." Just like there is skill involved, there is also a method to courtroom negotiating. Offer(s) will be made to your legal team for your lawyer to review and discuss with you. As you process the logic of each option, you can bet the other side will be watch-ing the clock. Remember the rush for intimacy and solidifying the relationship in the beginning? The same theory will be used when making you an offer; they will try to rush you into a decision before you're able to determine what everything means. This is your future so do not succumb to the pressure from your lawyer or soon-to-be ex. Compile level-headed groups as sounding boards, such as trusted family members or a divorce coach, who can read between the lines and help you weigh out all of the possibilities.

Once you have taken the time you need to decide the direction you wish to go, don't be surprised to learn that said offer(s) is no longer on the table. Welcome to the world of divorcing a narcissistic part-ner; you are a puppet and they pull the strings. The time you took to consider has become a clue to the narcissist. They now know what you will accept and how you might settle. The baseline has been estab-lished and the bar will get lowered. Hopefully your lawyer is familiar with this dance so your entire hand wasn't shown all at once. You do not want to be left with nothing to negotiate.

Finding leverage and the smoking gun

Divorce is about give and take. It is not wise to come out of the gate with your best offer because the other side's job is to negotiate, or reduce, based on what it appears that you want. Always start high to allow yourself room to move to where you would be willing to settle. This may seem like a game, and to some it is, but it's critical to leave wiggle room. Many have laid out their best proposal first only to lose a large percentage of what they really had hoped for in the bargain.

Do you have any financial leverage against your ex? Imagine they have a military pension as well as a 401k. You know that you are willing to settle for half of the pension but instead suggest that you want half of the 401k, which is substantially larger. You now have put yourself in the position to have the upper hand. Rather than just give it up, you "offer" the suggestion that paying off the joint credit card debt in addition to half of the pension would suffice. You would never enter a bargaining session without something you are willing to give back: I will give you my favorite yellow crayon if you give me three of your pencils.

Finding a smoking gun can also be a very helpful negotiation tool as it is the juice that can be used to influence your negotiating power. Many with a spouse who cheated believe this to be a good advantage but it doesn't hold any clout unless your spouse would not want the facts revealed. Chances are good that a pastor or prominent member of the community would prefer that this type of truth not be told. It may sound like blackmail but it is leverage that can be used by your lawyer at the right time to encourage them to agree to something you want. Another example could be your knowledge that they have hidden money from the IRS. Something to note about your smoking gun that I briefly mentioned in Chapter 7 is that it should remain secret until its use: if you reveal your hand prior to dropping the bomb, your spouse's team will have sufficient time to devise a defense strategy. Give your lawyer all the information and backing documentation that you feel will be helpful and let them determine the right time. When it works, it's brilliant.

The world of motion after motion

Prior to experiencing any divorce-related activity, you would have no idea that the term motion refers to anything more than a moving football, let alone legal steps taken in a courtroom. A motion is a request for the court to put in place any changes you are seeking. There are many types to familiarize yourself with prior to your lawyer becoming involved with them on your behalf. Each would be specific to your case so ask your lawyer for a full explanation of what they mean in your situation.

- » Emergency Motion for Sole Custody – based on a new situation, one side is asking for sole custody
- » Emergency Motion for Support – asking the court to order support payments
- » Motion to Modify – where either side can ask the judge to review an order
- » Motion to Compel Discovery/Order of Compliance – when a lawyer demands the judge make the other side do what they have already been ordered to do
- » Motion to Delay – when either side asks for more time from the judge
- » Motion to Sequester Non-Party Witnesses – bring in others to testify
- » Motion to Modify Child Support – asking the court to modify already approved support based on new information
- » Motion to Modify Custody – asking the court to change the custody
- » Motion to Enforce – asking the judge to enforce an order already stipulated

Pre-Trial Motions
When you first file for divorce, your lawyer can request to have a hearing to ascertain motions. This is an appeal, not something you are guaranteed, but it all starts with the "ask."

At the beginning of most divorces, basic decisions must be ironed out like who will live in the marital home, how much temporary support either party will get from the other, how much temporary child support will be given to the custodial parent, and what will visitation look like until the divorce is final. If you are unable to decide together, a judge will be given the task. If your spouse has a violent history and a restraining order needs to be enforced, motions should be sent to the judge to address it. If one spouse is moving out and needs to collect their personal property but the other side is not being cooperative, a motion can be entered to be decided by the judge. If you are fighting over the coffee maker now, that's an indication of the battle ahead.

Post-Trial Motions

To ask the court for any modifications to orders, your lawyer will need to file a motion. After the divorce, if your spouse hasn't complied with orders to pay you, sell property, or disburse assets, your lawyer must file a motion to make them act accordingly. Eventually, it could morph into a contempt of court order but the motions are the first step to get whatever is at stake in front of a judge. Review Chapter 11 regarding the hues of grey in the divorce decree to prevent these post-divorce motions from slowing down your ability to move on with your life narc-free. If you protect yourself with consequences for non-action in the original decree, much of this might be avoided.

Court Motion to Delay

A motion to delay is a request by either party to reschedule a hearing or trial date. Intentionally delaying hearings with the sole intention to slow down orders would be a concern if, for example, a spouse wants to push back the start date for paying temporary support. It's a huge inconvenience to the party requesting the money as this moratorium may leave them in dire financial straits. A motion of this nature usually needs a substantial cause to delay such as an unavailable essential witness, a death, or other excusable circumstance. To this point, the Trial Court Delay Reduction Act stipulates the requirement of courts to ensure prompt disposition of civil cases. They cannot drag on and on.

Changing of local counsel is typically an accepted reason for a delay because a new lawyer would need to get up to speed with their new client. Since this is an approved way to delay, narcissists are famous for changing lawyers. Most judges are aware of this angle and they are generally opposed to it. This doesn't mean that your spouse still won't try it a few times...like the old saying goes: "It ain't over till the fat lady sings."

The truth about contempt of court

What is contempt of court in family court? When we are seeking to understand the action that a judge will take if your ex doesn't comply with court orders, it can be very confusing. A judge has the power to impose a contempt of court charge on anyone who is being unlawful in their courtroom, disobeying their orders, or displaying uncooperative behavior. The line, however, gets blurred comparatively against what we think should happen versus what a judge's actions reflect.

Each state and country has their own guidelines regarding this charge. For example, the guideline for my state is as follows:

Colorado Rule of Civil Procedure 107(a) defines **contempt** *as: Disorderly or disruptive behavior, a breach of the peace, boisterous conduct or violent disturbance toward the court, or conduct that unreasonably interrupts the due course of judicial proceedings; behavior that obstructs the administration of justice; disobedience or resistance by any person to or interference with any lawful writ, process, or order of the court; or any other act or omission designated as contempt by the statutes or these rules.*

I have worked with people whose judge was forced to threaten the charge of contempt to their spouse to spur them to comply with the guidelines of paperwork and discovery. This is usually shot out as a warning for the lawyers to get their client to cooperate – it is strictly up to the judge whether or not they take action with jail time. No one should risk being in contempt of court but I can assure you that your narcissistic spouse will test the judge's patience with stonewalling and obstruction tactics, pulling away once they realize the judge means business. Expect them to push the envelope but they usually get a heads up from their lawyer when they are walking too thin of a line.

Contempt of court charges are more often seen as your legal recourse and filed when your narc-spouse defies orders post-divorce. If they don't pay child support or alimony or sell the house as they were ordered to and consequences have not already been established in the decree, your job will be to take them back to court to make them comply. The general sentence for contempt of court is to spend some time in an orange jumpsuit; that is it, after you've spent thousands of additional dollars just to get what has already been awarded to you. That is standard with a narcissist: they don't comply which forces you to file contempt charges and spend extra money to restart the process. Then, at the last minute, the alimony (or whatever the case) gets paid. You will drop the case, knowing the cat and mouse game will repeatedly occur. Fair warning: do not be upset when there are no penalties assessed for their noncompliance. When we await justice that never comes for repeated bad behavior, we find ourselves wounded again, this time by the court system. If due process is attempted, the judge will take the contempt charge into consideration and hopefully do what they can within the guidelines to favor you for doing the right thing. The only justice I saw in my case was in the end as the judge read his final ruling. He said that because my husband disobeyed his orders, he was granting me a larger piece of the pie.

What can you do to avoid this merry-go-round? As I have mentioned several times up to this point, do anything in your power to make your divorce decree as narc-proof as possible, with penalties if they don't pay or comply with the court orders. Take any opportunities that arise to use your new knowledge and forethought to beat them at their own game.

How to face them in court

Going up against your soon-to-be ex in a courtroom can be terrifying. After everything they have done to you thus far, you must now face them, maybe for the first time since the divorce started. Bolster your fortitude by bringing your own cheering section of friends and family.

Their presence and support will inject you with confidence. There is strength in numbers.

Something that can catch a victim off guard is the courthouse arrival. No matter how hard you try, it never fails that you both will arrive at the exact same time at some point during the hearings. Meeting a spouse at the X-ray machine is a real possibility. Prepare for it and arrange to enter with a friend or meet your lawyer outside so you can walk in together.

If you are unable to avoid walking in alone, have a strategy in place to meet your lawyer so you have a objective once you enter the building. Most courthouses have small rooms where lawyers meet with their clients prior to trials.

For your peace of mind, avoid eye contact with your ex, their family, or any of their supporters. In your vulnerable state, a trigger of this magnitude could have a negative effect on your mental preparation. You are already in a high stress environment so make every effort to not exacerbate the issue. When walking into the courtroom, divert your eyes away or to the friendly faces in your corner. Keep your mind sharp and positive for the happy future you are there to put into place.

If you take the stand, focus your attention on the judge and your legal team. Refrain from looking at your spouse's face in order to stay grounded. When they get on the stand, write down anything that you may want your lawyer to dispute later. Consider carrying a crystal or squishy ball that you can keep in your hand under the table to relieve the strain of being in the courtroom.

At one of my many hearings, I became so incensed by his lawyer's lies, coupled with the smirks on his and his parent's faces, I completely lost it. I did! There were no tears like so many times before. I thought I was being discrete – I guess I failed – but I gave them the finger. It wasn't the in-your-face finger but I did place my hand on my face with a particular finger fully extended. Not my proudest moment; I was harshly scolded by his attorney…and then the screaming started. The judge reprimanded me and I was warned against a repeat performance. I was blinded in that moment by rage and I vented my frustration without thinking it through. While I wouldn't do it again, because pissing off your judge is never a good idea, it offered me a flash of satisfaction and comfort. I recognize now how careless it was and that it could have cost me dearly. Never lose sight of who you are. Let the narcissist do their thing and bury themselves with their aggressive behaviors.

> **When you go to court, never interrupt the judge:** Nothing good comes from this. Maintain your credibility and wait for your turn to speak. Also, refrain from facial gestures, or grunting noises while your spouse or their attorney is talking to the judge.
>
> **Jason Levoy,** former divorce attorney turned coach, creator of DivorceU

Things to do once the divorce is final

Congratulations! I told you that one day this nightmare would be over. The fear you have struggled with will linger a bit longer until you get grounded in your new routines, but these will be happy times. I want to remind you of the steps you should take throughout the decoupling process to separate and sever all unfinished business. Take the time now to do everything at once or risk triggering yourself later if you piecemeal them out in small stages. Rip off the Band-Aid, feel the pain, and move on.

Is your plan to go back to your maiden name? If so, save yourself time and money by including it as part of your plan. You typically need to provide the divorce decree to legally change your name for some agencies and businesses but some states will automatically make the change with the finalization of the divorce. Use the decree where necessary to update your name on your driver's license, social security card, credit cards, and all other accounts from PayPal to Amazon. This would also be the best time to apply for a passport with your new name. So often the driver's license gets addressed but the passport gets forgotten, especially if it's not needed in the immediate future. If an opportunity comes up, you don't want the hassle then to make all your documents match. You can find the form online or at a post office and start the ball rolling before the need to travel arises. Update the car insurance to display your name only. This will give you control to register the car in your own name. While you're at it, streamline the car title, home insurance and healthcare package too. Follow the complete list I created in Chapter 5 for reference so nothing is forgotten.

Prepare new wills, both living and end of life. Remove your ex and assign your new beneficiary(s) for these as well as your life insurance, 401k, and retirement accounts. Contact a financial planner to establish an account for any money you may have been awarded in the settlement. Contact your employer to update your name and W-4 tax filing status. These might be easy to overlook considering all the details that will require your attention but in the event that something does happen to you, you want to be sure that whomever you choose gets the money or other benefits. If you have children, you may want to review who was assigned to be their guardian in your absence. That might need to be modified. Think carefully and choose the person who you trust implicitly to make any medical decisions in your stead. I am familiar with cases where this was not handled in a timely fashion and the ex-spouse showed up at the hospital to make the end-of-life decisions because they still had that original document. This can literally be a life-or-death situation.

While I'm sure the attorney that you choose will be well qualified, ensure that when your legal documents are rewritten, they include wording that supersedes all previous documents. If your children are older, give them copies of everything; reliable friends or relatives are excellent resources to safeguard current copies as well.

Did you know that your lawyer can request to have your divorce records sealed? If untrue things were said or you wish the financial exposure to remain private, the judge can take care of that for you. Speak up – no one will protect you better at this point than you. You are and always will be your own best advocate.

Notify your children's school that the divorce is final and ask that the teachers alert you if the kids appear to be struggling in any way. That can be a potential problem that you will want to nip in the bud immediately before it becomes a runaway train.

Finally, ask your lawyer for the electronic file of your divorce for your records. This small detail could save you from running up another legal bill later if you need any of the records going forward. While you are entitled to have the file, the onus will be on you to ensure you receive the complete package. It is your property, after all, so don't be afraid to ask for it!

Chapter 13

BACK TO NORMAL?

*"Universe, if you could just get my life back to normal – I will make it work." – **Tracy A. Malone***

Survivors always ask me, "When will my life go back to normal?" I usually respond with, "What did normal look like?" What might have seemed normal before you broke free from your narcissistic spouse may not be the normal you strive for now. Your goal should be to imagine, design, create, and implement a glorious new chapter going forward for your life.

"My normal was so abnormal that I normalized the crazy."
*– **Tracy A. Malone***

I believe that our lives are just like a book. Each period has chapters full of characters, locations, and things we accomplished. For example, if you look back, you might have lived a seemingly innocuous childhood in the same house, with your family and a pet, taking vacations in the summertime. Throughout your teenage years, school and friends may have topped the list, and if you are lucky, you remain friends with some of them to this day. It's natural that not all would have continued in your story; not everyone was intended to and that is okay.

> *"People come into your life for a reason, a season or a lifetime."*
> – ***Author unknown***

There will be friends, neighbors, coworkers, and people from your spouse's family as well as your own who may not continue into the next phase of your life. You may grieve some of these people and feel an overwhelming sadness for the losses, perhaps even anger at the injustice of it all. Why does the end of a marriage mean you may never talk to certain people again who have been a part of your life for years? I call these people casualties of war. Don't be fooled: these casualties happen in non-narcissistic divorces too. Either way, it hurts. Trust the universe that the people who stay in your life are the ones who are meant to be there.

As I was going through my divorce, my therapist repeated a quote so frequently that it became an automated internal message that I repeated to myself every time I felt sad about what I saw happening around me. I see it as my mantra and I keep it close, handwritten on my desk. I share it with clients who need to hear it.

> *"You don't know if you have been denied heaven or spared from hell."* – ***Author unknown***

It is easy to look back at your married life and overlook how unhappy you were much of the time. You may only feel sorrow that the happy times you *do* remember are gone. It is truly the end of a dream and a living nightmare, all in a single breath. The abandonment wounds that you carry with you will take time to heal as the scorched earth that the divorce leaves behind sprouts renewed life. Your past only defines you if you let it. This traumatic stage in your life will register as nothing more than a rough patch once you get through it. Letting go is scary but holding on will only cause more pain. Today is a new beginning.

This book has outlined many tricks narcissists pull during divorce.

Unfortunately, there are more not included here. There will always be more. What is experienced during a narcissistic divorce is not normal but you will survive to write your next chapter. What choice do you have? Focus on healing the feeling rather the actual details of the event.

By this time, I'm confident you can see that a drama-filled, verbally abusive marriage is unacceptable; wishing for a life with an abuser equates to killing your own soul. Sadly, the covert abuse I experienced in my marriage was my "normal," and without knowing anything different, my desire to get back to normal allowed me to be blindly scooped up by an evil sociopath. I do not want this to happen to you too.

Now is the time to imagine what your next era will look like and what you want your new normal to represent. Write down the goals you have for the future. They are endless. Tap into your emotions from this point forward. Visualize a perfect world full of the types of people you want to love, places where you desire to travel, and most of all, how you want to feel. Identify your future and believe that it will happen exactly as you dream it to be. Take one step toward that dream every day.

Finally, it is time to heal your wounds. There is no Betty Ford Clinic or cookie-cutter cure for narcissistic abuse recovery. While many of us may have similar divorce and co-parenting battle stories, the injuries we have suffered are vastly different based on what we had to endure and for how long. To add insult to injury, childhood wounds often get discovered during the recovery phase which adds an additional layer of pain. For me, I needed to look hard at my childhood in order to see how much healing was in my future. Taking accountability of what happened to me freed me from the victim status that I had waved like a flag my entire life. While this sounds like awful wisdom to gain, consider it a blessing. It is what separates us from someone with NPD as they will never take responsibility or learn from mistakes. I do not encourage you to look at your marriage as a mistake but rather as your opportunity to evolve into a healthier person. Grab your happiness with both hands and hold onto it with all your might. What did you learn?

I, personally, learned that letting my wounds go untended made me vulnerable and set me up as narc-bait. My boundaries were tested and my weaknesses were found and exploited. It has been scientifically proven that to not actively heal open emotional wounds can make you physically ill. Think back to any physical health issues you may have dealt with while you were with your narcissist. Do not discount the reality that the abuse you suffered caused those physical symptoms to manifest in ways that can be explained and understood. When you understand how you were made to feel in certain situations, you will recognize the symptoms as something much deeper and more importantly, something fixable.

I suggest that you study books like *The Body Keeps the Score* by Bessel van der Kolk or *Feelings Buried Alive Never Die* by Karol Kuhn Truman. Both outline how physical symptoms are caused from emotional trauma. During my marriage, I was diagnosed with irritable bowel syndrome (IBS). I was always unwell and my husband would make fun of me for being "sickly, just like your mother" (it was a passive-aggressive trigger that he knew would piss me off). Once I was free of his covert abuse, I never experienced those symptoms again.

I look back on my journey to recovery as a gift because through it all, I have acquired the self-help bug and I know that I will never stop my quest to continue evolving into a better person. It's not that I haven't healed and found my new normal, but I find that what I now consider normal fosters my own improvements. I practice self-love by educating myself to be the best me, for me. And what's more, I have found the voice and platform to help others do the same which is an unexpectedly beneficial happenstance that I had not even considered. It really is not a cliché to say that helping others is gratifying; I never lose sight of the fact that it is not about me but rather the person who has reached out for my help.

In the beginning, I studied narcissistic personality disorder and was rewarded with the first piece of my recovery puzzle: I understood who I had dated, who I had married, and most importantly, why. Once I determined that the attention shouldn't be focused on red flags and cycles of abuse but rather the direct question, "Why me?," I discovered I was raised by a narcissistic mother and an emotionally unavailable stepfather. This was the wound aching to be healed. I had my answer so I dedicated myself to solving the problem.

I worked with talented therapists, I took courses, and I constantly fed my soul a new diet of information that I never learned as a child. I read so many books that I stopped counting. As everyone does, I trusted YouTube to teach me that I was not alone or crazy. I attended every online summit I could find in my search for more pieces of *my* puzzle; and I grew stronger.

My healing process catapulted me forward once I shifted my concentration off the narcissists in my history and placed it squarely onto myself instead. There is a reason that I teach "understanding fear" at the beginning of each support group. Until we can successfully navigate and regulate our fear, we will never be in control of the pen to write our new chapters. We must face our fears, eyeball to eyeball, and understand their roots without a shadow of a doubt in order to create custom strategies to deploy whenever we smell them creeping back into our soul.

Stuck in ruminating thoughts

We can contemplate the good times or we can focus on the chaos and pain. At the beginning of your recovery, paramount to anything else will be validation for all of the terrible things that happened in your marriage and divorce. Once you *substantiate* the bad memories, begin the process of discrediting the good ones you are holding onto because unraveling this toxic period of your life must be addressed. Is there any truth behind your recollections? Were they really as good as you remember? We tend to hold on tightly to what is good and that is what keeps us trauma bonded to the person responsible for the damage sustained. You may recall a great vacation with the family, but how did your narcissist act? Did they ruin it? Are you idealizing those memories for any particular reason? In my recovery, it took years before I started to look more closely at my partner's abusive behaviors sprinkled into those times when I thought I was untroubled. While we experienced amazing holidays together, I was cherishing the ideal of a family together. Clinging to the acceptable moments will only keep you more deeply entrenched in the big lie and generate roadblocks to the healing process, but doing the work and dissecting them will help break the bond that holds your heart captive. Be brutally honest with yourself: allow yourself to really see the narcissistic behaviors for what they were and all the terrible things that were done to you, even during those "good times." You can more easily let go of the illusion and heal than if you continue to deny the truth. The further you step away from a situation, the less foggy the mirror becomes. The next time you have a ruminating thought playing ping pong in your mind, write down everything you can remember about it. Were all the responsibilities left to you from inception to completion? Did they get angry or sad or demand constant attention? Seeing the details on paper will be helpful to let go of the fantasy of that event.

How to heal emotional abuse

It is difficult to know where and how to start your recovery journey to your new happiness. My recommendation always is: educate yourself, understand your accountability, and accept your portion of the responsibility. Give yourself permission to not be perfect. You can visit the pain of the breakup or loss but do not live there. When you are ready to get help and move on, you will.

Learn to let go – The first step to begin the healing process is to let go of the fact that you will possibly never understand what happened to you or why. Giving up the need for vindication will also allow healing at an accelerated rate. Letting go of the idea that a narcissist will willingly give the requested closure is simply an illusion that will impede your recovery. What are you holding on to?

Be willing to fail – To fail at something does not make you a failure; never let it stop you from putting yourself out there. There is always a lesson. Seek it out to avoid making the same mistake twice.

Be your own best friend – Learn to appreciate the time that you spend alone and practice self-love. Find things to do that you enjoy. Be the best friend that you always wanted. Feeling happy and content when you are alone is the first step to move forward in your journey.

Learn boundaries – Define your boundaries, determine penalties when they are crossed, communicate them, and honor yourself by enforcing them. Don't be afraid to test other people's ability to respect your boundaries often.

Listen to your intuition – Accept the signs your body is telling you. Your inner child, or spirit, is warning you when something is not right. Stop and listen!

Determine your core beliefs – Write down your expectations and refer to them often. Love yourself, listen to your intuition, and never accept being taken advantage of again. If anyone violates the parameters you have set, evaluate and remove the offenders swiftly.

Find gratitude – Everything you have is a gift, from the stars and flowers to the rain. Give thanks every day. When you learn to have gratitude for what you have now instead of wishing for more or longing for the past, you will find that you have everything you need; peace will return.

Control your feelings – Understand that you have the power to turn bad emotions into positive ones. Similar to muscle memory, this is a skill that you must exercise daily to keep strong. If you find that emotions are ruling your life, look at rephrasing your story in order to keep that emotional calm and balance.

Understand fear – Everything you want is on the other side of fear. Move through it steadily and with confidence. Remember that fear steals tomorrow, it does not fix yesterday.

Work hard for tomorrow – No one owes you anything but you owe yourself everything. Take care of yourself and the world is yours.

Date and marry yourself – Learn to do things on your own. Be brave and enjoy time alone to do all the things that you wish to share with a future partner. In sickness and in health, learn to self-care, provide for, and love yourself. When you can care for yourself without the need of someone else to complete you, you will find happiness.

Take calculated risks – Be smart, do research, weigh benefits against risks, and listen to your intuition. Put yourself out there but be smart and keep your eyes open. Always take care of yourself first.

Live for today – Understand the past and forget the mistakes but always remember the lesson. When we live in the past, we are not living, we are reliving.

Accept that you cannot please everyone – Our job in life is to make our own joy, not to make other people happy. Let go of criticism directed at you; you can't control it anyway.

Perfection is not possible – Fairy tales are made up stories and Prince Charming is a Disney character. People are meant to have their own passions, not live vicariously through others. Don't be fooled by someone who claims to be more than your gut tells you that they are. If it (they) sounds too good to be true, it (they) probably is.

Life changes – The hills and valleys of life are just like chapters in a book: they begin and they end. Learn to accept the changes and roll with the punches. Revise your story to include new possibilities – you have the crayon to write the rest of your story.

Never lose your "happy" – Happiness is a state of mind which is completely controlled by your own thoughts. Practice mindfulness and always stay in the moment. You can't get the time back once it has passed.

Study forgiveness – Forgiveness is not about erasing or condoning bad behavior but rather detaching the emotional charge from the offenses so the negativity derived from them does not control your feelings. To heal your wounds, you must learn to forgive yourself and let go of the guilt that will weigh you down which will hinder your progress toward positivity. The lesson I learned was that I did not need to tell my narcissist that I forgave him – that was mine to release and it was only for me. It had nothing to do with him.

Keep dreaming – When you have a dream, set the goals to get there. Work hard to make them your reality. Without a plan, a dream is just a wish.

Trust again, learn to love yourself again, and believe in a brighter tomorrow.

Summoning emotional resilience

Initially, it's hard to reconcile the fact that you will be replaced as a spouse or a parent. In time, you will learn to deal with the new people in your ex's and children's lives even though much healing will be involved to come to grips with that reality. That is okay, it's all part of the process. When you're able to get past the fear of the unknown and understand the wounds and vulnerabilities caused by the abuse, you will finally find the resolve to make it happen. When you get there, you will be ready for it.

If you were the discarder, you will feel yourself growing stronger, building resilience, and see yourself gaining back your life. You will very possibly experience regret and wonder if you made the right decision. As long as you remember that the abuser cannot change, your life will be better without them. You made the right choice because now you can soar with no expectation to ever be held down again.

If you were the discarded, you may find yourself with abandonment wounds and trust issues. Each person comes into a new relationship with baggage so every direction for recovery will be different. This is when you should stop watching NPD videos and start studying healing with even more dedication and gusto than you gave to learning about the narcissist. Set practical goals and continually explore new topics to study and get stronger.

Recovery is like an iceberg: the depth of the problem will be unknown until you start the exploration. You won't really perceive what needs to be learned or what is most helpful until you broach different subjects to study. Some might be dead on and address exactly what you're looking for while others may offer only a nugget of useful material. My advice is to try everything. Don't give up just because a particular topic doesn't match up perfectly like you think it should. Knowledge is power, no matter how you slice it.

Explore ideas that are destined to help your soul thrive for the rest of your life. Finding happiness in yourself first is paramount; then look for what you need out of your next relationship. The erosion of our self and who we were was broken by the narcissistic abuse, but it can be fixed. Trust the process and build new skills so you have the courage and strength to move on into your new beginning.

People have identified the recovery journey after divorce as the hardest thing they've ever had to do. After the end a marriage with a narcissist, it's easy to see that Pandora's Box has been opened. In addition to learning that our childhood might be a contributing factor to our trauma, we may now also recognize other people in our lives who are unhealthy and realize that their dysfunction may have been part of the reason we never understood the abuse in our marriage. Toxicity spreads like a disease.

If you are wondering how long it takes to reach recovery, my answer is, it depends. It will be based solely on the speed at which you study and heal: if you only do the basic work and put out fires, expect the results to be delayed. This will not be a quick fix so do not be under that assumption.

Biting the bullet and going no contact will offer the benefit of faster healing; that is a proven fact. Unfortunately, not all people have this luxury. If you are co-parenting, the journey will assuredly last longer because you must keep that connection, even if it's limited. Once the kids are grown and you have no need to communicate with your ex again, you will be able to see the light at the end of the tunnel much more clearly. If you find yourself worn down from the co-parenting battle and feel your own healing is out of focus, fight the urge to give up and do nothing. Put on your oxygen mask first; by learning to manage your emotions and avoid being triggered, you gain stability. That is how you take back your life.

A key to healing comes with the comprehension that you had the strength to stand on your own all along. One of the cruelest side effects of emotional abuse is the ingrained belief that we are un-lovable because one person, who is incapable of long-lasting love, doesn't love us. We forget the multitude of loving and supportive family members and friends who do love us. Don't drink the poison. If you never love again, the poison worked; if you never trust again, the poison worked. Self-love is always the antidote.

Break the self-blame cycle with self-compassion: Narcissists love to blame other people for their mistakes and shortcomings. So, you've probably been blamed for things you couldn't control, accused of things you didn't do, and shamed into thinking you're inadequate or worthless. Unfortunately, when you're repeatedly exposed to this type of toxic behavior and thinking, you internalize it and learn to blame and devalue yourself. This is why divorcing your narcissistic spouse probably won't automatically free you from blame or restore your self-worth.

Self-compassion – being kind to yourself -- can help you break the cycle of self-blame: Self-compassion can include affirming your feelings, prioritizing self-care, accepting your mistakes, or giving yourself the benefit of the doubt. The first element of self-compassion is to acknowledge that you're struggling (perhaps feeling like a failure, feeling overwhelmed or tired) and recognize that everyone struggles and deserves compassion; no one is perfect or has it all together.

When you notice that you're being hard on yourself, take a few moments to write down exactly what your self-critical voice is saying: Next, acknowledge your self-critical voice and respond to it in a positive and caring way, like something you'd say to a friend. Here's an example: Self-critical voice: "You're so stupid. Why did you ask Travis to take Maggie to ballet class? You should have known he'd blow up!" Compassionate response: "I know you wanted Maggie to be able to go to class; ballet means so much to her. It's not your fault that Travis blew up." Practicing self-compassion exercises regularly, such as this one, can help you break the self-blame cycle and restore your sense of worth!

Sharon Martin, author, psychotherapist

Getting closure: it is different for everyone

We all seek closure to help us package everything up in a neat little bundle. It is human nature to want this but it doesn't always happen when dealing with a narcissist. When I speak with survivors, I ask them what closure looks like to them as it is different for everyone.

A common response is that they want to be heard, to be given the opportunity to tell the narcissistic ex exactly what they did to them, and they want them to listen. Others wish for an apology or restitution for the things that they said, did, or are currently doing. Asking for an apology from a narcissist never really works out well because in their minds, you are the problem, not them. If you had only... if you hadn't... then they wouldn't have been forced to do what they did. You have been demonized with their black-and-white thinking and it's all your fault. If they do apologize, they won't mean it. In the end, it won't make you feel better because you will see the obvious insincerity which will only stir your anger all over again. They might be sorry they got caught or that people were exposed to the truth about them during the court process, but they will never be sorry for what they did to you. The sooner you rid yourself of the delusion that they will ever come to their senses and ask for forgiveness, or somehow bring you peace, the faster you will lean in toward finding it on your own.

Since you will be unable to get closure from them, you must find it on your own for yourself. If you are just beginning this process and still full of anger from the divorce, getting to this point is unimaginable, and that is okay. Later in your recovery, as you can see the port through the storm, it will be the key to healing.

Closure is all about you. What would it look like to you? Can you let go of the anger? Can you forgive yourself? Can you forgive them and move beyond the hurt? Can you trust again? Do you trust yourself? Closure is personal and is directly correlated to how much time has passed since the trauma and betrayal. The last exercise I will suggest is to write out what closure looks like to you and set it up as a goal (or multiple goals, if that is what it will take to get you there). Allow yourself the space and patience to move at your own pace. Perform periodic check-ins to ensure you are moving in the right direction. It is an honor system and it is important that you respect yourself throughout the process because it will be long and it will be uncomfortable. The amount you will learn about yourself, however, will make it all worth it in the end.

Succinctly put, getting closure after narcissistic abuse is identifying your wounds caused by this abuse (and perhaps a lifetime of abuse), forgiving yourself, building trust again, and finding the strength to carry on to create the life you desire. You are a blank canvas and your goals are the paint. Dream big.

True recovery and the first year of firsts

The first year of firsts is hard. No matter how detached you feel you are at the end of your divorce, the triggers caused by the events of your life will never fail to raise the hairs on the back of your neck. The first solitary Valentine's Day or anniversary may be met with sadness or anger since they now represent all of the wasted years. The first birthday or Christmas morning that you don't wake up to see your kids' happy faces as they blow out candles or open gifts will be difficult as you learn to deal with the emotional roller coaster that divorce causes.

Calendar triggers are different from those generated by location or events. You can steer clear of your favorite restaurant where you became engaged or your friend's annual Super Bowl party to circumvent the memories of some especially significant occasions, but the calendar triggers are unavoidable. Like any trigger, they bring up memories, both good and bad: joy, excitement, hope, resentment, anger, sadness, as well as open the wounds of abandonment. What starts out as a simple date on the calendar suddenly places a spotlight on and amplifies feelings that you thought you had under control. You must go through this first year of firsts; it's part of the grieving process. You are grieving the loss of the times you had together and will never have again, the loss of a secure future with the person you trusted, and the loss of people who you expected to always be around. There will be sad days where you feel very alone and your mind will extrapolate fear of your unknown future, easily catastrophizing that you will be single for the rest of your life. Be aware if these thoughts come to mind, identify them, and give yourself a slap of reality. You have friends, you are loved, and you will only be alone if want to be. Build your new life. You have the power. You are the master of your universe.

I recall when I was going through my divorce and one of my best friends told me to get out my calendar and make plans in advance with friends on the days I knew would be hard. Distractions can help to create new traditions and new memories so that these calendar triggers become just another day. Memories hold the emotional charge. Our minds will play tricks on us so expect "the suck." If you are able to find a way to divert your thoughts from the importance of the day, you will walk away stronger. It is usually healthier to be distracted by others, if only for a few hours, than to suffer in silence. Resist the urge to "go it alone" and empower yourself toward a faster recovery from your first year of firsts. Talk to a therapist if things get hard, you can't recover as fast as you would like to, or have trouble dealing with the events as they unfold. There is never shame in asking for help.

My own journey to create new traditions has evolved over the years. At first, I felt like a third wheel crashing other family's traditions. I wondered why some people I thought were my friends didn't offer to take me in and that initially amplified my sadness and sense of abandonment. One thing I quickly learned was that I couldn't control how other people stepped up or, in my case, how many did not step up as I thought they might. I realized that when I set my expectations in relation to how I wished they would have acted, it made me feel sad and lonely. Instead of needing to be rescued on a holiday, I took control and invited others to be with me as I surged forward to establish my new sense of self. I love to cook and entertain so when I took back my kitchen and the joy of setting a holiday table, I knew I was living my new life.

My recovery journey – the next chapter

I refer to "my recovery" as a new chapter in my life because it has taken many years of learning, growing, and healing to get where I am today. I honestly love the peaceful and drama-free life I have painstakingly built for myself. I feel a deep appreciation when I get up in the morning, look out over the lake, and know that my day will be whatever I choose it to be. It excites me to continue to learn about spirituality, resilience, courage, and attracting the life that I want.

It is critical to remember, especially at the precarious beginning of your recovery, that everyone's wounds are their own; my prescription to become whole for the first time is not necessarily what your journey will encompass. The topics I studied had no order when I began. It was very much an educated approach: some things I tried helped me tremendously while others only a small part. I simply picked up another book and searched for the next piece that fit.

Many of the teachers I listened to made the claim that if you were abused, you must be codependent, so I started there; I even attended a CODA meeting. Codependency is a series of behaviors that often are adopted in an abusive situation as coping mechanisms. Once we are removed from the abuse, the strategies of people pleasing and the learned knee-jerk reaction to put other's needs before our own can be replaced with healthier coping skills. Through my research, I concluded that labeling every victim as anything specific could only be generalized at best and may not be inclusive for everyone. Certain things about it made sense but I needed to know more.

Learning about boundaries made me realize that I had never set any before which made me perfect supply for narcissists to abuse. I was not taught how to set boundaries by my family of origin nor was I familiar with the term people pleaser, although of all the things I discovered about myself, I find this one described me the best. I hear my mom's voice in my head telling me to be a "nice girl," and to put other's needs before my own. I now realize the irony of this lesson which came from a narcissistic mother who always had to have her needs met first. Narcissists are takers and hunt for people pleasers to be their slaves. In my relationships, I was always apprehensive, looking for the balance, but because of my people pleasing training, I was perfectly matched with men who would abuse my kindness. Life will change drastically when you learn to say no.

During and after the divorce, my body was in severe adrenal fatigue. The CPTSD, the anxiety, and the sleepless nights all brought me down and I was weak. I saw an amazing homeopathic doctor who helped get my system out of the adrenal fatigue along with the fight, flight, and freeze mode that was doing additional damage to my body and mind. That was another turning point in my recovery: my regular medical doctor had been solely treating my symptoms with drugs. While I firmly believe that meds have a time and place in recovery, I hated taking them and was glad to find a solution that not only masked the outward indications but also made my body stronger. Prior to finding my new path, I lost four pants sizes because I had no appetite; working with the homeopathic doctor, I found I could eat more, sleep restfully, and gain back the strength I needed to continue in my battle with gusto.

I sought out traditional therapy with multiple counselors and built a foundation of knowledge and validation for the abuse I had endured. I then attended my first therapist led support group and I learned the power of other survivors. Along with my new found homeo-pathic treatments, I incorporated acupuncture and light therapy into my health plan as well as energy workers who specialized in moving energy in the body. I even had my lymph nodes drained once a month – who knew this was a thing! I tried Brainspotting[26], had spiritual readings, Reiki sessions, and not willing to discount anything, agreed to have gong-like bowls[27] played over my head, as I wondered, "How can this possibly help me?" I did tapping sessions, family constel-lation work, and I studied the A Course in Miracles[28]. I cleared my energetic chakras and studied the power of crystals like it was my religion. I carried crystals in my pockets and truth be told, I often shoved a brown crystal into my bra as I was told that it would keep me grounded all day. I did energetic cord cutting sessions, I smudged my house with burning sage, and I even put salt in every corner of my house to clear out the negative energy that was attached to our marital belongings. I became addicted to Angel cards and the positive hope they gave me. CBD was a good find because it helped me sleep

---

26 According to Brainspotting.com, Brainspotting is a powerful, focused treatment method that works by identifying, processing and releasing core neurophysiological sources of emotional/body pain, trauma, dissociation and a variety of other challenging symptoms.

27 Tibetan sound bowls are used by tapping the bowl gently with a mallet and then circling the bowl with different amounts of pressure and speed to vary the sounds. Sound bowl healing works when the bowls are played to elicit prolonged sounds that emit varying vibrational frequencies.

28 Find this information at https://acim.org/

without any negative side effects. I learned to meditate, I practiced strategies to calm my fear and anxiety, and essential oils could be found in diffusers all over my house because they brought a sense of tranquility that I longed for.

I tried everything I could get my hands on and I believe they all helped in some way. Some of my efforts may seem very new age and way out of the realm of normal recovery, but where I live in Boulder, Colorado, we have many modalities to explore and I was willing to do whatever I could to help my life get back on track. Recovery is about learning new things and trying anything.

The practices that I engaged in were meant to support my body and mind, but they were just the beginning. Reading books and educating myself on healing topics helped me locate other critical pieces to my developing puzzle. Not everything works for everyone. Select the options that sound the best suited for you. Add to them as you wish. Try various combinations because everyone's recovery wounds are different.

Learning about the abandonment wounds created by my family enabled me to see how the decisions I had made my entire life were based on fear versus love. I always assumed that abandonment meant the obvious: that Daddy or Mommy disappeared. While this type of wound absolutely can be created by the loss of someone, it can also be instilled by rejection, betrayal, or neglect. Once I made the distinction and could check off all the pertinent boxes, I was able to search for the answers of how to examine the wound, claim it, face it, and heal it. I learned that the most significant person who had abandoned me was me. That instigated the opening of new doors all around me to facilitate other pieces to fall into place.

As I studied fear, I came across a book called *Feel the Fear and Do It Anyway* by Susan Jeffers. Another quote that can be found on a sticky note on my desk comes from her book – "Whatever happens to me, given any situation, I can handle it!" Fear has the tendency to paralyze us and lead us to believe that we can't handle things adequately; if you look at situations that you have experienced thus far in your life and how you got through them, you may find the confidence to push the fear down and see the light filtering through the clouds. Think about it: you have lived with a narcissistic abuser and you're still here to tell the story. That is impressive as hell and something to be proud of.

When you choose to fill your mind with positive healing strategies, you will be granted a respite from the pain and negative energy that has filled your soul. Your road to recovery will not follow the same path as mine but it will involve taking your mind off the negative and replacing hope where fear has always lived. Each of us has a final destination pre-determined and built for our individual voyage, full of highs and lows. Imagine flattening the curve in relation to how low your depression can go. Instead of remaining in bed for five days, consider it a win when next time it is only three days; how fast you can recover and begin the upward momentum is a good progress indicator. Do not think that life will not throw you more challenges, because it always will. No matter what, keep learning, never stop growing, and, most importantly, be kind to yourself without exception. If you regress back into depression, fear, or anger, and it is possible, learn that forgiving yourself is essential to finding inner peace. Read books by Dr. Wayne Dyer and Brene Brown, and study radical forgiveness, letting go, and moving on. Be inspired by TEDx Talks and listen to the imagination and positivity of commencement speeches. Find the courage to write your next chapter and leave behind those who no longer have a place in your life. Fill your heart with gratitude every day and relish the fact that you are free from the danger and drama of your old existence. Open your heart to tomorrow and plan accordingly.

I could go on all day listing the plethora of topics I studied to heal myself. As I said, your prescription will not be the same as mine. Turn the sherlocking skills you perfected inward to find the answers you need to help you heal and raise your energetic footprint that will repel the lower energy people with NPD. You will win because you always did.

The value of finding support

When my husband asked for the divorce, it blindsided me, which thrust me into a spiraling state of depression, anxiety, fear, and aloneness. A dear friend suggested I find a divorce support group right away. I joined a 12-week program with 40 others that met once a week for three hours and began the work before the actual papers were ever filed. Since everyone was in a different stage of the divorce process, the ones further along organically became mentors and lead us fledglings down the road of expectations. This was not a narcissistic abuse divorce group but the new friends I made became my lifeline.

After I learned what narcissistic abuse was, I joined a second smaller group of five women that was run by a therapist. That was immensely helpful and I was able to get validation for my specific challenges that I desperately needed. Unfortunately, due to my legal bills at the time, I was unable to sustain the cost involved so I decided to start my own group.

A big part of my recovery began when I formed my first in-person support group in 2016. I set the group up on meetup.com and I waited for people to find me. If you build it, they will come. About a month later, I received a call from a woman who asked when the group would begin. I hadn't realized that twenty people had signed up! So it began. I can admit that even though I started the group, each time I met with other survivors, I healed. I believe that leading the group pushed me to keep learning so I could help others. Now, I run two Colorado-based groups, one in Boulder and one in Denver. We meet at local libraries once a month where everyone looks forward to speak and learn strategies from others. In 2020, Covid shut down all in-person activities so I adjusted and transferred my groups online. Nothing compares to the friendships made in a group with a common struggle. Community is essential to healing.

Also in 2016, I started my resource website NarcissistAbuseSupport.com where I maintain a directory of support groups from all over the world[29]. Visit the website to see if there is one near you. Some

---

29   https://narcissistabusesupport.com/book-resources/

groups are run by therapists and may have charges associated while others are run at no cost by survivors and coaches like myself who have stepped up to bring people together to help each other heal. Sadly, some have found that there are no groups available in their vicinity when they look at the list. It's true: some show only one group in the entire state. Because of this, I have created an online course based on what I learned which teaches people how to start their own narcissistic abuse support group. You can also find that on the website[30]. I was far from an expert in the beginning so do not think that is a prerequisite; just step up and bring the people together and they will help you heal. The rest will fall into place. As my knowledge grew and I found my voice, I became a speaker at many online events. Many of these are free which I happily pass along to any and all who would be interested in learning more.

Another suggestion to find support is by joining a Facebook group. I started my Facebook group which now has over 15,000 members from all over the world. We are one of the smaller communities out there; I have a friend whose page has over 60,000. My admins are volunteers who have been with me for many years and they help moderate the conversations to ensure our rules are followed, for safety reasons. Day or night, you can pop into a group and get feedback, validation, and support. I want to thank them again for their tireless dedication to foster support for others with love and compassion.

Get Support: When we need support the most, we often choose to "go it alone." We do this for so many reasons. Maybe we're afraid of judgment, we're feeling shame, embarrassment or we're just not comfortable being vulnerable. It could also be that we're really comfortable giving to others yet we struggle with receiving. Well, now it's your time to receive. Think of how great you feel when you give to others. Choosing to keep pain to yourself is taking away that same opportunity someone could have to help you. Recovering after a painful breakup may also mean that you need support from a

---

30   https://narcissistabusesupport.com/book-resources/

qualified professional. Be careful here because someone not skilled in the specific area you need help with could do more harm than good. For example, if you broke up with a gaslighter or narcissist, someone unskilled could have you believing you were at fault (of course we need to take responsibility for our part in relationships, that's not what I mean). Or, someone lacking empathy could try to "help" by telling you to "put it behind you," "get over it," or "just move on." While well-meaning, you need to process your breakup and grieve the loss before you can put it behind you for good.

Self-Care: The stress from your divorce is likely to take a toll on your body, mind, and spirit. Left unchecked, that stress could lead to symptoms, illness, conditions, and disease. Take some time for self-care, whether that means more rest, eating healthier, moving, spending time in nature, beginning or restarting a daily practice of meditation, journaling, yoga, etc. Also, if your divorce is due to a betrayal, there's lots of cleanup left in the wake of this type of life crisis.

Write your coherent narrative: What's that? A coherent narrative is when you take what may have become your life story and turn it into a pivotal chapter of your story. You are learning to make sense and find meaning out of your experience by writing (either figuratively or literally) the story of your relationship and breakup. It's common that by the time you're done with this activity, you see the benefit in all you've learned, along with what you're no longer willing to accept or tolerate. It's also common to see how that person who hurt you was actually one of your greatest teachers; showing you what new boundaries need to be in place and just how lovable, deserving and worthy you are. Whether you give yourself sentence prompts like, "I learned…," "The benefit of this experience was…," or "What I'll do differently next time is…," this is an important activity that signals the body and mind that you're ready to heal.

Debi Silber, author, holistic psychologist, founder of The PBT (Post Betrayal Transformation) Institute

Finding peace by having faith

My family never went to church and we did not practice any particular religion but we celebrated Christmas, Hanukkah, and Easter. There was no spirituality in our home except when my mom pretended to be a church member or when she used the Lord's name in vain to yell at me and my sisters.

> If you had a Hijackal® parent, that is, one with narcissistic, passive-aggressive tendencies or worse, you may tend to overlook the red flags in other people's poor behavior. Get help so you won't continue to settle for the familiar, hooked on the hope that *this time* you'll be loved.
>
> Sadly, you cannot love a Hijackal out of behaving badly. No amount of bending to please will change them. They will twist, turn, and move the markers. Empower yourself by clarifying, expressing, and maintaining non-negotiable boundaries. Don't settle.
>
> **Rhoberta Shaler,** "The Relationship Help Doctor," host of the Podcast, Save Your Sanity: Help for Toxic Relationships

During my divorce-inspired garage sale, my neighbor from two doors down hugged me and asked if he could pray for me. I gratefully agreed. He and his wife were active in their church and they invited me to join them. Three years later, he baptized me in front of the entire congregation.

I have been actively going to church ever since and it has changed my life.

Before I found God, I hoped I would be okay. Hope to me was something similar to a wish but maybe a bit more serious. Once I found my church family in God, I learned that hope is okay but having faith in the knowledge that I would be fine was a much more powerful belief. I'm not insinuating that you can't find hope or peace or success without adding religion into your life. Spirituality does not always include weekly attendance in a building with other people; it can have vast differences as big as time and space. You simply need to determine what works for you. Have faith and do the work. I have a sign on my wall that says, "Faith is trusting in what we can't see." You may not be able to see a future beyond all the divorce drama but knowing you will be all right should be a solid guiding light.

Surround yourself with people who 'get it': Many narcissistic abuse survivors have suffered so much gaslighting during their marriages that the need for support in the form of affirmation and validation during and after the divorce becomes vital to building a resilient recovery. Family members and friends who have not experienced it often don't understand and will offer up the standard, garden-variety divorce wisdom and advice that doesn't fit the special kind of crazy you're dealing with. The effects of well-intentioned but misinformed comments like, "it takes two to tango" or "he/she can't really be that irrational" can set you back and derail your recovery. This is the reason why it's important to only discuss your divorce from your narcissistic ex with people who truly *get it*. Having at least one person in your life – a therapist, friend, or mentor- who empathizes can have a massive impact on your overall well-being and help you feel grounded and saner, at the same time providing the perspective needed to navigate the grueling, high-conflict terrain.

Bree Bonchay, author, psychotherapist, founder of World Narcissistic Abuse Awareness Day

When you do the work and heal your wounds, you become a surTHRIVER.

ABOUT THE AUTHOR

Tracy A. Malone is a narcissist abuse survival coach, author, and founder of NarcissistAbuseSupport.com, a global resource dedicated to empowering victims of emotional abuse which offers support and coaching to those trying to break the ties with the narcissists in their lives. Tracy is herself, a surTHRIVER of Narcissistic Abuse.

Tracy has authored multiple eBooks on narcissistic abuse to educate victims on various types of narcissistic relationships such as divorcing a narcissist, narcissistic spouses, narcissistic siblings, narcissistic parents, narcissistic children, co-parenting with a narcissist, narcissistic friends and a narcissistic boss or coworker. She is also an expert on destructive relationships. You can learn more from her online courses such as how to set boundaries, changing your story to stop attracting narcissists, and her newest course which explains how to create a narc-proof parenting plan.

Tracy, a frequent guest at summits and on podcasts, has a successful YouTube presence that currently includes more than 420 videos with an ever-rising subscriber base (currently around 24,000) whose reach has surpassed two million survivors. Her Narcissistic Abuse Support website offers resources to victims in excess of 145 countries and she is the founder of a Facebook group with over 15,000 members. Her inspirational quotes on Pinterest have more than two million monthly visitors.

Tracy is available for coaching, interviews, and appearances both nationally and internationally by arrangement and can be reached through her website.

NARCISSISTIC ABUSE TERMINOLOGY

Flying monkeys – people used by the narcissist to do their bidding, similar to the monkeys controlled by the witch to hurt Dorothy in the *The Wizard of Oz*. The monkeys can unwittingly be your friends or family or they may be people who willingly reach out to attack you on behalf of your spouse.

Future casting – exceedingly early in the relationship, narcissists talk in terms of "we" and "us." You are quickly thrust into the position to begin dreaming of a future together as they proclaim that you are the perfect mate and have searched for you their entire life. Subtle phrases such as "Let's go back to our place," or "Let's go home," when you are heading to their house. Each thing that makes you a "couple" is designed for you to envision a future with them.

Gaslighting – a form of emotional abuse and psychological manipulation where the abuser targets their prey into thinking they are crazy by making them question their own memory or reality.

Grey rock – this concept utilized by the victim promotes simple one-word answers that offer no details to be used against them in the future. It is most helpful for victims when contact is still necessary with their narcissist (i.e., coparenting situations).

Hoovering – to suck you back in, like a vacuum, usually with lies that they have changed or will do whatever it takes to make the relationship work. If it works, which it often does the first few times they try, you have been hoovered.

Love bombing – a manipulation that literally "bombs" the victim with compliments, texts, phone calls, flowers, and gifts that make you feel like you cannot live without them. They use this time to isolate you from your friends and family and slyly trick you into thinking that you want to spend all of your time with them until you have completely detached from all other relationships.

Narcissistic injury – created when a person with NPD perceives that someone has done them wrong. This is usually the point where, in their mind, you go from good to evil. Calling the police in defense of their abusive behaviors, telling the truth about them, filing for divorce, asking for your fair share of the marital property, or seeking custody of the children will all be perceived as viable threats against them.

Narcissistic rage – narcissists despise any challenge or affront and when they occur, they spew insults and become physically and emotionally aggressive with their partners.

Narcissistic supply – the benefit a victim gives their narcissist. The energy that feeds them can be positive, like your adoration of them, or negative, from the fear or anxiety they cause. All derive from the control they maintain over you.

No contact – when the victim "goes dark" and gives the silent treatment back to the narcissist, both verbally and electronically.

Projection – a manipulation tactic where the narcissist accuses the victim of the very thing(s) that they themselves are doing, i.e., cheating, laziness, insecurity, neediness, jealousy, or selfishness…the best one being when the narcissist calls the victim a narcissist. "The pot calling the kettle black" is very apropos in this situation.

Sense of entitlement – narcissists believe that the world owes them and they will lie, cheat, and steal to get it. Entitlement is said to be caused by deep rage and that fuels the conviction that they have a right to do, say, and have anything that they want.

Silent treatment – going dark and being unresponsive which brings the victim confusion and pain and is often used to control, punish, test boundaries, avoid responsibilities, and be spiteful, especially after the narcissist has groomed their victim to expect constant attention. This not only teaches the victim to not expect the frequent calls and texts but it also allows the narcissist to begin their second life with a new supply without the unwanted communication from their current victim.

Smear campaign – creating a series of lies, exaggerations, half-truths, suspicions, and false allegations about the victim's behavior which serve to undermine the victim's credibility and sanity to their friends, family, and acquaintances. The lies spread are meant to cause division and the loss of a support system.

Triangulation – a tactic used by narcissists to change the balance of power, pitting people against each other with lies and obvious favoritism.

Word salad – a circular exchange with a narcissist that includes irrelevant facts and meaningless logic meant to confuse and manipulate the victim. Imagine a blender with words flying around inside your head that make no sense and have no rationality to them. Narcissists use this technique of "doublespeak" to create verbal traps and impossibly unreasonable conversations.

Resources

Learn more helpful information to assist you through this process by visiting our book companion page: https://narcissistabusesupport.com/book-resources

CONTRIBUTOR BIOGRAPHIES

Donna Andersen

Donna Andersen has authored seven books, including *Love Fraud* and *Red Flags of Love Fraud—10 signs you're dating a sociopath* and has presented research to the Society for the Scientific Study of Psychopathy. She founded Lovefraud Continuing Education, which offers webinars to help professionals and survivors identify, escape, and recover from narcissists, sociopaths, psychopaths, and other manipulators. Donna has appeared on various tv shows including *ABC News 20/20, Who the Bleep Did I Marry?,* and *The Ricki Lake Show.* Learn more about Donna at www.lovefraud.com/.

Susan Ball

Susan Ball is an abuse recovery expert, disruptor, speaker, and best-selling author. Recovery After Abuse blossomed from Susan's own abusive relationships and is built on the belief that all women are entitled to live free, fulfilled, and fearless. Susan is on a mission empowering women to rise up, show up, free their voices, and move from the victim space to the courageous & healing space. Learn more about Susan at www.susanball.ca.

Anne Blythe

Anne Blythe, M.Ed. is Producer and Host of the *Betrayal Trauma Recovery* podcast. She and her team provide a daily support group, with multiple sessions a day in all time zones, for victims of emotional, psychological, and narcissistic abuse. Learn more about Anne at www.btr.org.

Bree Bonchay

Bree Bonchay, MSW, LCSW is a psychotherapist and narcissistic abuse recovery expert who specializes in helping people recover from toxic relationships. She is the founder of World Narcissistic Abuse Awareness Day and the highly regarded Survivor Empowerment Tele-summits. Learn more about Bree at www.linktr.ee/bree_lcsw.

Karen Covy

Karen Covy is a divorce advisor, attorney, consultant and coach who is committed to helping couples resolve their disputes as amicably and efficiently as possible. She is the author of *When Happily Ever After Ends: How to Survive Your Divorce Emotionally, Financially, and Legally*, the creator of the "Divorce Road Map" online program and has been featured on the Channel 7 News, WCIU You and Me This Morning, WGN Radio, MarketWatch as well as numerous radio shows and podcasts. Learn more about Karen at www.karencovy.com.

Lindsey Ellison

Lindsey Ellison is a relationship coach and narcissistic abuse survivor. Creator of the online course "Break Free from Your Narcissist," Lindsey is also a Huffington Post contributor, podcast host, has been featured on shows such as Dr. Laura and ABC News: Good Morning Washington, and author of *Magic Words: How to Get What You Want from A Narcissist*. Learn more about Lindsey at www.lindseyellison.com.

Randi Fine

Randi Fine is a pioneer in the narcissistic abuse movement and a Narcissistic Personality Disorder abuse expert. Author of the groundbreaking book, *Close Encounters of the Worst Kind: The Narcissistic Abuse Survivors Guide to Healing and Recovery*, the memoir, *Cliffedge*

Road, and blog, *Narcissistic Abuse Awareness and Guidance with Randi Fine*, she is also the host of the blog talk-radio show, *A Fine Time for Healing: A Sanctuary for Your Emotional Wellbeing*. Randi is a coach/counselor living in Ft. Lauderdale, Florida. Learn more about Randi at www.randifine.com.

Susan Guthrie

Susan Guthrie, nationally recognized as a top family law and mediation attorney, has been helping individuals and couples restructure their lives and families through the divorce process for over 30 years. Host of podcasts, *The Divorce and Beyond Podcast with Susan Guthrie, Esq.* and *The Learn to Mediate Online Podcast with Susan Guthrie, Esq.*, Susan has been featured in and on media outlets such as CNBC, Market Watch, Forbes, Eye on Chicago, and WGN, among others. Learn more about Susan at www.learntomediateonline.com and www.divorceinabetterway.com.

Rev Sheri Heller

Rev. Sheri Heller, LCSW is a NYC psychotherapist, freelance writer/author, and interfaith minister in private practice specializing in the treatment of complex trauma, narcissistic abuse syndrome, and addictive disorders. Learn more about Sheri at www.sheritherapist.com.

Jason Levoy

Jason Levoy, a/k/a The Divorce Resource Guy, is a former divorce attorney turned divorce coach who helps people navigate the system as inexpensively and efficiently as possible, with confidence and integrity. He is the creator of DivorceU as well as the host of *The Divorce Resource Guy* podcast, which covers everything divorce-related, from an attorney›s point of view. Learn more about Jason at www.jasonlevoy.com.

Rosemary Lombardy

Rosemary Lombardy is a financial advisor with over 35 years of experience as well as a domestic abuse survivor. She is the founder of Breaking Bonds, a free resource for abused women, and author of *Breaking Bonds: How to Divorce an Abuser and Heal—A Survival Guide*. Learn more about Rosemary at www.breakingbonds.com.

Jasmine Mann

Jasmine Mann (a.k.a M. J. Star) is a software engineer turned webcomic artist. She is a survivor of both Narcissistic Abuse and Endometriosis. More of her illustrations can be found at www.mjstarart.com.

Amy Marlow-MaCoy

Amy Marlow-MaCoy is a Licensed Professional Counselor and author of *The Gaslighting Recovery Workbook: Healing from Emotional Abuse*. Amy specializes in supporting adult children of narcissists in healing from toxic relationships and creating a healthier, happier life. Learn more about Amy at www.amymarlowmacoy.com.

Sharon Martin

Sharon Martin, LCSW is a licensed psychotherapist and codependency expert practicing in San Jose, CA. She specializes in helping perfectionists and people-pleasers embrace their imperfections and overcome self-doubt and shame. Sharon writes the popular blog *Happily Imperfect* for PsychCentral.com and is the author of the book, *The CBT Workbook for Perfectionism*. Learn more about Sharon at LiveWellWithSharonMartin.com.

Victoria McCooey

Victoria McCooey is a transformation coach, motivational speaker, and creator of The Reclaim Your Power System™. She works with women who are in controlling or otherwise abusive marriages to help them stand up to their abusers and regain control of their lives. Victoria has helped hundreds of women (and some men) acquire the skills, mindset shifts, and courage necessary to stand up to an abusive partner and create a better, more joyful life for themselves and their children. Learn more about Victoria at www.victoriamccooey.com.

Jessica McCrea

Jessica McCrea, Psy.D. is a licensed clinical psychologist and integrative business coach in Boulder, CO. She offers a relational and experiential approach to healing, informed by attachment-focused trauma work and hypnotherapy. Learn more about Jessica at www.jessicamccrea.com.

CONTRIBUTOR BIOGRAPHIES

Kate Parry

Kate Parry, actress, Audible book narrator, Assistant Director and Kids Acting Coach at Prodigy Talent Training enjoys working with authors in order to bring their books to life by understanding the world through their lens. She thinks books are important and her passion is to help reach as many people as possible through this medium. Learn more about Kate at *www.bookkateparry.com*

Suzanna Quintana

Suzanna Quintana is an abuse survivor, feminist, divine rebel, single mom of three sons, and author of the new book, *You're Still That Girl: Get Over Your Abusive Ex for Good!* After escaping nearly two decades of abuse at the hands of a diagnosed narcissist, she now helps other women recover, heal, and leave the pain behind them for good. Learn more about Suzanna at www.suzannaquintana.com.

Patricia Riley

Patricia Riley is a former Family Lawyer turned divorce mediator. 30 years of practicing law taught her that mediation is equally successful in a much shorter amount of time. Learn more about Patricia at www.rileymediations.com.

Duane Robert

Duane Robert is the host of the Podcast, *Break the Cycle with DSD,* as well as the YouTube Channel, *Dad Surviving Divorce.* Duane has built a community helping men and women with the struggles of toxic high-conflict divorces. His content has helped many viewers improve relationships with their children and implement techniques to help deal with their narcissistic ex. Learn more about Duane at www.dadsurvivingdivorce.com/.

Rhoberta Shaler

Rhoberta Shaler, PhD, "The Relationship Help Doctor," helps clients worldwide navigate the journey from recognizing to recovering and rebuilding after toxic relationships with Hijackals®. She hosts the podcast, *Save Your Sanity: Help for Toxic Relationships* and the *ForRelationshipHelp* channel on YouTube. Learn more about Rhoberta at www.Hijackals.com.

Joyce Short
Joyce Short is leading the way to define consent in society's awareness and the laws that protect us against sexual assault. She is the Founder of the Consent Awareness Network (CAN), the author of *Your Consent – The Key to Conquering Sexual Assault,* a TEDx Talk Presenter, a "Woman of Distinction" Honoree by the New York State Assembly, and a three-time sexual assault survivor. Learn more about Joyce at www.ConsentAwareness.net.

Debi Silber
Dr. Debi Silber, founder of The PBT (Post Betrayal Transformation) Institute, is a holistic psychologist. A health, mindset, and personal development expert, she's also an award-winning speaker, coach, and author of the Amazon #1 Bestselling book: *The Unshakable Woman: 4 Steps to Rebuilding Your Body, Mind and Life After a Life Crisis* as well as the book's companion guide workbook, *The Unshakable Woman,* and others. Debi has also contributed to FOX, CBS, The Dr. Oz show, TEDx (twice), and The Huffington Post, to name a few. Learn more about Debi at www.pbtinstitute.com/.

Babita Spinelli
Babita Spinelli, LP JD is a Psychotherapist and Certified Coach. She is the CEO of Opening the Doors Psychotherapy and the Babita Spinelli Group. Babita works with individuals who are experiencing significant life transitions and couples looking to transform or rebuild their relationships and specializes in narcissist abuse, toxic relationships, infidelity, divorce recovery, and mental health in the workplace. She is frequently featured in the media as a guest expert and provides consultation to entrepreneurs and fortune 500 organizations worldwide. Learn more about Babita at www.openingthedoorspsychotherapy.com.

Alisa Stamps
Alisa Stamps, MSS, LCSW is a licensed clinical social worker in private practice in Philadelphia. Alisa specializes in working with adult children of narcissists, and runs a support and recovery group for these individuals entitled, "Shattering the Mirror." She also has

experience in the treatment of eating disorders and complex trauma. Learn more about Alisa at www.alisastamps.com.

Tina Swithin

Tina Swithin is the author of the "Divorcing a Narcissist" series, founder of One Mom's Battle, and the High Conflict Divorce Coach Certification Program. Continuing to champion children's rights through her family court advocacy, Tina is working to raise awareness on narcissistic abuse, post-separation abuse and the issues in the family court system through her latest project; the Family Court Awareness Month campaign. Learn more about Tina at www.one-momsbattle.com/.

Debbie Tudor

Debbie Tudor, BS, MA is a Licensed Professional Counselor-Supervisor and Life Coach with more than 23 years of experience helping adults through difficult life situations, such as divorce and dealing with toxic parents. She is the author of *Its Not You, Its Them: 30 Days of Hope and Help for the Adult Child of a Narcissistic Parent*, a workbook for recovery and relationships. Certified in Narcissistic Abuse Recovery by Dr. Karyl McBride, Debbie owns Rockwall Counseling, PA. Learn more about Debbie at https://rockwall-counseling.com/.

Rebecca Zung

Rebecca Zung is one of the nation's top 1% of divorce attorneys, having been recognized by U.S. News & World Report as "Best Lawyer in America" and "Legal Elite" by Trend Magazine. Author of the bestselling book *Breaking Free: A Step-by-Step Divorce Guide for Achieving Emotional, Physical, and Spiritual Freedom*, Rebecca has also been featured by *Extra TV, Forbes, Huffington Post, Newsweek, Time, Dr. Drew, and NPR Talk Radio*, among others. Currently based in Los Angeles, she continues to serve through her law and high conflict negotiation coaching practices, her on-demand courses, as well as through her YouTube channel and podcast. Learn more about Rebecca at www.rebeccazung.com.

BIBLIOGRAPHY

American Psychiatric Association: Diagnostic and Statistical Manual of Mental Disorders: Diagnostic and Statistical Manual of Mental Disorders, Fifth Edition. Arlington, VA: American Psychiatric Association, 2013.

Cambridge Dictionary. (n.d.). Pathological Liar. In *Cambridge.com Dictionary*. Retrieved January 27, 2021, from https://www.dictionary.cambridge.org/us/dictionary/english/pathological

Jeffers, Susan. *Feel the Fear and Do It Anyway*. New York, NY: Ballantine, 1988. Print < https://amzn.to/3w0F4gr >

Kuhn Truman, Karol. *Feelings Buried Alive Never Die*. Salt Lake City, UT: Olympus Distributing, 1991. Kindle Edition < https://amzn.to/2QEGRaX >

Merriam-Webster. (n.d.). Stonewall. In *Merriam-Webster.com Dictionary*. Retrieved February 4, 2021, from https://www.merriam-webster.com/dictionary/stonewall

Merriam-Webster. (n.d.). Survive. In *Merriam-Webster.com Dictionary*. Retrieved February 4, 2021, from https://www.merriam-webster.com/dictionary/survive

Merriam-Webster. (n.d.). Victim. In *Merriam-Webster.com Dictionary*. Retrieved February 4, 2021, from https://www.merriam-webster.com/dictionary/victim

"Moms: We know you're worth it. But how much is "it" really worth?" *Salary.com*. January 2021. Web. February 4, 2021.

van der Kolk, Bessel. *The Body Keeps the Score: Brain, Mind, and Body in the Healing of Trauma*. Westminster, London, England: Penguin Books, 2015. Kindle Edition < https://amzn.to/3vXXCOr >

CPSIA information can be obtained
at www.ICGtesting.com
Printed in the USA
LVHW051125090322
712905LV00012B/782